Handbook for Communication and Problem-Solving Skills Training

An Einstein Psychiatry Publication

Publication Series of the Department of Psychiatry
Albert Einstein College of Medicine of Yeshiva University
New York, NY

Editor-in-Chief   Herman M. van Praag, M.D., Ph.D.
Associate Editor   Demitri Papolos, M.D.

Editorial Board

Handbook for Communication and Problem-Solving Skills Training

A Cognitive-Behavioral Approach

JEFFREY R. BEDELL

and

SHELLEY S. LENNOX

John Wiley & Sons, Inc.

New York • Chichester • Brisbane • Toronto • Singapore • Weinheim

Copyright © 1997 by John Wiley & Sons, Inc.

Library of Congress Cataloging-in-Publication Data:

Bedell, Jeffrey R.
    Handbook for communication and problem-solving skills training : a
cognitive-behavioral approach / by Jeffrey R. Bedell and Shelley S.
Lennox.
        p.   cm. — (An Einstein psychiatry publication ; 14)
    Includes bibliographical references.
    ISBN 0-471-08250-3 (cloth : alk. paper)
    1. Problem-solving therapy.   2. Mentally ill—Rehabilitation.
3. Social skills—Study and teaching.   I. Lennox, Shelley S.
II. Title.   III. Series.
    RC489.P68B43   1996
    616.89′14—dc20   96-24667

Printed in the United States of America

10 9 8 7 6 5 4 3 2 1

To my family—Paul, Irene, Paul, Gene, and Carol—the foundation of my life, and Lynne Cascio who makes everything better.

J.R.B.

A Note on the Series

Psychiatry is in a state of flux. The excitement springs in part from internal changes, such as the development and official acceptance (at least in the United States) of an operationalized, multi-axial classification system of behavioral disorders (the *DSM-IV*), the increasing sophistication of methods to measure abnormal human behavior, and the impressive expansion of biological and psychological treatment modalities. Exciting developments are also taking place in fields relating to psychiatry; in molecular (brain) biology, genetics, brain imaging, drug development, epidemiology, experimental psychology, to mention only a few striking examples.

More generally speaking, psychiatry is moving, still relatively slowly, but irresistibly from a more philosophical, contemplative orientation to that of an empirical science. From the 1950s on, biological psychiatry has been a major catalyst of that process. It provided the mother discipline with a third cornerstone, that is, neurobiology, the other two being psychology and medical sociology. In addition, it forced the profession into the direction of standardization of diagnoses and of assessment of abnormal behavior. Biological psychiatry provided psychiatry not only with a new basic science and with new treatment modalities, but also with the tools, the methodology, and the mentality to operate within the confines of an empirical science, the only framework in which a medical discipline can survive.

In other fields of psychiatry, too, one discerns a gradual trend toward scientification. Psychological treatment techniques are standardized and manuals developed to make these skills more easily transferable. Methods registering treatment outcome—traditionally used in the behavioral/cognitive field—are now more and more requested and, hence, developed for dynamic forms of psychotherapy as well. Social and community psychiatry, until the 1960s were more firmly rooted in humanitarian ideals and social awareness than in empirical studies, profited greatly from its liaison with the social sciences and the expansion of psychiatric epidemiology.

Let there be no misunderstanding: Empiricism does *not imply* that it is only the measurable that counts. Psychiatry would be mutilated if it would neglect that which cannot be captured by numbers. It *does imply* that what is measurable should be measured. Progress in psychiatry is dependent on ideas and on experiment. Their linkage is inseparable.

This Series, published under the auspices of the Department of Psychiatry of the Albert Einstein College of Medicine, Montefiore Medical Center, is meant to keep track of important developments in our profession, to summarize what has been achieved in particular fields, and to bring together the viewpoints obtained from disparate vantage points—in short, to capture some of the ongoing excitement in modern psychiatry, both in its clinical and experimental dimensions. The Department of Psychiatry at Albert Einstein College of Medicine hosts the Series, but naturally welcomes contributions from others.

Bernie Mazel originally generated the idea for the series—an ambitious plan which we all felt was worthy of pursuit. The edifice of psychiatry is impressive, but still somewhat flawed in its foundations. May this Series contribute to consolidation of its infrastructure.

—HERMAN M. VAN PRAAG, M.D., PH.D.
Professor and Chairman
Academic Psychiatric Center
University of Limburg
Maastricht
The Netherlands

Preface

Social skills training and cognitive therapy have created a renaissance in mental health treatment. Proponents of these approaches have proven the treatments are effective for persons with a wide range of psychological problems. "Talk" therapies have had remarkable and unprecedented success in the areas of depression, anxiety disorders, and schizophrenia. In addition to being effective, these methods work rapidly and are amenable to short-term applications—a prized feature in the current climate of managed care and cost containment. This particular program emphasizes objective, structured treatments that focus on learned patterns of thinking, feeling, and behaving in the here and now.

The treatments follow a new philosophy that affirms the basic goodness of human beings and views clients in a positive light. We can openly collaborate with our clients, forming a partnership that enhances the process and outcome of therapy. People can learn to understand and modify the dysfunctional aspects of their lives, therefore taking control and becoming empowered.

Social skills training and cognitive therapy stress objective forms of treatment that can be translated into standardized procedures and presented in a handbook to guide the practitioner. We have found that practitioners, regardless of years of experience or discipline, are usually aware that social skills and cognitive therapy are the therapies of the 1990s. Many are attempting to improve their skills by learning the theory and practice behind these techniques. They are eager for practical training and for written materials that will aid them in learning new approaches and helping their clients.

This book reflects these trends in mental health. We have created a guide for the practitioner that focuses on both theory and practice. We have blended social skills training and cognitive therapy into an innovative and practical program of treatment. Social skills training and cognitive therapy are naturally complementary, the former focusing on objective behaviors and the latter on subjective thoughts and feelings. Whereas one treatment without the other is incomplete, combining them creates a complete and unified whole. Thus, we describe our work as a cognitive-behavioral approach to skills training.

We hope the reader will find this book useful as a guide to clinical practice, as a classroom text, and for other similar purposes. Professionals such as psychologists, psychiatrists, social workers, recreation therapists, and activity therapists should find the models of treatment described here relevant to their clinical work. Applications include clients with mild, moderate, and severe disorders stemming from anxiety, depressed mood, and thought disorder. These techniques should also help persons with dysfunctional interpersonal styles of behavior. Our intent is for this handbook to be a convenient reference source to skills training in areas of self-awareness, communication, assertiveness, problem-solving, and coping with inhibitory anxiety.

This volume also can serve as a textbook. We have used these materials as the basis of graduate level therapy courses and seminars at universities. The book actually came out of a training program for postdoctoral psychologists who were studying cognitive-behavioral social skills training techniques. These courses have mostly been for psychologists, but have also included psychiatrists, social workers, and other allied mental health professionals. The innovative teacher and practitioner will find many applications of this text.

JEFFREY R. BEDELL
SHELLEY S. LENNOX

Acknowledgments

The material in this book is the product of nearly two decades of development, testing, and refinement. During that time, important contributions from many people ultimately made this book possible. I hope to acknowledge the contributions of these creative, hard-working, and dedicated individuals.

In the beginning, at the Florida Mental Health Institute (FMHI), Larry Weathers provided the spark of creativity without which this book would not exist, and so I owe much to this man. Other important contributors from the FMHI include Herbert Marlowe, Joseph Ferrandino, John Ward, Barry Naster (Hamid), Stephen Hinricks, Carmen Bermudez, Susan Fertig-McDonald, Eileen Edmundson, Robert Archer, and Kathi Penner.

During my tenure at the Albert Einstein College of Medicine (AECOM), my co-author Shelley Lennox played an essential role in advancing these ideas to their current level of development. Also participating with us on social skills training at AECOM were Robert Gervey, Frederick Foley, and Jeffrey Frank. In addition, nearly 20 psychology trainees tested procedures with clients and helped shape these treatments.

Most recently, at the Mount Sinai College of Medicine and Elmhurst Hospital, James Rivera has assisted in the final refinement of the program in preparation for publication.

A number of people have helped with the preparation of the present manuscript. Lynne Cascio reviewed and edited every chapter, with the skill of a journalist and the patience of a saint. James Rivera prepared the sophisticated figures in this book and provided essential input into many of the concepts. Alec Cecil reviewed early versions of several chapters and helped to shape the final form of the manuscript. George Mavrolefteros did a highly competent job with the research reviews and reference list. Raquel Gutierrez provided word processing support and translated our handwriting into English, not always an easy task.

Sincere thanks to all these talented people for contributing to this project.

J.R.B.

Contents

xiii

Introduction

This book provides the practitioner with a practical model of treatment to develop client skills in self-awareness, empathy, making and responding to requests, assertiveness, problem-solving, and coping with anxiety. As explained in Chapter 9, these skills can be combined in a comprehensive program or individual skills can be taught independently. A program based on two or more skills is also possible by merging various chapters.

Each chapter focuses on how to teach a specific skill and presents an example of a skill training program in enough detail to serve as a treatment manual. To facilitate learning, many of the chapters include structured learning activities based on games such as crossword puzzles and bingo. We have found that practitioners who have been exposed to this material appreciate the detailed "how to" explanations that make the conceptual models of treatment more real.

To assist the reader in understanding the structure of this book, the following paragraphs summarize the material in each chapter.

In Chapter 1, we describe the background, effectiveness, and structure of this social skills training program. We also discuss "nonspecific" treatment issues traditionally referred to as resistance, transference, and countertransference.

Because social skills training and cognitive therapy are empirically based treatments, an extensive research literature supports their effectiveness. Since literature reviews are easily obtained elsewhere, Chapter 1 simply provides an overview of some of the more remarkable applications of social skills training methods.

Any treatment is more than a set of procedures—it is also a set of attitudes, beliefs, and philosophies that direct the clinician. To help readers understand the philosophical and conceptual underpinnings of this treatment approach, we describe influences from psychology, education, and psychiatric rehabilitation.

The structure of a social skills training program is also presented. This model includes four interrelated components:

1. Instructional material explaining the skill concepts.
2. Supervised practice activities.
3. Feedback.
4. Methods for independent practice of skills outside the therapy setting.

Chapter 1 also addresses therapist-client relationship issues from the viewpoint of social skills training and cognitive psychology. Social skills trainers must be able to do more than perform a set of procedures based on learning principles. They must also deal with treatment resistance and irrational components of this relationship.

Chapters 2 and 3 present the core concepts and procedures of this skills training approach. These chapters provide a model for developing awareness of wants, expectations, and feelings of the self and other. Effective social behavior is dependent on these skills. In Chapter 2, thoughts, feelings, and behaviors are defined in ways that help the client monitor these events. An explanation of the way thoughts, feelings, and behaviors interact and influence each other culminates in a set of diagrams that depict a model for understanding and changing dysfunctional thoughts, feelings, and behaviors.

The concepts that explain how thoughts, feelings, and behaviors interact are applied to the understanding of others in Chapter 3. The practitioner is shown how to teach empathic skills and given a model that shows how to effectively express empathic understanding. The package of self-awareness and awareness of others may be used as an independent module of treatment for clients who need to develop these skills.

In Chapter 4, the client is taught how to make an effective request in different situations including those where there is conflict or when one wants to change another person's behavior. The chapter outlines procedures for teaching clients how to use language to influence others and get what they want. These skills are important because they enable persons to exercise control over the environment and influence the reinforcements they receive in life. Such people function better in life than those without these skills. Chapter 4 ends with an example of a skills training program directed at developing request-making skills.

Chapter 5 extends the request-making skills to the related situation of responding to requests from others. Chapters 4 and 5 may be used together as a training module focused on these complementary skills. A request always carries three options: It can be granted or refused, or an alternative offered. Skills in these chapters focus on not only how to make these three kinds of requests, but also how to determine which of the three responses is appropriate in a given situation.

This skills training program is based on assertiveness. Modern presentations of assertiveness include the related concepts of aggressiveness and passivity, so in Chapter 6 we describe the verbal and nonverbal aspects of assertive, aggressive, and passive behaviors. The verbal aspects focus on stating one's own wants in a clear and direct manner while showing consideration of the wants and feelings of others. The nonverbal components of assertiveness include eye contact, posture, hand gestures, distance between the parties, latency of response, and voice quality. This chapter also applies cognitive-behavioral theory to understand the short- and long-term consequences of assertive, aggressive, and passive behavior.

The problem-solving skills presented in Chapter 7 focus on identifying problems, defining them in a solvable form, generating alternative solutions, evaluating the alternatives, selecting an alternative for implementation, and determining the effectiveness of the problem-solving plan. The cognitive-behavioral orientation of this chapter is especially helpful in the areas of identifying problems since thought, feeling, and behavioral cues can be used to facilitate the problem-solving process. In this chapter, we present seven basic principles of problem-solving to guide the process and improve outcomes.

The therapy approaches in this book are effective in developing skills, but as experience has shown us, clients may not fully use them in everyday life. Chapter 8 provides a number of active approaches to reduce the inhibitory anxiety that clients often experience when attempting to change habitual ways of thinking, feeling, and acting. This chapter explains the role of global self-defeating beliefs such as thinking one cannot change or is biologically destined to behave in certain ways, and suggests methods to overcome or modify these cognitive styles. Additionally, cognitive coping techniques are presented based on a four-part model:

1. Recognition of irrational and unrealistic wants and expectations.
2. Evaluation of these wants and expectations to see if they involve catastrophizing or overestimating potential consequences.
3. Substitution of more realistic wants and expectations for the irrational ones.
4. Learning to reward oneself for engaging in positive cognitive coping activities.

Although the development of cognitive coping skills should reduce the anxiety associated with the performance of new skills, coping strategies that work directly on the client's physiological arousal are also helpful. Therefore, two methods of relaxation are presented—diaphragmatic-slow breathing and progressive muscle relaxation. Finally, we explain the benefits of gradual exposure to feared situations and the clinical application of a stimulus hierarchy.

In Chapter 9, we describe several applications of the skills training procedures in this book. A wide range of applications have developed over the years due to the program's versatility and adaptability. It has been our experience that almost every person can benefit from all or part of this training.

The treatment methods can be used in both time-limited and open-ended group therapy, as well as individual cognitive-behavioral therapy. It is also appropriate for recreational, activity, and family therapy. These programs have also been used in a highly effective supported employment project that placed and maintained clients in competitive employment.

Applications to case management programs are also described, especially in areas where peer counselors are part of the treatment program. The program has also been applied to several special populations, including persons experiencing their first hospital admission, clients being sent to a state hospital for extended inpatient treatment, and patients with multiple sclerosis who also have cognitive impairments.

A wide range of related treatments are presented in this book. They may be used in their entirety or in part, as appropriate to meet the treatment needs of the client. We hope these topics and procedures will enhance the skills of practitioners working with clients who have skill deficits in self-awareness, empathy, making and responding to requests, assertiveness, problem-solving, or coping with anxiety.

1

Key Concepts of Communication and Problem-Solving Skills Training

SOCIAL SKILLS TRAINING: PRACTICAL AND VERSATILE

The concepts and procedures described in this book are the product of nearly two decades of clinical and research experience with communication and problem-solving skills training. During this time, we have found this approach to treatment to be extremely versatile and effective. We have applied it to patients with severe disabilities to reduce hospitalization and with persons having mild and moderate disorders to improve functioning, well-being, and quality of life.

Because of this versatility and effectiveness, many mental health professionals provide social skills training. These practitioners need to be able to base their clinical work on clear theoretical and practical models. This book addresses this need and provides a guide to the concepts and practices of social skills training. This book has chapters on self-awareness, empathy, making and responding to requests, assertiveness, problem-solving, and coping with anxiety that inhibits the use of new skills. All these skills can be taught in a comprehensive program of treatment, or individual skill modules can comprise one or more chapters of this book. We will say more about applications of these programs in Chapter 9.

This chapter describes some of the research that demonstrates the effectiveness of social skills training, how social skill is best defined, and the contributions of psychology, education, and psychiatric rehabilitation to social skills training. An overall structural model of the process of social skills training is provided. And, the nonspecific therapy factors of resistance, transference, and countertransference are reviewed and explained in terms of social learning and cognitive-behavioral theory and practice.

The Effectiveness of Social Skills Training

Social skills training is an empirically based approach to treatment. During the past 20 years, social skills training has evolved into an effective mental health intervention, heralded by initial reports demonstrating its effectiveness (e.g., Goldsmith & McFall, 1975; Goldstein, 1973). There are now applications of social skills training to distressed marital couples, school problems, vocational decision making, anxiety disorders, drug and alcohol abuse disorders, personality disorders, depression, and schizophrenia. In fact, there have been over 100 published evaluations of social skills training, most of which demonstrate the effectiveness of this approach.

In addition to these studies, six comprehensive critical reviews of research on social skills training have been conducted. These reviews concluded that investigators have found strong evidence to support the effectiveness of this paradigm of treatment (Brady, 1984; Hersen & Bellack, 1976; Ladd & Mize, 1983; Morrison & Bellack, 1984; Robertson, Richardson, & Youngson, 1984; Wallace et al., 1980). Most recently, Benton and Schroeder (1990) reported the results of a meta-analysis of 27 well-designed studies evaluating the effectiveness of social skills training for persons with schizophrenia. In their review, these authors included only studies with controlled designs, clear social skills training methods, and a variety of objective outcome measures. Using sophisticated statistical techniques, these authors discovered that research on social skills training reliably showed six effects:

1. There was significant improvement in assertiveness, anxiety, and other specific behaviors.
2. The social skills learned in therapy generalized to natural real-life settings.

3. Compared with other treatments, social skills training produced superior social functioning with treatment differences increasing over long periods of time.

4. Social skills training resulted in superior hospital discharge rates.

5. Social skills training resulted in lower rates of relapse compared with other treatments.

6. The superior effects associated with social skills training were the same with schizophrenic samples and samples comprising a heterogeneous mixture of mentally ill patients.

Although widespread research has shown the effectiveness of social skills training, there is little consensus regarding what constitutes an effective training program. For example, Benton and Schroeder (1990) defined social skills training according to the treatment procedures used rather than the skills to be learned. An intervention was defined as social skills training if it employed techniques such as instructions or coaching, live modeling, taped modeling, simple rehearsal, role-play rehearsal, verbal feedback, videotaped feedback, interpersonal reinforcement, and homework assignments.

In comparison, most social skills training programs have been defined by the skill being taught. Many reports have identified problemsolving as the targeted skill (e.g., Bedell, Archer, & Marlowe, 1980; Bedell & Michael, 1985; McFall, 1982; Penn et al., 1993; Trower, Bryant, & Argyle, 1978; Wallace, 1982). Still other programs have focused on communication skills and assertiveness (e.g., Bellack, Morrison, & Mueser, 1989; Brown & Carmichael, 1992; Wallace, Liberman, MacKain, Eckman, & Blackwell, 1992). Many effective programs have trained communication and problem-solving skills as a package (Hogarty et al., 1986; Wallace & Liberman, 1985).

Social skills training programs that used a combination of communication and problem-solving skills training appear to have yielded some of the most impressive outcomes. For example, research reported by Wallace and Liberman (1985) and Liberman, Mueser, and Wallace (1986) evaluated the effects of communication and problem-solving skills training for schizophrenic patients living with families high in Expressed Emotions (Leff & Vaughn, 1980). These families were highly critical of the patient, a factor found in previous research (Leff & Vaughn, 1980) to increase the presence of disruptive symptoms and relapse. A 9-week program of treatment emphasized training in various elements of communications skills, including how to attend to relevant social cues, process social information to develop appropriate responses, and to make skilled behavioral responses. In this program, the skills training focused on effective use of communication to make requests and respond to the requests of others. In addition, clients were taught problem-solving skills that focused on teaching them to generate and evaluate alternative solutions to problems, and to choose an effective response. Extremely positive outcomes resulted from this program on a variety of meaningful treatment outcome measures. Reduced rehospitalization rates were also reported during a one-year follow-up period.

Hogarty et al. (1986) reported the results of a treatment that similarly employed training in communication and problem-solving skills. Additionally, this treatment established a low-stress environment and provided social support and empathy from staff. Compared with an active control consisting of socialization and stress management, this treatment reduced the rehospitalization rates of schizophrenic patients by nearly 50 percent. Even better results were obtained when families also learned effective communication skills. Recently reported applications of these skill training approaches for individual psychotherapy also emphasize communication and problem solving skills development (Hogarty et al., 1995).

A third study (Bedell & Ward, 1989) evaluated a treatment program based on nearly identical versions of the communication and problem-solving procedures presented in this book. Training in social skills was combined with active medication and behavior management techniques (Ward & Naster, 1991). Clinically significant findings were obtained, demonstrating the efficacy of a program based primarily on communication and problem-solving skills training. The subjects receiving this treatment showed a dramatic reduction in length of hospitalization (32 vs. 150 days) and a significantly reduced rehospitalization rate during most of the 30-month period following discharge. In addition, a substantial reduction in the cost of an episode of treatment was observed ($4,130 vs. $13,282).

Communication and problem-solving skills training has also been used successfully in family therapy. Falloon, McGill, Boyd, and Pederson (1987) describe a program of behavioral family therapy that has greatly influenced treatment of families of persons with severe mental disorders. These clinicians provided communication and problem-solving skills training to patients and family members in the home environment, ruling out the necessity for treatment in a clinic or hospital setting. Results revealed improvement in symptoms and social adjustment, and a reduction in hospitalization.

These empirical findings demonstrate that skills training programs that have combined both communication and problem-solving skills training are remarkably effective. Consistent with these findings, the program described here focuses on these elements. It teaches communication and problem-solving using the most current concepts of social learning theory and cognitive-behavioral treatment.

The Definition of Social Skills

Because the definition of social skills on which a program of treatment is founded will dramatically influence its practices and procedures, we have reviewed the various definitions in the literature (Bedell & Lennox, 1994). Based on this review, and a recognition of the importance of the cognitive elements of social skills, we suggest that social skills include the abilities to (a) accurately select relevant and useful information from an interpersonal context, (b) use that information to determine appropriate goal-directed behavior, and (c) execute verbal and nonverbal behaviors that maximize the likelihood of goal attainment and the maintenance of good relations with others. This definition implies that the term *social skills* denotes two sets of abilities, cognitive and behavioral. Cognitive abilities are the social perception and information-processing skills that define, organize, and guide social skills. Behavioral abilities are the verbal and nonverbal behaviors that implement the decision derived from the cognitive processes.

Nevertheless, there is little consensus in the field regarding the definition of social skills. Commonly, social skills are defined in terms of the description and function of instrumental behavior. These definitions typically focus on the rate and volume of spoken language and nonverbal behaviors such as facial expression, posture, and hand gestures. These behaviors are often referred to as "microskills," or "microbehaviors" small components that combine to form global skills. Training is offered on each small component behavior with the ultimate goal of assembling the microskills into chains of socially appropriate actions.

The value of the microbehavior approach is that it enables the targeted behaviors to be well specified. Consequently, training procedures can be carefully focused on small discrete behaviors. The disadvantage of this approach is that not all the microbehaviors that constitute skilled performance are known. And skilled behavior appears to comprise more than a chain of small behaviors. The skilled person must be able to determine what behaviors to engage in and how to construct a series of microbehaviors into a socially appropriate chain. The latter are cognitive processing skills.

Some definitions of social skills have focused on their function in determining the outcome of specific social interactions. Social skill training programs based on this definition of social skills may provide training in global skills designed to achieve certain interpersonal goals. For example, persons may be trained in heterosexual interactions, how to initiate and maintain a conversation or how to act assertively. As was the case with microskills, this global approach makes it easier to focus on well-defined target behaviors. A limitation, however, is the extent to which these global behaviors are generalizable to different circumstances. Additionally, the person must be able to determine which global behavior is appropriate for each different social situation. This involves cognitive processing as well as global skills.

Increased awareness of the critical role of social perception and information-processing skills in the development and maintenance of socially skilled behavior has led to the inclusion of these skills in training programs (Bellack, Morrison, & Mueser, 1989; Liberman, 1982). Social perception and information-processing skills include those cognitive abilities that enable one to (a) recognize relevant and essential information in the environment and (b) process this information and decide the appropriate way to act in the situation. Only after learning to function in these areas can the person perform the most suitable microskills and global skills.

The current program uses this three-part cognitive-behavioral model of skills training and includes the following components: (a) information gathering, (b) information processing/decision making, and (c) behavior.

Foundations of Social Skills Training

The concepts, procedures, and practices of communication and problem-solving skills training are described in detail in the following chapters. Understanding the philosophical, theoretical, and practical underpinnings of the program is also essential. Any comprehensive program of treatment is held together and organized by its philosophical and theoretical roots. Clarifying these issues will help the reader to better understand how this program was constructed and how the components fit together. Therefore, we will describe the key concepts that underlie the present program.

General Orientation of Treatment

Social skills training is an uplifting enterprise concerned with the betterment of the human condition. It is based on the belief that people can grow psychologically and better themselves. An individual is helped to pursue life in a way that results in the maximum amount of reward and the least stress, punishment, and unhappiness. When people learn effective communication and problem-solving skills, they will be better able to interact with others to achieve positive outcomes and avoid or minimize the negative ones.

Any discussion of what makes a person's life "better" is not based entirely on factual or scientific criteria, but also includes value judgments of good and bad. Who ultimately decides what social behavior is "better" and what is "worse" for a given individual? Since value judgments are inherent in social skills training, it is important to carefully analyze the values, goals, and desires of the provider and recipient of the training. It is essential that the recipient of this training "choose" to participate; the patient and therapist should agree that learning better communications and problem-solving skills is in the client's best interest. Otherwise, issues of control and coercion will cloud the uplifting potential of social skills training. When it appears to the therapist that a client would benefit from social skills training but the client is resistant, it is appropriate to educate the client about social skills training and to encourage participation. It is also appropriate to encourage the client to try a brief exposure to social skills training that will demonstrate its value. Ultimately, however, the decision to participate in this treatment rests with the client.

Skills training also assumes the innate ability of people to grow and change. Change may be encouraged and supported by external influences such as a skills training program. Skills training is based on an optimistic view of human nature and of the positive collaboration that is possible between the provider and recipient of treatment. The social skills trainer hopes to facilitate the positive growth of the individual.

The social skills training methods described in this book should not be viewed as a "one size fits all" approach to therapy. A program of social skills training is most properly seen as an attempt to match an available set of behavior change strategies with the needs of the individual. While skills trainers use treatment procedures that are based on an extensive body of scientific and practical knowledge, they should not be employed in a rigid fashion. The procedures and practices of social skills training are best seen as guidelines for learning effective behavior. They will be helpful for most people but may need to be revised and modified to fit the needs of a specific individual.

Influence of Psychological Theory and Practice

Social skills training is clearly grounded in psychological theory and practice. The present program is based on principles of learning and behavior change associated with cognitive-behavioral therapy and social learning theory. The value of teaching social skills emerged in the 1960s as practitioners began to understand the role of learning in the development and maintenance of pathological behavior. Early researchers such as Libet and Lowensohn (1973) discovered that the social skills of depressed persons were critical to the development and maintenance of this syndrome. They were among the first to show that people with depressive patterns of behavior were deficient in the social and interpersonal skills needed to elicit positive reinforcement from the environment. In fact, the environment of depressed people often reinforces dysfunctional behavior. The modification of social skills to increase reinforcement from the environment and to break dysfunctional patterns of interaction makes it possible to alter the course of personal and interpersonal problems. Zigler and Phillips (1961) were among the first to explain how social skills deficits were a significant factor in a wide range of psychiatric disorders. Their work suggested that the debilitating effects of many psychological disorders could be reversed by teaching social skills to overcome these deficits.

As therapies based on learning theories evolved, various principles, practices, and procedures were amalgamated into contemporary skills training approaches. Many of these principles are implicit in the procedures described in the various chapters of this book. A brief chronological overview of the major psychological models that form the foundation of the present social skills training program will be helpful in explaining the orientation of this program.

Between 1960 and 1970, principles of operant learning were discovered and applied to clinical practice. Although this work is appropriately associated with B. F. Skinner, a large group of behavior therapists developed the clinical applications (see Ullmann & Krasner, 1965; Ulrich, Stachnich, & Mabry, 1966). A basic principle of operant learning is that the individual's behaviors are strengthened or weakened depending on their consequences in the environment. This concept of behavior was divergent from the intrapsychic and psychodynamic models dominant at the time. The conception that the modification of behavior is important in its own right became the foundation of social skills training. The goal of social skills training was to establish behaviors that were socially effective and would enable the individual to receive reinforcement from other persons. The unskilled behaviors exhibited by persons with psychological problems were seen as being ineffectual in generating positive reinforcement. In some cases, behavioral patterns resulted in aversive or punishing consequences. Therefore, according to operant learning theory, the individual who learned to behave in a socially skilled way was more likely to receive rewards and avoid punishments from the environment.

The "applied behavior analyst" of this period was primarily concerned with overt behavior to the exclusion of cognition and affect. This orientation influenced social skills training to focus on objective behaviors. The concepts of social skills and behavior were sometimes viewed as synonymous. As the field has matured, however, social skills training has increasingly emphasized a three-part model of skills development that includes thoughts, feelings, and behaviors. Bellack, Morrison, and Mueser (1989) reviewed the role of cognitive factors in social problem-solving skills and criticized the once-popular "Motor Skills Model" as being outdated. Bellack et al. (1989) correctly suggest that a strictly operant behavioral model is inadequate as the conceptual basis for understanding interpersonal behavior. The role of cognitive and affective aspects of social skills and social competence appears to be the current focus of development in social skills training (e.g., Bedell & Lennox, 1994; Liberman, 1992; Liberman & Bedell, 1989; Liberman & Green, 1982; Wallace & Boone, 1984).

The cognitive elements of social skills training were advanced by the development of social learning theory (Bandura, 1969, 1977) in the 1970s. This research demonstrated the cognitive mediational processes involved in the development and maintenance of patterns of behavior. The influence of concepts of observational learning and modeling developed by social learning theorists is fundamental to every modern social skills training program. In fact, as mentioned earlier, the use of modeling procedures as a method of teaching social skills has sometimes been used to define social skills training programs (Benton & Schroeder, 1990).

The influence of cognitive variables such as "wants" and "expectations" on behavior is based on social learning theory. In the present program, the recognition and ability to process these kinds of cognitive material are paramount in directing the individual toward skilled social behavior. The ability to identify wants and expectations is fundamental to understanding social interactions. The concepts of "the want" and "the expectation" are woven into the fabric of every communication and problem-solving skill in this book.

Cognitive therapy has been the most recent contributor to social skills training. The work of Beck (1976; Beck, Rush, Shaw, & Emery, 1979), Ellis (Ellis & Grieger, 1978), and Meichenbaum (1977) has demonstrated the effect that thoughts and beliefs have on mood and behavior. Ellis has shown that irrational beliefs, such as the need for perfection, fairness, or getting one's way, are the basis of many psychological problems.

According to the cognitive therapy model, a person who performs in a skilled manner according to community standards still may feel anxious and depressed because of an irrational belief that his or her performance should somehow be better. For example, the person may have unrealistically high standards and expect to win the approval of everyone. If performance does not produce these unrealistic results, the person believes it to be unacceptable and deficient. Since expectations of perfection and universal approval are impossible to fulfill, the individual experiences failure, no matter how well he or she performs.

Similarly, Beck has identified a core group of "cognitive distortions," such as overgeneralization and catastrophizing, that influence affect and behavior. Beck recommends identification of these cognitive distortions and learning to substitute more realistic and adaptive appraisals. This approach is referred to as cognitive restructuring and will be addressed more fully in Chapter 8.

Consistent with these different theories, the present program has attempted to present a clear, cohesive, and useful model of how thoughts, feelings, and behaviors interact and influence each other. Chapter 2 includes an explanation of the concept of the "Thought-Feeling-Behavior Triad," which has its roots in cognitive therapy.

Contributions from Education

Many educational practices have been incorporated into social skills training treatment. These methods typically use structured curricula, lesson plans, didactic teaching, and exercises to facilitate the learning of new skills.

In educational settings, it is standard practice to divide the overall domain of instruction into separate courses, such as mathematics, English, and history. Similarly, a social skills training program will be divided into separate courses such as communication, problem-solving, and assertiveness. The presentation of educational courses is further structured and a teacher develops a set of daily lesson plans that determine the content of each classroom meeting. Similarly, a social skills trainer follows a structured set of lessons that define the learning goals of each meeting.

Consistent with these educational practices, the present program limits its focus to two courses: communication skills and problem-solving. Each chapter in this book contains material that could be likened to a teacher's lesson plan including text that can be organized as a didactic lecture to explain the basic skills to be taught and practice exercises to facilitate rehearsal of the techniques presented in the lecture.

The roles of the client and therapist in social skills training also demonstrate the influence of educational practice. The client's role is similar to that of a student who is an active participant in a positive learning experience (skills enhancement). The therapist is a teacher.

Because of the collaborative relationship between teacher and student, the latter is identified as "client" not "patient." In the student role, the client takes an active part in his or her own treatment and may also assist others in learning new behaviors. In this way, the client is both a recipient and provider of skills training.

Most emphatically, participants in social skills training are not passive recipients of a treatment or "cure" but are responsible for their own development. They may be expected to take responsibility for gathering information and practicing skills between formal skills training sessions. They will not be supervised in these tasks but will complete "homework" assignments independently. Much of their learning is expected to occur outside the formal sessions, where these clients will have more of an opportunity to apply the principles in the natural environment.

The therapist's role as teacher merits some discussion. The therapist assumes the role of educator, trainer, and behavior change consultant. As an educator, the therapist uses the treatment situation as an instructional setting to teach both the knowledge and performance of all aspects of social skills. The therapist actively interacts with the members of the skills training group. The therapist explains concepts, demonstrates new ways of thinking and acting, and is actively involved with clients. The blending of therapeutic and educational practice also implies that professionals from a wide range of educational backgrounds can effectively conduct skills training.

Contributions of Psychiatric Rehabilitation

Psychiatric rehabilitation has influenced contemporary social skills training methods. Psychiatric rehabilitation recognizes that many chronic and severe mental disorders can rarely be cured. Nonetheless, people with these disorders can learn skills that will enable them to live active and reward-filled lives despite the disability. Psychiatric rehabilitation does not focus on personality restructuring as do some older models of treatment. Rather, it concentrates on the development of functional behaviors and the teaching of skills.

Social skills training is one of the core practitioner activities associated with psychiatric rehabilitation (Anthony, Cohen, & Farkas, 1990). Although psychiatric rehabilitation has not focused on developing models of skills training, it has influenced the values and philosophy of skills training. Every social skills practitioner should be guided by the following key values of psychiatric rehabilitation (Farkas, O'Brien, Cohen, & Anthony, 1994):

- *Person Orientation.* Social skills training focuses on the whole person, and takes into account both strengths and weaknesses. The person's living environment, including family and friends, may be part of the treatment. Consistent with the person orientation, the focus of social skills training is on enhancing skills rather than eliminating symptoms.

- *Self-Determination.* Highly trained and experienced professionals sometimes begin to believe they can make decisions for clients. Though understandable, since the professional has expertise in psychology and social functioning, this belief is viewed as fallacious. Respect for self-determination involves the recognition that individuals, including those with disabilities, have the capacity and the right to make decisions for themselves. As we mentioned, the failure to support the client's self-determination will undermine the positive orientation of social skills training.

- *Consumer Empowerment.* Social skills training, by its very nature, empowers its recipients. This type of intervention enables individuals to be effective in their environment and to get wants met. It is essential, however, that this philosophy of empowerment permeate all aspects of the training program. For example, a client who can use newly acquired communication skills to disagree with the therapist may be learning the meaning of empowerment. A passive, unquestioning, and submissive patient, although treatment compliant, is not empowered.

- *Everyday Activities.* Psychiatric rehabilitation places high value on the facilitation of functioning in everyday activities. It is less concerned with issues associated with psychiatric diagnosis and symptoms than many other forms of treatment. The field identifies four convenient areas of everyday activities that may be the focus of treatment: living, learning, working, and leisure. Social skills training can be directed toward developing skills for use in these areas.

- *Outcome Orientation.* The behavioral psychology tradition of social skills training focuses on the goals of treatment as well as the process. Thus, communication and problem-solving skills are only effective if they lead to a therapeutic outcome, such as the ability to obtain reinforcements from life. If the prescribed process does not prove to be effective in realizing a given client's treatment goals, changes are appropriate. Treatment should focus on desired treatment goals, not process.

THE STRUCTURE OF SOCIAL SKILLS TRAINING

Now that we have presented the foundations of social skills training, it is appropriate to discuss the general methods and process. Social skills training has four interrelated, but clearly distinguishable, components: Instruction, Supervised Practice, Feedback, and Independent Practice.

Instruction

A distinctive element of this training approach is the clear delineation of the Instruction component. While other social skills training models described in the literature have included instructional components (e.g., Bellack, Turner, Hersen, & Luber, 1984; Liberman, DeRise, & Mueser, 1989), the potential of this aspect of training does not seem to be fully appreciated or used. The current model places emphasis on the Instruction component and provides a foundation for the other three skill training components—Supervised Practice, Feedback, and Independent Practice. The Instruction phase focuses on the systematic teaching of many of the cognitive aspects of social skills and setting the standards for performance and feedback. The cognitive elements of instruction (referred to as "skill concepts") provide standards to help the individual decide what behavior is appropriate to match the situation and then to organize and guide performance.

Instruction may involve both verbal description and behavioral modeling. For clarity of presentation and to emphasize the similarities and differences between verbal instruction and behavioral modeling, we will discuss these two methods of instruction separately. In practice, the therapist uses verbal instruction and behavioral modeling concurrently.

Instruction with Verbal Descriptions

For each social skill being taught, the trainer uses verbal instruction to *define, organize,* and *guide* performance. First, the behavior being taught is *defined* by providing an operational definition of the skill and its major components. For example, when teaching clients how to make an empathic statement (see Chapter 3), we define it as "A statement that expresses our understanding of another's wants and/or feelings." This definition specifies that the empathic statement describes the wants or feelings of *another person* and not those of the speaker. Learning the meaning of concepts such as "want" and "feeling" is part of this skills training program, and these terms would also be taught to the client (see Chapter 2).

The *definition* of empathic statement delineates three types: (a) a statement that reflects the wants of another person, (b) a statement that reflects the feeling(s) that another person is experiencing, and (c) a statement that reflects both the wants and feelings of another person.

The trainer defines the skill being taught by differentiating it from other behaviors with which it might be confused. For example, the trainer might differentiate between an empathic statement and a sympathetic statement by stressing the concept that a sympathetic statement and an empathic statement differ in terms of whether the want(s) and/or feeling(s) of the sender or the receiver of the message are being described. This explanation would clarify the difference between stating another's wants and feelings and one's own.

Information also is provided that will help clients *organize* thinking and behavior associated with a social skill. In the example of the empathic statement, the skilled individual must be able to organize the vast array of information in the environment and attend to those aspects that will help in understanding the wants and/or feelings of the other person. To help clients do this, trainers present five recommendations. Each recommendation focuses on one way an individual can acquire information about another's wants and/or feelings:

1. Listen to the verbal information the other person provides about his or her want(s) and feeling(s).
2. Observe the behavioral cues provided by the other person.
3. Be aware of situational cues.
4. Imagine what you would want or feel if you were the other person.
5. Remember past experiences with the other person. How did the other person feel and what did the person want in prior similar situations?

The trainer then provides templates that the individual can learn to use to *guide* performance. For the empathic statement, clients would be given a guide for patterning these statements with an introductory phrase such as "It seems like . . . ," "I know you . . . ," or "It sounds like. . . ." These "guiding phrases" would help clients begin to communicate an empathic statement. After verbalizing this guiding phrase, clients would learn to complete the statement by indicating the want or feeling attributed to the other person. (e.g., "It seems like . . . you want to get home in a hurry," "I know you . . . are upset about losing your wallet," "It sounds like . . . you are angry and want to get even with your brother.")

The verbal instruction component may also provide guidelines for the appropriate time and place to use a particular social behavior. An empathic statement, for example, is appropriate when (a) an individual wants to show active interest in what another person is saying, (b) when making a request, and (c) when refusing a request from another.

In addition to *defining, organizing,* and *guiding* thinking and behavior, it is often useful in the Instruction phase to describe the possible *consequences* of using the skill being taught. For example, we suggest to clients that the use of the empathic statement promotes the development and maintenance of close positive relationships with others.

Instruction Using Behavioral Modeling

Modeling is also used to teach clients how to define, organize, and guide behavior. In the current program, the therapist uses modeling to provide an example of the behavior he or she has verbally described. The ramifications of social behavior can inordinately complicate a verbal description that covers every element of the skill being taught. For this reason, the main elements are described (defined) verbally, and modeling is a beneficial supplement. The truism, "a picture is worth a thousand words," is applicable, although it is important to mesh verbal instruction and the modeling. Since the overall goal is to help the client develop a clear cognitive map that defines, organizes, and guides behavior, the modeled behavior should illustrate the same concepts that were presented verbally. When teaching the empathic statement, for example, the therapist defines the behavior by modeling empathic and sympathetic remarks that demonstrate the distinguishing characteristics. The three kinds of empathic statement are modeled as well, introduced by the guiding phrases previously mentioned.

Purely cognitive skills, such as the attempt to understand the want or feeling of the other person, are difficult to role-play. In these instances, the instructor verbalizes the thinking process used by the model to demonstrate it (Meichenbaum, 1977).

Combining verbal descriptions and behavioral modeling of skill concepts helps to link cognitive and behavioral aspects of skilled functioning and demonstrates how they augment each other. For example, to demonstrate cognitive and behavioral linkage a model may first recall from memory the definition of an empathic statement (a statement that expresses the wants and feelings of another person) and then make a statement that matches this definition.

In each chapter of this book, we will provide an outline and suggestions for material to present in the Instruction phase. This outline can be developed into a complete presentation by using the information in the chapter.

Supervised Practice

In the Instruction component, the therapist defines a behavior for the client and helps the client understand how to organize information and direct the behavior. In the Supervised Practice component, the trainee has an opportunity to *match,* both cognitively and behaviorally, the model's demonstration of skill concepts. Having received instruction in new ways of thinking and acting, the patient attempts to think and act in the ways described.

Cognitive Aspects of Supervised Practice

Most skilled social behavior requires some cognitive activity prior to performance. This "thinking" component enables the individual to (a) select the appropriate behavior for the situation (e.g., Should I make an empathic or sympathetic statement?), (b) organize behavior (What information do I need to make an empathic statement?), and (c) sequence behavior (What should I do or say first, second, third . . . ?). A proficient, socially skilled person may not need to mentally review all these factors to speak appropriately because well-learned behavior becomes routine and, ultimately, "automatic" (Beck, 1976). For someone learning a new skill, however, the thoughts that define, organize, and guide behavior must be systematically recalled and practiced.

The therapist supervises these cognitive activities by having the client verbalize them. For example, in response to a vignette, the client might engage in the following sequence of thoughts and verbalize them to the therapist (and other therapy group members):

> In this situation, first I have to decide what I want to do. I want to show Bob that I am hearing what he is saying to me and am "tuned in" to him. To do that, I will make an empathic statement. That means I express my understanding of *his* wants or feelings. I don't want to be sympathetic and express *my* feelings. Next, I have to figure out how he feels. I can tell by his behavior that he is fearful (he is talking very fast and said something that sounded like he expected something bad was going to happen to him). Also, my prior knowledge of Bob reminds me that he felt afraid the last time he had a meeting like this with his boss. To be empathic, I'll comment on his feeling of fear. I'll say, "Bob, it sounds like you are really scared of what will happen when you speak to your boss tomorrow."

Behavioral Aspects of Supervised Practice

Systematic behavioral practice is the hallmark of social skills training and is the aspect most frequently described in the social skills training literature (Bedell & Weathers, 1979). In the present model, practice only occurs after the skill concepts that define, organize, and guide behavior have been taught. In our example, the trainee's task is to enact the empathic statement decided on in the cognitive plan, which is, "Bob, it sounds like you are really scared of what will happen when you speak to your boss tomorrow." Repeated practice and observation of others engaged in the same task are provided in two ways. Most commonly, clients use multiple practice vignettes to role-play situations that require performing the social skill being learned. It is also possible to use procedures borrowed from activity therapy and recreational therapy (Ward & Naster, 1991). In this way, the skill to be learned is embedded in a game or recreational activity and practice occurs as the game progresses. This method facilitates repeated practice in a format that reduces the tedium of repetition. Many of the suggested procedures for supervised practice in this book will be based on a cognitive-behavioral application of recreational therapy. Each chapter includes detailed descriptions of activities that will facilitate supervised practice. In many cases, a specially designed game or activity provides the context for conducting supervised practice. In other chapters, vignettes will prompt the practice of an appropriate skill. The supervised practice material throughout the book has been thoroughly tested with clients and has proved effective.

Feedback

Learning cannot occur without feedback to cue clients about their performance. Feedback is provided to the individual from self and others. It is useful to teach clients a specific feedback model for evaluating both one's own performance and that of others.

Feedback is based on an appraisal of the match between one's performance and the skill concepts that define, organize, and guide that behavior. When teaching clients how to give feedback, it is especially important to emphasize the usefulness of commenting on specific aspects of behavior. Feedback should cite the degree to which performance *matched* the skill concepts governing that behavior. Statements such as "that was good" or "I liked what you did" or "I did a nice job," while enhancing motivation do not effectively provide information about specific skills. Comments about specific behaviors (e.g., "Your empathic statement was good because it stated the other person's feeling and not your own") are more efficient forms of feedback.

We also emphasize using feedback that describes ways the behavior *did* and *did not* match the skill concept. When teaching or learning a new skill, the participants often tend to comment only on the deficits of performance. Our Feedback model encourages the individual to comment first on a positive aspect of performance, (i.e., a way it matched or approximated the skill concept), and then to provide a *specific recommendation for change* that would improve performance (a way to more closely match the skill concept). For example, with our empathic statement, an individual might make an erroneous response that does not match the skill concept by saying "Bob, you have so many problems, I feel sorry for you." Appropriate feedback would be "I liked the way you looked directly at Bob as you spoke, and your voice was supportive. However, since you stated how you felt, you made a sympathetic statement. Your statement would have been empathic if you expressed your understanding of how Bob was feeling, not how you were feeling about Bob."

As the preceding comment shows, the Feedback component may include nonverbal as well as verbal behavior. Since communication is defined by how something is expressed as well as what is said, the motor (i.e., facial expressions, body movements) and paralinguistic (rate, volume, pitch of voice) elements that accompany the spoken words are of tantamount importance. Also, when evaluating one's own performance, it is possible to provide feedback on cognitive skills as well as behavioral skills. Thus, when providing self-feedback, a person has access to more information than is available when providing feedback to others.

Finally, though Supervised Practice and Feedback are conceptually distinct phases, in practice they are integrally interwoven. Their combined purpose is to hone skills and maximize proficiency in their use, albeit in a limited environment. To achieve this goal, practice is followed by feedback, which is then incorporated into additional practice. This sequence proceeds until performance is satisfactory.

General guidelines for feedback are provided in each chapter of this book. However, therapists must individualize feedback according to the performance of clients in the therapy setting.

Independent Practice

Independent Practice is the final phase in learning a new skill. This component requires the individual to independently perform all the cognitive and behavioral skills learned in the previous components. Thus, the client acquires experience performing the behavior in the "natural environment" without supervision, supportive guidance, or assurance of a positive response. In this component, as in all the others, there are both cognitive and behavioral elements.

Cognitive Elements of Independent Practice

The cognitive component of Independent Practice requires that the individual recall the skill concepts that help define, organize, and guide behavior. Cognitive aspects are employed prior to actual performance of the skill to prepare and "rehearse" the response and to create appropriate positive expectations. After performing the behavior, the person orients cognitions toward evaluating performance and providing self-feedback. All these cognitive activities are performed by the client without direct supervision and support from the therapist.

Behavioral Component of Independent Practice

The primary goal of the behavioral component of Independent Practice is for the client to actually perform the social skill behaviors without direct supervision or feedback from the therapist. Clients are encouraged to practice the new behaviors in a series of increasingly difficult settings, not only in terms of the situational characteristics, but also in the degree of positive reaction the client is likely to receive. Practice settings are graduated, beginning with situations that have high probability of successful performance and positive outcome, to those situations that are more difficult and problematic. For example, "Joan," who has just demonstrated mastery of the empathic statement concept, is faced with the challenge of learning to use it in day-to-day practice. The therapist may first assign the task of making an empathic statement in a setting outside the therapy group to a staff member who is associated with the skills training program. Next, Joan may try out her new skills on a staff member not associated with the skills training program, but known to be warm and supportive. As Joan is successful, she may practice with a "socially skilled" person in her social network. The process proceeds as Joan practices her new skills with other individuals who are naive to the social skills program. She avoids practicing the skills in a setting with a high probability of conflict and rejection until the skills become well integrated into her repertoire. When Joan can perform the desired communication and problem-solving skills in the natural environment, treatment for these skills is considered to be complete. Long-term follow-up and support may help her maintain the skills.

In the following chapters, we provide suggestions for structuring independent practice. It is important, however, to direct independent practice of skills to the individual treatment goals of each client.

Although these four components are considered to be separate, sequential steps in the training process, they usually are intermingled in actual practice and it is difficult to discern their sequence. For example, feedback is generally provided after the Instruction phase and during the Supervised Practice phases. This is followed by the Independent Practice phase. However, it may be desirable to repeat the Instruction, Supervised Practice and Feedback phases of training a number of times before proceeding to the Independent Practice phase. In general, however, trainers adhere to the basic training sequence, as it is both practical and logical, and maximizes skill acquisition. Information relevant to the skills initially presented didactically and learned conceptually (Instruction phase) are practiced in the protective, corrective environment (Supervised Practice and Feedback), and then applied in the natural environment (Independent Practice) until the skilled behavior reaches the desired criterium of performance. In this process, many of these steps may need to be repeated.

NONSPECIFIC ASPECTS OF SOCIAL SKILLS TRAINING: RESISTANCE, TRANSFERENCE, AND COUNTERTRANSFERENCE

The preceding section described the recommended structure and process of social skills training. As with every model of psychotherapy, however, other significant "nonspecific" treatment factors must be considered. Resistance, transference, and countertransference are integral factors in treatment, yet skills training programs seldom describe these three topics because they are concepts developed in the psychodynamic tradition, which has quite different goals and procedures. We have included them here, however, based on our experiences teaching professional staff about social skills training. Many professionals who are interested in learning about social skills training are not well educated in the social learning and cognitive-behavioral models that underlie these procedures. They are trained in psychodynamic approaches and are accustomed to formulating therapy from a dynamic perspective. Resistance, transference, and countertransference are central to psychodynamic therapy.

Individuals trained in these models have difficulty accepting the validity of any therapy that does not include these concepts. Trainees have often commented that, although the skills training approach seems well formulated, it is of limited sophistication since it does not appear to focus on important issues in the relationship between patient and therapist. Worse yet, the failure to include information on resistance and transference is interpreted as meaning that social skills trainers know nothing about these concepts and do not use them in treatment.

People reach these incorrect conclusions because presentations of social skills training often do not include information about the interpersonal processes and nonspecific treatment components. These process variables, however, exist in skills training therapy and play an important role in treatment. Every effective skills trainer is knowledgeable about and deals with resistance to treatment and interpersonal issues between the patient and therapist. It is a serious mistake to think that skills training treatment is simply a set of practices involving instructions or coaching, live modeling, taped modeling, simple rehearsal, role-play rehearsal, verbal feedback, videotaped feedback, interpersonal reinforcement, and homework assignments (as described in this book). Skills training is an active, dynamic, therapeutic milieu containing all the elements of other forms of individual and group therapy. The social skills trainer is expected to be knowledgeable and sophisticated in interpersonal process issues. The following sections describe how the social skills trainer approaches resistance, transference, and countertransference.

Considered broadly, the phenomena of resistance, transference, and countertransference are integral to any social interaction, including those that occur in skills training therapy. The construct of resistance deals with the observation that some clients, although apparently motivated to learn new skills and behaviors, also act in ways that interfere with treatment and disrupt progress. Transference describes a process in which the client relates to the therapist and other treatment components in an inappropriate and dysfunctional way based on beliefs and expectations carried over from prior learning situations. Countertransference describes a similar process in which the therapist responds to the client according to unrealistic beliefs and inappropriate expectations not based on an accurate perception of the client.

The broad concepts that are the basis of resistance, transference, and countertransference are just as valid and important to the social skills trainer as they are to the psychodynamic therapist. Inevitably, the skills trainer will be confronted with each of these three phenomena at some point in treatment and must deal with them effectively if the client is going to obtain the maximum benefit from treatment. Simply having competence in the technical skills needed to carry out the communication and problem-solving procedures in this book is not enough. An effective skills trainer must also be able to deal with dysfunctional interpersonal situations that arise during treatment. The significant elements of resistance, transference, and countertransference can be well understood and treated within the social learning and cognitive-behavioral models that underlie this program. There is no need to resort to the psychodynamic interpretations of these concepts to understand and use them therapeutically.

Therapists should become comfortable in understanding and using social learning and cognitive-behavioral concepts when dealing with resistance, transference, and countertransference. Using psychodynamic language and concepts to explain events that occur in a social skills training program implies that the social learning and cognitive-behavioral models are inadequate to describe and treat these phenomena, which is not accurate. Additionally, this practice will prevent therapists from developing full competency in diagnosing and treating these problems with a learning theory model. To gain competence in the use of these models, therapists must study and apply them where appropriate.

Moreover, in the context of a communications and problem-solving skills training program, interpersonal and resistance problems should be resolved through use of the skills being taught. The emergence of resistance, transference, and countertransference provides an ideal opportunity to demonstrate the utility and effectiveness of social skills applied to real problems that exist in the client's life.

In the following sections, we will explain the constructs of resistance, transference, and countertransference in terms of both the original psychodynamic concepts and the social learning and behavioral model. We will also describe methods of dealing effectively with these issues using the communication and problem-solving models advocated here.

Resistance

Social skills trainers, and indeed all psychotherapists, have observed the tendency of many clients to reject their helpful efforts. The clients have usually expressed an interest in participating in the skills training program and appear to be motivated to improve their current level of functioning. Yet, they engage in various subtle and overt actions that undermine and sabotage the therapist's efforts.

There are many examples of such behaviors. Patients may constantly attempt to socialize or discuss topics not relevant to the training material. Or they may continually introduce other psychological problems not related to the current content of the program. Despite having pervasive communication problems, the client may be unable to think of personal examples of communication or problem-solving difficulties that could appropriately become the focus of the skills training group. The client may "forget" to do homework assignments designed for practice of new skills and may shift from topic to topic, making progress impossible in any one area of desired change. Irregular therapy attendance may interfere with the continuity of treatment. These behaviors, frequently referred to as resistance, indirectly interfere with the process of skills training and the recipient's learning of adaptive skills.

The therapist cannot ignore resistance or treatment goals will not be attained and the new behaviors will not be learned. However, it is not appropriate to dismiss the individual as "a treatment-resistant patient" and accept the lack of therapeutic progress. Nor is it appropriate to blame the client or determine that the person's disability is the cause of any lack of progress. It is also incorrect to exclude from treatment a client identified as treatment resistant. The problem of resistance pervades psychotherapy and has no simple or widely accepted solutions. A skilled therapist will recognize and understand the basis of the resistance and take action to overcome it. Some recommendations follow for understanding and working with this phenomenon.

First of all, therapists should determine whether the observed behavior is best characterized as resistance or some other factor. What seems to be resistance to treatment may be the client's general response style in diverse non-treatment-related situations. Apparent treatment resistance may actually be a stable pattern of behavior that demonstrates how the individual copes with stress.

A social skills training group undoubtedly produces stress, as does any psychotherapeutic intervention. The skills training program, by its very nature, presents threats and pressures. Simply being enrolled in a skills training program implies communication or problem-solving difficulties and can trigger feelings of incompetence and low self-esteem. In the skills training program, clients are expected to learn new ways of understanding thoughts, feelings, and actions and how they interact with each other. They are expected to talk about thoughts, feelings, and behaviors, role-play unfamiliar skills, receive feedback on performance,

and try new behaviors in situations where a negative reaction is anticipated. Although the therapist tries to introduce material at a rate clients
can manage and, in other ways, reduce the stress of the program, this is
an anxiety-provoking situation for anyone.

From a cognitive-behavioral perspective, resistant behavior may also
result from an *expectation* that participation in treatment may result in
something undesirable such as failure or criticism. This expectation
leads to avoidance of the behavior that is possibly associated with the
undesired outcome. When the individual's expectation seems to be irrational or unrealistic, it may be considered to be resistance.

It is inevitable that the social skills trainer will encounter resistant behaviors at some point. What can be done? First of all, it may be helpful
to reveal to the client the observed pattern of resistant behavior. The description should objectively identify the problem behaviors in a nonjudgmental way, not as signs of failure, manipulation, or ill intent on the
part of the client. They exist in the behavioral rapporteur because of
prior learning experiences. It should be emphasized that some degree of
resistance is a normal reaction to change, which includes acquiring self-
awareness and learning new communication and problem-solving skills.
It is usually helpful to validate the client's fear by pointing out the wide
variety of new things the person is being called on to do (e.g., talk about
problems, think about things in a cognitive-behavioral way, role-play in
front of others).

The therapist should stress to the client that fear and anxiety dissi-
pate with repeated exposure to new experiences. Also, as skills are acquired, self-confidence increases and anxiety diminishes. Therefore,
clients can expect their fears to decrease as they progress through the
skills-training program.

Clients may be encouraged to recall past experiences that illustrate
how exposure and practice reduced anxiety and avoidance. This information will add to the credibility of the therapist's prediction that things
will get better. The therapist may also point out that clients must experience some anxiety and discomfort if they are going to change and improve. It would be unrealistic to expect to uproot ingrained behaviors
without some effort and difficulty.

The therapist needs to direct this kind of attention to client resistance
on a regular basis. Clients will benefit from observing the therapist's con-
viction that the skills training process will work and that people can improve themselves. This approach is likely to change negative expectations

to those of success and improvement and will help overcome the resistance. A fundamental attitude of optimism is an essential characteristic for a social skills trainer and is critical in dealing with resistance to treatment.

The attitudes, beliefs, and demeanor of the therapist are important in helping clients to cope with and learn from resistance. The therapist who is discouraged, angered, and dismayed by resistance will communicate this attitude to clients in subtle but discernible ways. The pessimism of the therapist will reinforce and validate the negative expectations and fears of clients, perpetuating and perhaps strengthening their resistance.

Resistance is also related to a fear of making choices based on the individual's deep-seated belief that he or she is incapable of making them. Throughout this book, we mention issues of "client choice." Choice is a fundamental value in social skills training; a primary goal is to give people the skills that will enhance their ability to make choices in life. The belief that one cannot make choices is usually unrealistic, self-destructive, and limiting. To the extent that clients believe they have choices and learn to make them in a way that maximizes their well-being, the need to resist treatment will diminish.

A final recommendation is for the therapist to provide appropriate feedback about observed changes in resistance over time. When the client makes progress, the therapist should acknowledge it. Also, positive changes should be noted and remembered by the therapist. This information will be useful at a future time, when the client may be feeling hopeless about treatment. A reminder of the positive changes that the client has accomplished in the past will help disconfirm the patient's hopelessness.

Transference

As we mentioned, transference is not typically associated with social skills training therapies. And, the behavior therapy and rehabilitation models on which social skills training is based do not employ this concept. However, an application of the broad concepts related to transference is appropriate and beneficial to the social skills trainer.

Transference is a concept derived from psychodynamic theory. The relationship between patient and therapist is of central importance to all practitioners of psychodynamic therapy. Within this model, transference is the process in which the patient reacts to the therapist as though he or she were some other important person in the patient's past, such as a mother or father. The patient essentially performs a mental substitution of one person for another. In dynamic theories, transference is considered to be a process involving a *reactivation* of attitudes once harbored toward others and now brought into the relationship with the therapist.

Early theorists wondered why people would react toward their therapist as though the therapist were someone else. Transference was variously believed to (a) arise from a basic human tendency to return to previous states of organization (Freud, 1942), (b) represent the reemployment of patterns of behavior previously associated with the avoidance of anxiety (Sullivan, 1953), and (c) be a carryover from earlier relationships with the family doctor, dentist, or minister (Fromm-Reichmann, 1950).

Within a learning theory model, transference is considered to be the process by which a person overgeneralizes from one situation to another. Expectations that are appropriate in one environment are transferred to another where they are inconsistent with reality. A behavior or attitude may be learned in response to one situation (comprising people, places, and activities) that provides certain rewards and punishments. The pattern of reward and punishment in this situation results in certain behaviors being strengthened and retained, and others being eliminated. In learning this pattern of outcomes, the individual develops the expectation that similar patterns are present in other similar situations. Where the situations are in fact similar, in that contingencies of reinforcement are the same, the transfer of expectations is appropriate. Known as generalization, this process is adaptive, because the person does not have to relearn how to think and act in every new situation but instead, can apply prior learning to similar new situations. Inappropriately applying expectations and associated behaviors to a situation that is not like the original one, however, is overgeneralizing and results in inappropriate behavior for the new situation. This behavior may be referred to as transference.

Processes described as transference may occur in any interpersonal situation and are therefore a normal part of human interaction. Nevertheless, people differ in the degree to which they overgeneralize or fail to discriminate and thus respond inappropriately to a person or situation.

Although the specific etiology and meaning of transference phenomena may vary between cognitive-behavioral and psychodynamic therapists, there can be no doubt that the relationship between the therapist and the client is an important element of both types of treatment. The relationship is important above and beyond the specific psychodynamic and cognitive-behavioral treatment techniques employed.

Many similarities are apparent in the interpersonal dynamics that develop between the therapist and client in skills training and psychodynamic therapy despite their differences in the form, process, and goals. Most important, the two types of therapy establish an interpersonal situation in which two or more people meet for the purpose of changing the client's patterns of thinking, feeling, and acting. This interpersonal situation involves a power and authority differential between the therapist and the client. The therapist is the expert who directs the treatment and is believed to have the greater knowledge and skill about the change process. It is easy for the client to perceive the therapist as an authority figure and to respond accordingly.

At the same time, there are expectations that the client will reveal "dysfunctional" aspects of thinking and behavior. In this situation, the therapist usually does not explore his or her own dysfunctional attributes, so the relationship is unbalanced. And, to overcome dysfunctional habits, the client is required to function in new, unfamiliar, and unaccustomed ways, a process usually accompanied by both success and failure. The latter is likely to arouse feelings of inadequacy and frustration in both the client and the therapist, but more so in the client. Other dynamics, too numerous to mention here, are set in motion by the therapy milieu. But even considering only those factors mentioned, skills training therapy is a complex interpersonal process that gives rise to complicated goals and expectations. At the least, skills training is stressful and likely to arouse anxiety in the client.

Initially, clients may reasonably be expected to relate to the therapist in the same way they learned to relate to other authority figures. The way they relate is based on expectations developed as a function of experiences (rewards and punishment) with other authority figures. People vary in how they relate to authority because of varying prior experiences, which lead to response differences. Clients who have had prior relationships that were uniformly positive, supportive, and nurturing will have expectations consistent with this history. They will be relaxed and confident in the therapy setting and will expect to be treated positively. Clients whose previous relationships have primarily been critical and punitive will expect to be criticized and punished and will be tense and anxious. A client who has had a range of experiences with varied authorities may be more flexible than the individual who has had more restricted experiences. The expectations people bring to the therapy or skills training situation will reflect the multitude of different learning experiences in their background.

Clients' expectations and patterns of behavior will be those that have seemingly enabled them to maximize pleasure and minimize pain. Because of the apparent "success" of these beliefs and behaviors, they are brought into the new and untested relationship. Clients, especially those with severe psychological problems, may rigidly hold to stereotypic expectations, distorting all information that is inconsistent with these predetermined beliefs. Also, they may primarily focus on those elements of the current situation that support these unrealistic expectations.

For example, "Joe," the social skills trainer, may tell clients he will provide feedback on their performance so that they can learn the skills being taught. "Bill," a client who has learned that authority figures are sources of punishment may interpret this statement to mean that Joe wants to be critical and punitive. Bill would then respond as though Joe were threatening him rather than attempting to be helpful. Also, Bill might narrow his focus and selectively attend to the information provided by Joe. This biased focus might cause him to put inordinate weight on one or two critical statements made by Joe. These few statements may both activate the expectations that the authority figure will be punitive, and support its validity. This perception of Joe as critical and punitive would thus continue although Joe is generally positive, supportive, and complimentary toward Bill.

Functionally, it makes no difference whether Bill's distortion is overly positive or negative. It is no better for the client to expect therapist feedback to be consistently accurate and helpful than it is to assume it will always be faulty and of no value. Neither distortion is likely to match reality. Joe, the therapist, is not all knowing and perfect any more than he is incompetent and ignorant. The two sides of transference are positive and negative, neither of which is adaptive. The goal of skills training is to enable the individual to respond to a relationship in an accurate and realistic way.

The goal of the social skills trainer, therefore, is to be alert to client behavior that may reflect distorted expectations of the therapist's intentions and performance. When such behavior is observed, the therapist should (a) attempt to empathize with the client, (b) provide feedback including a description of the behavior as well as its effect on the therapist, and (c) ask the client to explain the basis of the expectation.

For example, Bill may refuse to participate in the role-play practice portion of the training program, stating that he does not like to perform in front of others. Joe's response would be different according to when this reaction occurs. If it happens during the initial sessions, it might not be considered a transference reaction since many people respond this way at first. If the hesitation readily subsides, there is no interference with treatment.

During early therapy sessions, a refusal to participate would result in a description of role-play procedure to ensure that Bill understands what is expected. The therapist would emphasize the importance of the role-play in the learning of communication and problem-solving skills. Bill's reluctance would be accepted as an understandable concern that may have been based on prior distressing classroom-type situations. The therapist would clearly explain, however, that this skills training group is carefully designed to be supportive and helpful and will not overload Bill with tasks he cannot perform. In addition, Joe would stress that Bill will eventually be expected to participate in the role-play practice just like every other member of the skills training group because repeated exposure to the therapist, the group, and the procedure will, in time, allow him to become comfortable in that situation. Finally, Joe would ask Bill to observe other group members as they role-play to see whether their actions disconfirm the concern that is the basis of his reluctance. Bill will observe the therapist behaving in a way that will demonstrate caring, objectivity, and helpfulness rather than punitiveness.

Suppose, however, that Bill is not willing to participate in the role-play practice even after long exposure to the group. At this point, it may be suspected that transferential issues are at work; Bill appears to be relating to the therapist and the group in a way that is inconsistent with his actual experiences in the group. Bill is apparently acting on beliefs and expectations from some other experiences in the past that have a deleterious effect on treatment. This conclusion would be based on the assumption that the actions of the therapist and the group do not justify the client's response.

In this situation, Joe would initially empathize with Bill, indicating that he understands how difficult it is to be evaluated in public, then give him feedback by describing the behavior to be changed, and its negative effect (Bill's reluctance to role-play limits the benefit from group, isolates him, and prevents him from contributing to others). Finally, Joe would ask what he, the group, or Bill could do to facilitate his performance. At this point, Joe might ask Bill to (a) describe his wants and expectations regarding his participation in the role-play practice, (b) describe the experiences of the clients he has observed participating in this activity, and (c) indicate how much his wants and expectations coincide with these observations. If he expects Joe to give him a task he cannot perform, he would be asked to indicate if there is any evidence to support this expectation, based on his observations of how Joe interacted with other group members during the past therapy sessions. If Bill indicates that there has been no evidence but expects he would be treated differently from the others, this expectation would also be questioned on its validity. Bill would be asked why he thinks he would receive different treatment than the others. If, after going through this process, the client changes his expectations and looks forward to having the same positive experiences, this would be reinforced and supported, and the role play would be planned.

If Bill continues to expect to have a negative experience, he will be expected to test these expectations within the group. At this point, Joe may give Bill the firm but supportive directive that he will be expected to participate in some way, even minor, in a role-play during the next meeting of the skills group. Joe would explain that part of the purpose of having Bill engage in the role-play is to see if his expectations and concerns will be confirmed or disconfirmed.

When Bill engages in the role-play, Joe should ask him to choose how he wants to participate. Different ways of participating, such as being the main character, secondary character, or observer who only gives feedback, will differ in the amount of stress the client experiences. Different types of participation may also differentially arouse the transferential material. Offering a choice also provides the client with a degree of control over what he does, an experience that is beneficial in its own right.

In addition, this procedure allows Bill to experience a gradual and progressive exposure to the role play. He may start as an observer who gives feedback, then act as the secondary character, and finally, act as the main character. Perhaps he will be the observer giving feedback five times before progressing to the next level. Perhaps he will begin his participation by only reading the role-play vignette and setting the scene. The rate of progression will vary according to the person.

This procedure will change Bill's unrealistic expectations by allowing him to have a personal disconfirming experience. Progressive exposure will not overwhelm Bill with an overly difficult task he cannot perform, which would likely reinforce the concern that is the basis of the transference. After the role-play, it would also be important to have Bill (or any client with transference difficulties) state how his experience disconfirmed prior beliefs and expectations.

If the procedure described, with its firm but supportive demand for performance, were not followed, Bill likely would continue to avoid participation. The reduced feelings of anxiety associated with the avoidance of a feared task reinforce the belief that the only way to cope with the transference issue is through avoidance. Also, the self-observation of failure to perform in an area where other group members are able, would support a self-defeating and self-deprecating pattern of thinking. Both of these unfortunate outcomes should be prevented if possible.

Transference of this type can be taxing for the therapist. A cognitive-behavioral therapist, as any other, would be expected to work with this client with sensitivity and patience. However, any therapist faced with a difficult case can become frustrated and angry, and subtly act out these feelings toward the client. Support and patience may give way to impatience, sarcasm, and resentment. These feelings and actions represent countertransference, the topic of the next section.

Countertransference

The concept of countertransference, originally conceived by psychodynamic therapists, is relevant to social skills trainers. The phenomenon of countertransference is considered to be an interpersonal development analogous to transference. In fact, Ruesch (1961) indicated that counter-transference was transference in reverse. In its original conceptualization, it was believed to be an unconscious process in which the therapist distorted his perception of the client or experienced some unrealistic reaction to him. The function of countertransference, it was proposed, was to enable the therapist to maintain self-esteem, prestige, and approval, and to avoid the anxiety experienced when these states of being were threatened.

Psychodynamically, countertransference may occur, for example, when a young inexperienced therapist fails to recognize the extreme dependence of a client, a characteristic apparent to any objective observer. The therapist sees strengths where none exist and ignores indications of vulnerability. This distortion is hypothesized to reflect the therapist's unconscious fear of being unable to satisfy all the client's needs. Thus, the countertransferencal distortions of the client's behavior protect the therapist from anxiety related to the fear of failure.

From a cognitive-behavioral perspective, we can expand the concept of countertransference to include any beliefs or expectations the therapist has about the client that are unrealistic or are not supported by objective observations. In psychodynamic models, countertransference is considered to be an unconscious process. In the present system, irrational or unrealistic beliefs are often "automatic" (Beck, 1976) because they are so well learned. They are generally in the preconscious, not currently in consciousness, but always available to it.

Irrational or unrealistic beliefs about a client in a given situation are a product of overgeneralization based on the therapist's inappropriate application of beliefs and expectations from prior learning experiences. The therapist is perceiving more similarities between past and present than actually exist.

Countertransference can occur in many ways, but the stereotyping of individuals is a common element. Thus, in the classic examples of countertransference, the therapist responds to the client as though he were a child, friend, or lover from the past. In the present model as well, this form of countertransference may develop by generalizing beliefs and attitudes from former relationships to current ones.

In mental health, diagnostic assignment to categories can provide general information to the therapist about potential characteristics of the client. Diagnostic labels, however, increase the risk of stereotyping. This occurs when the therapist begins to base beliefs and expectations about a client on membership in a class or group, rather than on the individual's unique attributes. Thus, the therapist's expectations of the client are based on a general belief about how the group to which the patient has been assigned thinks and acts. To maintain the accuracy of these generalized expectations, the therapist may selectively attend to those client behaviors that support the expectations. For example, the therapist may diagnose a client with schizophrenia. A therapist who believes schizophrenic individuals have cognitive deficits that prevent them from developing social skills may be overly influenced by observations supportive of this view when perceiving such a client. In reality, however, the client may exhibit a broad range of behaviors, only a small portion of which are unskilled. Moreover, the client could improve in this area of functioning with the proper training.

As just described, countertransference occurs when a therapist perceives the client as representative of a pathological group with a diagnostic label. But why would therapists use diagnostic categories in this inappropriate and harmful way? One reason is that they give therapists the illusion of knowledge about their clients. This fund of information empowers therapists with a belief in their ability to predict, and possibly control, a client's behavior. In addition, this fund of information, based on a sophisticated classification system, supports therapists' superior authority. These perceptions of prediction, control, and authority (among others) tend to reduce anxiety and provide a sense of well-being. So, a therapist may benefit psychologically. But since the therapist's perception of the client is not based on the actual skills and abilities of the person, this distortion will potentially interfere with treatment.

Countertransference is also likely when the therapist works with individuals who have severe and persistent disabilities or skill deficits. Clients who do not respond as expected to therapeutic efforts can stimulate a countertransference reaction if the therapist attributes lack of progress to his or her own incompetence, or responds with feelings of frustration and anger.

Bill, the client who refused to participate in role-play practice is a good illustration. He maintained a false belief that he would be punished or ridiculed if he attempted to perform in front of others and maintained this transferential belief despite the best therapeutic efforts. Such a situation can be difficult for the therapist. Joe—the therapist—might have questioned his skills or felt frustrated and angry. While the helping relationship requires maintenance of the therapist's warmth, empathy, and unconditional positive regard, countertransferential issues may limit, or even preclude, this occurrence. Joe might have become overly critical of Bill and failed to recognize Bill's attempts to change his behavior. Alternatively, Joe might have overlooked significant skill deficits and expected Bill to progress according to the therapist's timetable. It is even possible that Joe would terminate treatment because Bill did not progress at the "expected" rate.

While it is important to be alert to the development of irrational and distorted beliefs about the motives and abilities of the client, it is equally important to not suppress or deny feelings of frustration, or feel compelled to hide them from the client. Nor should the therapist think it is wrong to be frustrated by a client who is not responding to treatment as hoped and expected. Instead, the therapist should evaluate these thoughts and expectations to determine whether or not they are reasonable and realistic. If they are not, they may be countertransference and should be modified to be more realistic. If, however, the therapist's feelings and expectations seem to be based on realistic information about the client, it may be assumed that they resemble the experiences of others who interact with the client. Thus, an awareness of these reactions can be a useful part of therapy and may facilitate the skills training process.

For example, "Susan," a therapist, could become aware of her increasing annoyance at "Ellen," her client who refused to take any kind of leadership role in the skills training group. Whenever requested to do so, Ellen would demur saying that she did not understand the information well enough to take such a role. She always claimed that someone else would do a better job. The therapist's observations contradicted this self-appraisal because Ellen appeared to be quite intelligent and comfortable expressing herself in other social situations. When Susan described her reaction to this inconsistency in Ellen's behavior, Ellen admitted that she had been told this by other people in her life. Her reluctance, it was later learned, was based on a fear that, if she did well in the skills training group, people would begin to expect more and more of her and she would eventually fail and disappoint everyone. Ellen believed that it was better to do poorly so that people would not expect much and, therefore, could not become disappointed and angry with her. The therapist's feeling of annoyance had helped to identify this client's irrational and self-limiting belief, which extended to other parts of her life. Correcting this self-defeating belief could now become a positive goal of treatment in the skills training program. The treatment approach described in Chapter 8 would appropriately be adapted for use with this type of problem.

As illustrated in this example, the therapist should always evaluate his or her own reaction to a client's behavior. If the therapist then determines that a response to the client is relatively typical of others, and not grossly distorted, then the client's behavior may become the target of social skills training. The therapist would (a) initially attempt to empathize with the client, then (b) give feedback regarding the effect of this behavior, and (c) request a behavioral change and ask how the therapist and others could help.

A therapist whose feelings are due to countertransference, would handle the situation somewhat differently. The therapist may point out the countertransference to the patient in a constructive way that would give the client feedback. The therapist might say, "When you continually refuse to participate in the role-play practice part of the training, I feel frustrated and angry. I realize this is an overreaction, and my expectation of you to perform publicly right now is unrealistic. You must feel pressured, which only adds to your anxiety. If we work together, I'm sure we'll be able to help you learn all the necessary skills at a pace that is comfortable and appropriate for you. Meanwhile, if you continue to feel pressured, or observe behavior that reflects my anger, please give me feedback so I can change accordingly." In this response, the therapist (a) admits being in error (b) expresses empathy, and requests from the client both (c) collaboration in helping the client achieve goals, and (d) feedback about any repetition of the countertransferencal error under discussion.

This kind of communication demonstrates the therapist's openness, honesty, and genuine desire to help clients resolve their difficulties in an optimally safe environment. When handled in this way, issues of countertransference can add to the credibility of the therapist and facilitate the therapeutic process.

SUMMARY

In this chapter, we have presented the philosophical and historical roots of social skills training, the structure of treatment, and some of the nonspecific interpersonal aspects of skills training therapy. This information should help the reader understand the chapters that follow. Each chapter builds on the ones before, adding more tools to the therapist's repertoire. In Chapter 2, we will explore methods for teaching self-awareness skills. The chapter also includes a detailed example of how to conduct a skills training session teaching these skills.

2

Self-Awareness
A Foundation for Communication and Problem-Solving

SELF-AWARENESS

One need only be human to know that people constantly monitor the events going on around and inside themselves. People evaluate, organize, analyze, and plan in a stream of contemplative activity. These complex functions occur over long periods and involve information related to past and present events. Over the course of a lifetime, the individual develops a system for organizing and understanding information that determines his or her view of the world and the self. This process of reviewing, understanding, organizing, and making sense of internal events, and the way they influence interaction with the environment, is what is referred to in this book as self-awareness. This chapter presents a cognitive-behavioral system for self-awareness that facilitates effective communication and problem solving.

Because self-awareness provides the individual with a perception and understanding of thoughts, feelings, and behaviors, it requires vigilance and observation of internal and external events related to the self. This watchful alertness enables the person to draw inferences and create understanding about the self in the past, present, and future. The more real

41

and emotion-laden this process, the more potent will be its impact (Yalom, 1995).

As defined here, self-awareness is related to, but different from, insight and self-understanding. Insight often results from unconscious processes, and when attained, it leads to overt changes in personality and behavior (Beck & Freeman, 1990). In comparison, self-awareness is a conscious and purposeful process that does not have an automatic impact on behavior. Rather, it provides the material that is the basis of behavior control and change. Self-awareness goes beyond intellectual understanding to involve awareness also at the affective and behavioral levels.

Communication

Communication may be broadly defined as the transmission of information and the exchange of ideas. Communication skills include abilities to initiate conversations, maintain social interactions, express one's thoughts and feelings to others, and accurately comprehend the expressions of others. This book does not attempt to deal with all areas of communication, an extremely broad concept that permeates all aspects of human social functioning. Rather, it focuses on a set of skills that will enable the individual to use language to (a) obtain rewards with the greatest frequency, (b) perform undesirable tasks at a minimum, and (c) develop and maintain mutually supportive and beneficial relationships. Fully functional people use communication for these purposes.

Conceptual Plan of Self-Awareness Training

Although this approach to communication skills is designed to help people obtain rewards and avoid performing undesired tasks, it does not foster selfish, overbearing, or self-serving behavior. Quite to the contrary, this program is based on principles of assertiveness, empathy, and cooperation. Helping people use communication to obtain the things they want from life enables them to develop self-efficacy expectations (Bandura 1969; Bandura & Walters, 1963). As people develop social skills that are effective in obtaining rewards from the environment, they begin to have positive expectations of success and control. This sense of self-efficacy is generally associated with adaptive functioning. The ability to communicate effectively is inexorably tied to the development of self-efficacy.

Attaining a degree of self-awareness, which is the first step in learning effective communication skills, involves the recognition, labeling, and organization of one's own thoughts, feelings, and behaviors. To facilitate awareness of these complex phenomena, we will attempt to simplify them. The simplification process strengthens the individual's ability to use internal information, sharpens his or her focus on a few sources of useful information, and helps the person avoid attending to irrelevant information.

The first step in simplification is to provide a small number of categories for placement of information. In this program, three broad kinds of information are of interest: thoughts (cognitions), feelings (affect), and behaviors (actions). Thoughts, feelings, and behaviors are considered to be the totality of self-information available to the individual. Defining thoughts, feelings, and behaviors so that they represent meaningful and useful categories is the subject of much of this chapter.

Once we have developed the basic categories of thoughts, feelings, and behaviors, we will discuss the interaction and interrelationships among them. Understanding these interrelationships helps to provide predictability and order to these phenomena. It also helps clients use information about one type of experience (e.g., thoughts) to understand another (e.g., feelings); if certain expectations are known to be paired with certain feeling states, the knowledge of either the expectation or the feeling will provide information about the other member of the pair. The chapter concludes with the organization of self-awareness information into a series of thought-feeling-behavior triads.

BASIC ELEMENTS OF SELF-AWARENESS

The Concept of a Thought

We have tried to develop a useful definition of a thought that enables people to understand and organize the plethora of cognitive events that occur throughout the day. There is no one accepted definition of a thought, and we do not claim that the one used here is "scientifically correct." Our emphasis here is on providing practical, useful information that will assist people in developing self-awareness.

When discussing thoughts (and feelings and behaviors, as well), it is important to remember that they are constructs, not factual events. As noted by Nunnally (1967), a construct describes a variable that is abstract, rather than concrete. Such a variable "is something the scientist puts together from his own imagination, something that does not exist as an isolated, observable dimension of behavior" (p. 85). Therefore, a thought has been defined as "a message from the brain that expresses a want, expectation, comparison, description, or evaluation." To be aware of thoughts, the individual listens to the mind's internal dialogue and learns to recognize the five kinds of mentation: wants, expectations, comparisons, descriptions, and evaluations. The following are examples:

1. *Want.* "I want Jim to like me," "I want to make a clear presentation at the meeting tomorrow," "I wish I could get this job," "I would like to earn more money," "Before going to the grocery store, let's stop at the post office."

2. *Expectation.* "I am going to have fun at Sally's party," "My parents will be angry if I am late," "If I do a good job, people will respect me," "Don't worry, I can take care of that."

3. *Comparison.* "This book reminds me of the one I read last year," "I like being with Bill better than Pete."

4. *Description.* "This is the fifth time I have tried this phone number," "The people sitting at that table are wearing black and white skirts."

5. *Evaluation.* "I don't like this party," "These people are fun to be with," "This test is hard."

Classifying thoughts into these five categories helps people gain control over their internal dialogue. With categorization, they move from viewing mentation as random, uncontrolled and, perhaps, bewildering, to realizing that mentation can be organized, classified, and analyzed to better understand the inner workings of the self.

To identify the type of thought, it is often helpful for people to ask themselves, "Is this a want?" "Is this an expectation?" "Is this a comparison" and so on until the information fits and the answer is "yes." In many cases, the cognition may be an evaluation or description of a feeling or behavior, such as "I feel anxious" or "I avoided Jim at the party last night." An evaluation, comparison, or description of a feeling or behavior is still a thought; wanting or expecting to feel or act in a certain way is also a thought.

Reorganizing thoughts by defining them as wants, expectations, comparisons, and so on may be likened to learning to use a library. Like the mind, the rows and stacks of books in a library contain valuable information, but the sheer amount of information (and the number of books) is overwhelming. How can a person access all this information? Once he or she learns that the books may be classified into fiction and nonfiction and arranged by subject and author, the information is less overwhelming and becomes potentially usable. This is the process employed in the present system of self-awareness training. In the case of thoughts, the information is placed into one of five categories. Each category tells the individual what process is occurring (e.g., comparing, evaluating) and thus provides self-information.

The Primacy of Wants and Expectations

Of the five kinds of thoughts identified, *wants* and *expectations* are central to understanding the self from the perspective of cognitive therapy and social learning theory. Therefore, much greater emphasis is placed on these two categories of thought than the other three.

The Want

When people want something, they experience a desire. Words such as wish, desire, crave, and demand express the concept of a want. The want is a cognitive representation of a situation or object that, if it occurs or is obtained, results in the experience of *reward*. For example, if a man wants his roommate to accompany him to the grocery store, he will feel rewarded or satisfied if that circumstance comes about. If, on the other hand, the want is not realized, the person experiences a state of deprivation or frustration.

The object (or circumstance) wanted (the reward desired) functions as an incentive. Developing increased self-awareness of wants helps people to better understand those phenomena and circumstances that are rewarding, motivating, and frustrating. Because of its relationship with reward and motivation, recognition of wants helps clients to be goal directed toward the satisfaction of unmet wants and the concurrent experience of reinforcement. As will be presented in Chapter 7, the facilitation of goal-directedness is an important part of the problem-solving process.

Learning to recognize and understand wants involves both subtle and sophisticated processes. The man who wants his roommate to accompany him to the store may have a number of simultaneous wants, some of which are implicit. The man may want to be assertive enough to ask the roommate to accompany him to the store. He may want the roommate to volunteer to come. If he asks his roommate to accompany him, he would also want compliance with his request, and perhaps a cheerful response at that. Moreover, the man may want the roommate to be good company on the way to the store. Success or failure obtaining any one or combination of the many wants associated with this simple situation may result in the experience of reward and satisfaction or deprivation and frustration. At this point, an important step toward self-awareness is to help the person unravel the complexity of wants, which requires him to become accustomed to thinking about "wants." Multiple related wants can be listed and differentiated one from the other. Multiple wants can also be evaluated and prioritized.

In our example, this man would use the concept of "want" to develop the list of desires related to the trip to the grocery store. Next, he would decide which of the many related wants is most important. He would ask, "What do I most want from my roommate with regard to this trip to the grocery store? Do I want company? Do I want him to volunteer to go? Do I want my roommate to entertain me? Do I want to assert my authority?"

Accurately determining which of the many related wants is the "primary want" is an important piece of awareness that will guide the man's subsequent behaviors. If the primary want is for companionship, he would approach the situation differently than if it were to obtain money from the roommate. Without accurate knowledge of the primary want (this concept is elaborated in Chapter 7), the person may pursue the wrong goal. In the present example, the man may get money from the roommate for groceries but not do the things necessary to obtain the companionship that is more highly desired.

The Expectation

Expectations constitute the other critical class of thoughts in developing self-awareness. An expectation is a belief that some future event will occur. In particular, people develop expectations of reward and punishment. Expectations are similar to wants in that they may provide an understanding of the motivation for behavior in many situations. As first observed by Bandura (1969; Bandura & Walters, 1963), the expectation of reward or punishment is the prime motivation for behavior. A person's expectations may dramatically influence social functioning and communication. A woman who expects to fail in an interaction with another person will be anxious and fearful about communicating and will be likely to avoid the interaction. If, on the other hand, she expects her comments to be warmly accepted, she will have positive feelings about the interaction and be attracted to it. In some cases, the person's expectations for the outcome of a social interaction will influence behavior more than actual prior experience.

Although the concepts may seem alike, want and expectation are not interchangeable. A want always has a positive valence, whereas an expectation may be positive or negative. Moreover, a want may already be obtained (e.g., a person who is living with a roommate thinks "I want to live with a roommate"), whereas an expectation is always of a future occurrence. Even when the want is of a future event and the expectation is of a positive occurrence, the concepts are distinct. The want does not imply a prediction about its fulfillment, and the expectation, by definition, does. The expectation of a positive outcome does, however, imply the presence of a want.

A person's expectations may or may not be (a) consistent with the actual future outcome, (b) based on evidence relevant to the future outcome, and (c) based on a biased interpretation of evidence relevant to the future outcome. Thus, our expectations may or may not be rational. However, it is a central proposition of cognitive therapy that a person's expectations regarding future events affect him or her as though the expectations were valid. For this reason, our expectations may cause our feelings and greatly influence our actions. A woman who expects to be criticized by a coworker will feel and act in a way that is consistent with that expectation. She will feel anxious and may try to avoid any interaction with that person. Alternatively, if the woman expects to be praised by that coworker, she will feel happy and probably seek to interact with her.

That wants and expectations are central to self-awareness may seem overly simplistic. It might appear that all a person needs to do to identify his or her own thoughts is to ask, "What do I *want?*" or "What do I *expect* will happen?" In fact, however, the understanding of wants and expectations is a sophisticated skill, requiring much effort and practice to master. Most people are not cognizant of their thoughts, nor do they realize wants and expectations motivate behavior and affect feelings. Moreover, people do not typically structure their thinking to distinguish wants and expectations from other cognitive activity. Learning to do this is an important part of self-awareness that lays the foundation for more sophisticated skill development.

At this point, it is sufficient to provide a functional definition of the construct of a thought and to stress that wants and expectations are the two kinds of thought most central to self-awareness. Finally, thoughts do not occur in isolation, but are associated in reliable ways with feelings and behaviors. These associations will be discussed later in this chapter.

The Concept of a Feeling

The experience called a "feeling" consists of two parts: physical and cognitive. Although these two intertwined aspects of a feeling are often difficult to separate, it is useful to do so. The physical aspects of feelings are the bodily sensations associated with autonomic nervous system arousal, such as the "knot" in the stomach, the dry "cotton mouth," the pounding of the heart, tightness in the chest, lightheadedness, heaviness, weakness, sensations of depletion, and "lightness and energy." Sensations are the rudimentary components of feelings and do not allow the individual to discriminate well among them because many feelings share the same sensations. For example, a racing heart may indicate fear, anger, or eager anticipation, three very different emotional states.

In the development of self-awareness, physical sensation's provide cues for the cognitive aspects of feelings. The cognitive components are the thoughts (wants and expectations) that accompany the physical sensations. This cognitive aspect is associated with greater power to describe feelings and discriminate among them. For example, fear comprises a state of general physical arousal (e.g., rapid heartbeat, sweating) plus a specific kind of *expectation* (something bad is going to happen). The expectation that something bad is going to happen is a specific and reliable indicator of the feeling of fear.

To develop accurate awareness of feelings, it is also necessary to consider certain situational factors and appraisals. Since the process that creates a feeling is somewhat complicated, we have described it in a flowchart. Figures 2–1 and 2–2 illustrate the processes that create feelings, starting with the initial want or expectation and ending with a terminal feeling. The steps of the process include (a) experience of a want or expectation, (b) awareness of what happened "in the real world" regarding the want or expectation, and (c) the individual's appraisal or evaluation of what happened "in the real world" regarding the want or expectation.

Understanding the Process That Results in a Feeling

Two kinds of thoughts lead to feelings: wants and expectations. Figure 2–1 shows the sequence of events for an *expectation*. The expectation of something "good" creates an initial feeling of hope and happiness, and the expectation of something "bad" results in fear. These initial feelings continue to be experienced until there is an outcome in the "real world" regarding the expectation. As shown in Figure 2–1, there are only two possible outcomes: The expected event occurs or the expected event

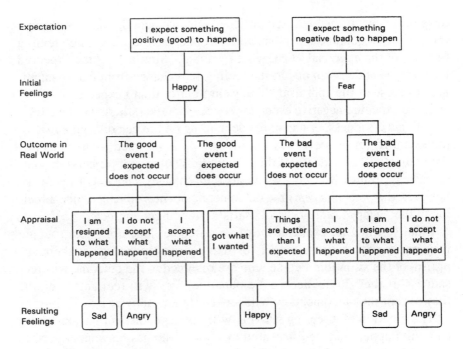

Figure 2–1. The process that results in a feeling, starting with an expectation.

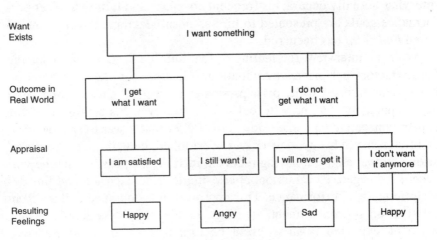

Figure 2–2. The process that results in a feeling, starting with a want.

does not occur. If the expected positive outcome actually occurs, the initial feeling of happiness persists and will become the "resulting" feeling because of the appraisal "I got what I wanted." Similarly, if the expected negative event does *not* occur, the feeling will change from fear to happiness because of the appraisal "Things are better than I expected."

If the expected negative event *does* occur, however, there will be a feeling of anger, sadness, or happiness depending on the person's appraisal of the event. If, for whatever reason, the person is resigned to the outcome, the feeling will be sadness. If the person does not accept (rejects) the outcome (e.g., thinks it unfair, wants another chance), anger will result. If, however, the person *accepts* the outcome, he or she will experience a feeling in the "happy" family such as satisfaction or contentment.

Finally, when an expected positive outcome does *not* occur, people may experience sadness, anger, or happiness, depending on their appraisal of the situation. People who are resigned to the outcome will feel sadness. If they do not accept the outcome, they will feel angry; and if they accept the outcome, they will feel content (happy).

The creation of a feeling starting with an expectation that something bad will happen may be illustrated by a man who has his annual performance evaluation scheduled at work. He knows that he has been absent and tardy frequently and, despite hard effort, has not met several of his performance goals. Looking ahead to the evaluation, he *expects* to receive an "unsatisfactory" evaluation (a negative event) and thus experiences the *initial feeling* of anxiety (fear). This initial feeling of fear lasts, perhaps for several weeks, until the interview takes place. When the interview actually occurs, his frequent absences and failure to meet performance goals are presented to him as unsatisfactory; thus the anticipated *bad event* has occurred.

After the interview, the feeling of fear subsides and he appraises the unsatisfactory performance evaluation. If he does not like the evaluation but resigns himself to it, perhaps saying to himself that nothing good ever happens to him, he will feel sad. If, however, his appraisal of this expected negative outcome leads to the belief that it was too derogatory, and that some of his good work was overlooked, he will reject the evaluation and feel angry at having received it. It is also possible that he will accept the negative evaluation, appraising it as an accurate and fair description of his performance. This appraisal of acceptance will result in satisfaction or contentment—feelings in the happiness family. Thus, when an expected negative event occurs, feelings of either sadness, anger, or happiness will be experienced, depending on the person's appraisal of the outcome.

If, on the other hand, the man who was expecting the bad evaluation was told that his job performance was acceptable (the expected *bad event does not occur*), he would appraise the situation thinking something like "Things are turning out better than I expected" and he would feel relief and happiness as the *resulting feeling*.

A similar example can be used to illustrate what would happen if a person has an expectation that something positive will happen, as shown at the top of Figure 2–1. Suppose a woman has a job performance interview scheduled and expects to be praised for good attendance and productivity. Looking forward to the evaluation, she *expects* to receive an "outstanding" evaluation (a positive event) and thus experiences the *initial feeling* of happy anticipation. This initial feeling of happiness lasts until the interview takes place. When the interview occurs, her good attendance and hard work are praised, and she receives an outstanding evaluation. She appraises this situation saying, "I got the good thing I expected" and the resulting feeling is happiness.

If, on the other hand, the woman was told that her job performance was merely "average" (the expected *good event does not occur*), her initial feeling of happiness might change, depending on her appraisal of the employer's comments. If the employee simply resigns herself to the bad news, she will feel sad. If, however, she rejects the opinion of the employer, she will feel angry and resentful. If the employee is able to accept the evaluation of the employer as valid, she will feel satisfaction or contentment. Thus, the feeling that ultimately results from an expectation varies depending on its actual occurrence and the person's appraisal of the situation.

Real life is not as clear-cut as the situation depicted in Figure 2–1. This figure is linear whereas life is more chaotic. The appraisal of an outcome may vary among resignation, rejection, and acceptance—the person may partly accept and partly reject an outcome. In such a situation, the person may experience more than one feeling in response to a situation, and the feelings may fluctuate as the appraisal of the situation changes. However, the concepts depicted in Figure 2–1 are still useful because they help people understand the sequence of events that occur, and the relationship between cognitive appraisal and the affect experienced. When appraisals fluctuate, so will feelings. As appraisals become more focused on resignation, rejection, or acceptance, feelings will settle on sadness, anger, or happiness, respectively. The more people can learn to accept the real-world outcomes that occur, especially those they cannot change, the more likely they are to experience happiness.

Figure 2–2 shows the process by which *wants* determine feelings. When a want is present, one of two events eventually will happen: It will be obtained, or it will not be obtained. If the want is obtained, the appraisal is "I am satisfied" and the resulting feeling is happiness. If, however, the want is not satisfied, either anger, sadness, or happiness is experienced, depending on the individual's appraisal of the situation. If the appraisal encourages the person's persistence in the want, feelings of anger will result over the current failure to obtain it. If, however, the appraisal suggests that pursuit of the want is fruitless, the person will give up hope of getting it and feel sad. If the individual decides he or she no longer wants what was desired, the result will be happiness (or at least contentment).

Suppose a man wants his roommate to share in the household cooking by preparing a meal every other day. If the two of them discuss this desire, they may decide to alternate days preparing meals. If the man returns home in the evening the first day this plan is in effect to find a meal prepared, he will feel delighted and happy because he wanted something and he got it, and he will appraise the situation saying something like "I am satisfied." If, however, he finds no meal prepared, he will be frustrated and angry as long as his appraisal of the situation results in a continued desire to have the roommate perform this task. If, on the other hand, he appraises the situation as hopeless ("I will never get my roommate to prepare meals on a reliable basis"), he will give up on the plan and feel sad and discouraged. If he reappraises the situation and decides it is not important for the roommate to share in the cooking and he no longer wants him to prepare meals, he will experience happiness and contentment.

The process described in Figure 2–2 is a simplification of real life, as was Figure 2–1. People can fluctuate in their appraisals, alternatively still wanting something and giving up hope on getting it. This situation results in the often-observed vacillation between anger and sadness. Other combinations of appraisals and affect are possible. Like Figure 2–1, this figure is useful because it helps people organize and gain control over their feelings by understanding the sequence of events that can occur.

As can be seen in both Figures 2–1 and 2–2, the formation of a feeling starts with a thought (a want or expectation). There is then an outcome in the real world regarding this want or expectation. Depending on the outcome and its appraisal, a feeling is created. This process applies to all the "basic feelings" (fear, anger, sadness, and happiness), a definition and discussion of which follows shortly.

Therefore, based on the preceding presentation, a feeling can be defined as an internal state or experience that (a) frequently *results from* a want or expectation, (b) motivates (but does not determine) behavior, and (c) may be experienced as either pleasant or unpleasant.

As was shown, feelings and thoughts (wants and expectations) are linked together, and there is a strong tendency for a feeling to follow a want or expectation. The motivational aspect of feelings is also highlighted by this definition. For example, feelings of fear or anxiety motivate a variety of "flight" reactions. Angry feelings, on the other hand, motivate people to "fight." Finally, happiness motivates "positive approach" behavior. This definition also indicates that certain feelings, such as happiness, are experienced as pleasant. Other feelings, such as fear and sadness, are experienced as unpleasant.

Basic Feelings

The preceding definition of a feeling gives a good general understanding of the construct, and helps to differentiate it from a thought and a behavior, the latter to be discussed subsequently. By itself, however, this definition does not provide enough specific information to assist people optimally in developing self-awareness of their feelings. One way to accomplish this goal is to decrease the universe of feelings to a manageable number. Toward this end, we have established a small set of "basic feelings" proposed to be representative of all feelings. The basic feelings are fear, anger, sadness, and happiness. Knowledge of these four feelings provides the specific information necessary for increased self-awareness.

There is ample rationale for developing a list of basic feelings. First of all, there are too many fine distinctions among feeling states for the average person to monitor. In fact, there may be as many as 717 feelings, according to one study (Averill, 1975). Increasingly subtle distinctions among feelings make the meanings of many feeling words notoriously imprecise (e.g., Clore, Ortony, & Foss, 1987). Since we are attempting to enhance accurate self-awareness, conciseness and precision of feeling terms are desirable.

A review of the full array of feeling words reveals that many terms represent subtle differences in intensity. Identification of a basic feeling that could represent these different intensities helps to simplify self-awareness. As shown in Table 2–1, the words irritated, irked, annoyed, mad, burned up, furious, and others describe various intensities of anger (see, e.g., Spielberger, 1988; Spielberger, Jacobs, Russell, & Crane, 1983; Spielberger et al., 1985). Similarly, pleased, satisfied, glad, joyful, elated, and cheerful all describe different intensities of happiness.

Also, many feeling words are nearly synonymous. Here again, use of a basic feeling to represent the family of synonyms simplifies self-awareness. For example, a person who feels "good" at a party is also "happy." The "tense" feeling that accompanies a mathematics exam is a variation of the feeling of "fear," and the statement "I feel down" is similar to "I feel very sad."

Other words represent combinations of basic feelings. "Excited," used to describe the feeling experienced when given a new and challenging work assignment, may express a feeling comprising fear and happiness, two basic feelings. Feeling depressed is sometimes a combination of sad and angry feelings. Hate, jealousy, and envy have been described as combinations of two basic feelings—fear and anger (Kemper, 1987).

Because feeling words often are synonymous, or describe different intensities of the same feeling or combinations of more fundamental feelings, we find that a number of feelings share the characteristics of a basic few. Therefore, it is reasonable to develop a short list of "basic" or "primary" feelings. Many researchers have endeavored to identify such

TABLE 2–1
Four Basic Feeling Categories and Those Difficult to Categorize

Fear	Anger	Sadness	Happiness	Difficult to Classify
tense	irritated	hopeless	pleased	upset
anxious	irked	bleak	satisfied	shy
afraid	annoyed	discouraged	glad	confident
worried	mad	down	joyful	inadequate
terrified	burned up	tired	elated	insecure
nervous	furious	unhappy	cheerful	crazy
jittery	tense	depressed	good	quiet
dread	bitter	sorrow	content	dissatisfied
fright	insulted	joyless	gratified	bad
uneasy	boiling	tragic	satisfied	awful

a set of "basic emotions." Results of these efforts have varied according to the conceptual model and the methodology used. Plutchik (1994) reviewed the research in this field and concluded that almost all the theorists who have written on the subject agree that anger, fear, joy, and sadness should be considered basic emotions; the vast array of feeling words in the English language, for the most part, describe different intensities or combinations of these four feelings. Other feeling words may be viewed as synonyms. In this program, happiness is used in preference to joy since it better describes a moderate intensity of this positive feeling.

Complex feelings such as hate, jealousy, and envy are not easily placed into one family of feelings. As these words describe feelings that are a combination of two or more basic feelings, self-awareness is facilitated by breaking them down into their constituent parts. The relative strengths of the different basic feelings that make up the complex feeling can then be assessed. Hate, for example, is composed of fear and anger. An individual experiencing this feeling can determine if it is mostly fear, mostly anger, or a balance of both basic feelings. This type of analysis allows the person to comprehend complex feelings using the basic four, thus keeping the self-awareness process relatively simple and manageable.

It is also possible for a person to experience two or more basic feelings at the same time or in the same situation. A mother may be happy and sad at her daughter's wedding. She is happy because she wanted her daughter to meet a nice man and get married, and she is getting that want fulfilled. At the same time, the mother may be sad because she wants the companionship of her daughter and knows that this will now be significantly diminished.

Thus, reduction of the vast number of feelings into a basic few makes gaining awareness relatively straightforward; it enables clients to readily identify the relative strength of different feelings and the wants and expectations on which they are based. This sorting process helps to keep clients from being overwhelmed by confusing and perhaps contradictory feelings.

Linking Wants, Expectations, and Outcomes to the Basic Feelings

Since wants and expectations in relation to real-life outcomes determine feelings (see Figures 2–1 and 2–2), it is useful to define the four basic feelings in terms of these factors. Having the following clear and concise definitions of the four basic feelings makes it easier to use this information to increase accurate self-awareness:

1. *Fear.* The feeling that is experienced when there is an *expectation* that something undesirable (unwanted) is going to happen.

   Examples If I tell Arthur that he is being rude to me, he will not be my friend any more.

   If I ask my roommate to pay more money for the groceries, she will tell everyone that I am cheap.

2. *Anger.* The feeling that is experienced when a person *wants* something and *does not get* it, and still *wants* it.

   Examples I wanted Arthur to be polite to me and he wasn't, he was rude.

   My roommate said he would chip in on the food bill, and now he says he spent all his money. He should make good on his promise, even if he has to borrow money.

3. *Sadness.* The feeling that is experienced when a person *wants* something and *does not get* it, and has *given up hope* of ever getting what was *wanted.*

   Examples I want Arthur to treat me with respect but he is always rude to me; he will never change.

   My roommate, who never has any money, said he would help pay for the groceries and now he is broke. I'll have to pay for everything myself, as usual.

4. *Happiness.* The feeling that is experienced when a person *wants* something and he or she *gets* what is *wanted.*

   Examples I wanted Arthur to treat me with respect, and he just offered his seat to me so I would not have to stand.

   My roommate said he would chip in on the groceries, and when I got home from the store, there was a 10-dollar bill on the counter with a note thanking me for doing the shopping.

These examples show the interaction between the cognitive state and a potential or actual environmental occurrence. This cognitive reaction to the potential or actual outcome determines the feeling state.

Therefore, accurate labeling requires awareness of wants, expectations, outcomes, and reactions to outcomes.

Feeling Words That Do Not Facilitate Self-Awareness

Some labels that people use to describe feelings are difficult to translate into one of the four basic feelings. These problematic feeling words (see Table 2–1) are usually general and vague and may describe more than one basic feeling family. It is best to avoid use of these words when describing internal states.

The word "upset," which is a cue or signal that something undesirable is being experienced, is in wide use although it is not suitable for the present model. It indicates a state of arousal and is usually experienced as unpleasant. Upset could mean that the person's basic feeling is fear, anger, or sadness. Someone who is upset may (a) be expecting something bad to happen, (b) have an ongoing unmet want, or (c) have given up hope on an unmet want, three very different situations.

To gain a useful level of self-awareness, people must translate the upset feeling into one of the four basic feelings by determining whether there is an unmet *want* and/or a negative *expectation.* Labeling the affective state will suggest goal-directed and adaptive actions. Just feeling upset leaves a person aroused and feeling distressed, but without any further understanding of the relationship of this feeling to wants and expectations and with no guide to adaptive behaviors.

Experience with this model has revealed that people can learn to substitute appropriate basic feeling words for "general" words. For example, a person who feels upset may search for any other words to describe the present feeling that will fit into one of the four basic feeling families. If this line of inquiry is not productive, the individual can attempt to identify wants and/or expectations. By using the "thought-feeling" dyads presented earlier, the appropriate feeling family can be discovered.

Use of the Relationship between Thoughts and Feelings to Increase Self-Awareness

Since wants and expectations occur in pairs with feelings, knowledge of either member of a pair can serve as a cue for the identification of the other. If Bill is aware that he is feeling angry toward his roommate, he can use this information to deduce that he wants something from the roommate that he is not getting (see definition of four basic feelings). He can ask himself, "Since I am angry at my roommate, what do I want from him that I am not getting?" The answer may be that Bill wants his roommate to pay half the grocery bill and he has not done so. In this way, the angry feeling signals to Bill that he has an unmet and persistent want that is the basis of the angry feeling. This anger could be experienced as annoyance, irritation, or any feeling in the anger family.

Having gained the self-awareness that he has an unmet want, Bill can evaluate the rationality of the want. If it is reasonable, he can devise a plan for satisfying it. If the want is not reasonable, he may decide to modify or abandon it. More will be said in Chapter 8 about this process of evaluating, modifying, and attaining wants.

Similarly, a person can use awareness of a want or expectation to identify a feeling. For example, a woman may become aware that her roommate has not cleaned up the kitchen as agreed. She could engage in a self-awareness process in which she thinks, "My roommate has not fulfilled our agreement and I would like her to do so. When people have an ongoing want that is not met, they feel angry. Yes, I am feeling angry at her for not cleaning up."

This process can be used for any of the four basic feelings because wants, expectations, and feelings are associated in pairs as described earlier in this chapter. Knowledge of one member of the pair automatically identifies the other member. More will be said about the pairing of thoughts and feelings in subsequent sections.

The Concept of Behavior

The third aspect of the self about which a person can be aware is behavior. Unlike thoughts and feelings, behaviors are public events and can be defined in relatively straightforward and objective terms. Thus, a behavior is defined as an action that can be seen or heard. Examples of behaviors are walking, sitting, humming, and speaking. Although it might appear easy to recognize a behavior since it is directly observable, many errors are made in their identification. Research evaluating the ability of people to identify behaviors in social interactions indicates that, when asked to do so, 58% of subjects' responses identified either a thought or feeling (Bedell & Lennox, 1994).

Part of the difficulty in identifying behaviors is that they are often given the name of feelings with which they are associated. Laughter or laughing (a behavior) may be mistakenly identified as a feeling because it is closely associated with happiness. Similarly, yelling and shaking one's fist (two behaviors) may mistakenly be called feelings because of their association with anger (a feeling). It is important to make the distinction between the behavior and the feeling. Although certain behaviors and feelings often occur in pairs, they are not the same phenomenon.

Although feelings and behaviors should not be confused, that they frequently occur together can aid self-awareness. The observation that behavior-feeling pairs occur leads us back to the previous discussion about thought-feeling pairs and the conclusion that knowledge of one member of a pair permits identification of the other.

The Thought-Feeling-Behavior Triad

If each thought-feeling dyad is likely to be consistently associated with a certain behavior, a thought-feeling-behavior triad (TFB triad) is formed. *Expectations of negative consequences,* that produce *fear* or *anxiety* are frequently associated with *avoidance behaviors* such as staying away from certain people or situations. Similarly, feelings of *anger,* defined in terms of *wanting something, or expecting something desirable and not getting it,* are likely to be associated with *negative approach behaviors* such as aggressively moving or leaning forward, *raising voice volume, pushing, and so on. Sadness,* the feeling resulting from *unmet wants that are expected never to be met,* may frequently be associated with inaction or *psychomotor retardation.* Finally, *happiness,* which occurs when *wants are satisfied* or fulfilled, is accompanied by *approach behaviors* such as seeking out and approaching the source of the happiness. Kemper (1987) has suggested that happiness is associated with "up" behaviors. He observed that posture is upright, facial muscles are pulled upward, and the voice volume and tone are elevated. Sadness, on the other hand, is associated with "down" behaviors. These TFB triads are summarized in Table 2–2.

TABLE 2–2
The Four Thought-Feeling-Behavior Triads

Thought	Feeling	Behavior
Expecting something bad	Fear	Avoid
Wanting something and getting it	Happiness	Positive approach
Wanting and not getting it, and still wanting it	Anger	Negative approach
Wanting and not getting it, and giving up hope	Sadness	Inactive or slow action

These behavioral patterns can be influenced by other variables. As behavior is under voluntary control, a natural behavioral tendency can be modified. A person who becomes angry may suppress the tendency to yell or otherwise aggress and instead engage in avoidance. A fearful person, rather than avoid the threatening situation, may approach and fight when honor or pride are to be upheld.

Although these examples may suggest that the relationship between thoughts, feelings, and behaviors is unreliable, they also indicate that there are frequently competing wants in a given situation. The behavior *observed* may be consistent with the most important, or primary, want. When Bill wants his roommate to clean the kitchen and the roommate fails to do so, Bill may experience anger. Rather than engage in "negative approach" behaviors, he may leave the room, thus engaging in avoidance. However, avoidance may be consistent with a want that is more important than getting the kitchen cleaned. That is, Bill may want to maintain a positive relationship with the roommate and maintain companionship. He may fear that the positive relationship would be jeopardized by expressing anger. Thus, anger and fear are both present in the situation, and avoidance behavior indicates that the feeling of fear is stronger than the feeling of anger.

As may be seen, the sophisticated use of the TFB triads can facilitate self-awareness. As identified previously, the four basic behaviors to which people should become vigilant are (a) avoidance, (b) negative approach, (c) positive approach, and (d) inaction (or slowed action). The associated feeling with each is fear, anger, happiness, and sadness, respectively.

Although hardly describing behaviors in detail, these four families of behaviors have the important virtue of being readily monitored. Behavioral observations also help people develop awareness of wants, expectations, and feelings through the development of TFB triads (Table 2–2). Here, knowledge of either a thought, feeling, or behavior helps the person become aware of the other two phenomena.

The Thought-Feeling-Behavior Triad: An Example

The following example shows how thoughts, feelings, and behaviors are interrelated, or linked, in a given situation. This example also illustrates how thoughts (wants or expectations) in a particular situation *determine* feelings and *influence* behavior as well as how knowledge of one component of the triad reveals the other two.

Imagine that a man is walking down the street in a large city. In the distance, he sees a person on the corner asking people to sign a petition condemning a foreign country for human rights violations. The man dislikes signing such petitions and doesn't want to sign this one. He thinks the petitioner is going to approach him and talk him into signing it. He doesn't think he'll be able to say no, because he will probably stutter if he attempts to do so. Then, he expects the petitioner and everybody nearby will snicker and think he is stupid.

As he gets closer to the corner, the man begins to expect the petitioner to approach him. He will probably begin to feel *fearful* because, he *expects* that something "he doesn't want" is going to happen (he will be asked to sign something he doesn't want to sign, and will stutter, and people will think he is stupid). When he begins to think (expect) that he will not be able to say no because of the reasons specified, his feeling of *fear intensifies* as the undesirable outcome seems more likely. At this point, what behavior does he engage in? He will probably choose *avoidance behavior* by either crossing the street or walking on the other side of the sidewalk.

In this example, the man's expectation that the petitioner would approach and that he would not be able to refuse the request (and would be embarrassed) led to a feeling of fear and, in turn, to avoidance behaviors. This scenario is consistent with the fear TFB triad described in Table 2–2.

Now imagine the same situation except, in this case, the man has confidence in his ability to say "no." He has refused similar requests on a number of occasions, knows how to do it, *expects* to be able to do so now, and *wants* the opportunity to express his beliefs about signing such petitions. As he begins to *expect* the petitioner to approach, he will probably *feel* somewhat neutral at first. As he begins to *expect* to be able to refuse the request and look forward to the opportunity to express his beliefs, the man's *feeling* may change to *happy anticipation* because he *wants* to be able to express himself. Regarding *behavior,* he will probably *approach* the person, or at least not go out of his way to avoid contact.

As illustrated by this example, different thought processes (wants and expectations) in identical situations lead to different feelings and behaviors. Similar examples could also be presented to illustrate the other TFB triads. For example, what would be the effect if the man in the preceding example wanted to express himself to the person with the petition but his companion prevented him from doing so?

The "Thought-Feeling-Behavior" Circle

It is useful to think of the TFB triads as circles (TFB circle), as illustrated in Figure 2–3. The circle expands the concept of the interrelationship of thoughts, feelings, and behaviors from a straight line with a beginning and an end to a continuous figure without any beginning or end. That is, the process of the thought-feeling-behavior triad does not necessarily start with a thought and end with a behavior, as illustrated in Table 2–2. Rather, the process may begin with awareness of any one of the triad members—a thought, a feeling, *or* a behavior. After identifying

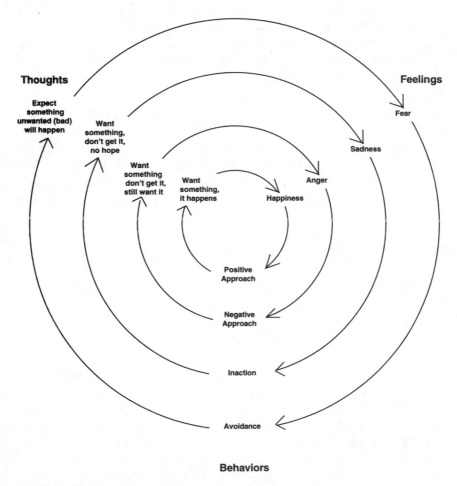

Figure 2–3.   The thought-feeling-behavior circle.

one component of the triad, a person can deduce the other two and complete the circle. This model also suggests that the self-awareness process may continue around several times with changes in thoughts, feelings, or behaviors occurring as time passes and more information is processed.

Imagine the situation described previously about approaching the man with a petition. As presented, the expectation of being embarrassed came first, followed by the feeling of fear and then the avoidance behavior. However, it is also possible that the man may have first become aware of the feeling of fear, followed by awareness of the expectation and finally the behavior. Or, he may have become aware of crossing the street (behavior) before paying any attention to the feeling or expectation. The TFB circle illustrates this process better than a linear model.

The circle can also illustrate how an individual can switch from one ring of the circle to another and change thoughts, feelings, and behaviors. In the situation with the man and the petition, he may have engaged in coping processes once he recognized that the avoidance behavior was due to the feeling of fear and the expectation of a negative outcome. Perhaps he would remind himself that because he had just completed an assertiveness course and knew how to handle such situations, his expectation of embarrassment unfounded. This realization would change his expectation and, therefore, his affect and behavior. Continuing around the circle for the second time, the self-observation of less avoidance may increase the expectation of success even further. This change in expectation would lead to additional change in affect, and so on around the circle until the situation ended. The TFB circle could also be used to describe how negative feelings escalate and maladaptive behaviors increase in a spiraling circle as expectations of negative events move in a "catastrophic" and increasingly frightening direction.

Using the concept of the four-ringed circle, self-awareness at any point within one ring will provide understanding of the rest of the ring. One element of a ring of the circle may also influence and change the other two elements that compose the ring. It is important, however, to keep the self-awareness model as simple as possible. If it becomes overly complex, its practical utility will diminish. To facilitate self-awareness, users of the circle should understand that they can enter the circle at any point representing one of the basic cognitive components, feelings, or behavioral tendencies. The circle must be followed through at least one rotation on one ring to obtain a complete picture of self-awareness. Completing the information that comprises the three parts of the circle will facilitate self-awareness because it structures the information in a meaningful and understandable way.

How to Change from One TFB Triad to Another

So far, this chapter has focused on the development of *self-awareness* through the use of cognitive-behavioral concepts of linking thoughts, feelings, and behaviors. At this point, it is appropriate to discuss concepts related to the *modification of maladaptive* thoughts, feelings, and behaviors. A more complete presentation is provided in Chapter 8.

The TFB circle helps to change thoughts, feelings, and behaviors. First of all, it is useful to assume that, in most cases, *thoughts (wants and expectations) determine feelings and influence behavior.* As indicated, a person may become aware of either a problem thought, feeling, or behavior and, therefore, enter into the circle at any point. However, awareness of wants and expectations is always essential for change. Change in the individual is greatly facilitated by understanding and, if necessary, modifying the way he or she thinks (wants or expects).

Sometimes, wants and expectations can be modified directly, by getting the person to evaluate thoughts more realistically. In the previous example about the man with the petition, the person who expected others to think he was stupid for stammering, could be helped to see that this *expectation* led to *feelings* of anxiety and avoidance *behaviors.* Also, by reevaluating this expectation more realistically, he could change it, along with the companion feeling and behavior. If this man re-evaluated the expectation that others would think he was stupid, he might realize this is an excessively negative appraisal and that people do not necessarily imply lack of intelligence from stammering. He might also evaluate the importance of the street petitioner's evaluation. Does he care what this stranger thinks of him? Deciding that the evaluation of a total stranger he will never see again is not very important could lessen the feelings of anxiety. Finally, he might also look at his prior behavior in similar situations. Does he have a history of stammering or is this just an imaginary expectation? If there is no prior history, this realization will lessen the anxiety.

This factual evaluation and debate of an unrealistic *expectation* can change it to a more realistic one. Rather than expecting to engage in a series of embarrassing behaviors and being ridiculed by a stranger, the man might expect to handle the situation reasonably well and would replace the expected catastrophic outcomes with more realistic ones.

Once the expectations become more realistic, there is usually less to fear. It may take time and effort to accomplish the desired reappraisal of expectations, but the model is valid and is the basis of cognitive therapy.

The same process may be applied to wants. That is, suppose a person is angry because she did not get a want met and still has the want. Evaluation of the want may modify the feeling of anger. Is it realistic? Should it be modified? If the want is modified, the affect will change. For example, the woman may be angry because her friend has refused to give her a ride to a party. Reevaluation of the want (to be given a ride to the party) may reveal that it is unrealistic. Perhaps the friend would have to drive five miles out of her way to provide the desired ride. Realizing this, the woman may reappraise her want and, taking the other person into consideration, decide that what she wants creates a burdensome chore for her friend. Her anger would then disappear.

It is not always necessary or desirable to directly debate the expectation or want. It is sometimes possible to bring about a change in thinking (wants and expectations) by having the person *behave* differently. Refer again to our example of the petition. To modify the person's expectation that he would not be able to say "no" to a request, he might first need to demonstrate to himself that he could perform such a task (say no to such a request). If he practiced refusing requests, he ultimately would be able to do so effectively, and thus change his current belief that he cannot perform this task. The revised expectation that he *would* be able to say "no" would cause him to feel less fearful in such a situation. Avoidance behaviors would also be reduced and positive approach behaviors would be increased.

Finally, change in a want (or expectation) can also be brought about by a change in the feeling associated with it. In our example, the man's expectation that he would stammer could be due to feeling extremely tense. In that case, he could be taught a method of relaxation (e.g., slow breathing; see Chapter 8) to reduce his overall level of arousal. Gaining control over the anxiety would change the man's expectation that he would stammer.

So, although we must change our thinking to change ourselves in any meaningful way, it's not always necessary for the change in thinking to occur first. Because of the interrelationship among thoughts, feelings, and behaviors, modifying of any of these phenomena can bring about a change in the other two.

A SKILLS TRAINING PROGRAM FOR
INCREASING SELF-AWARENESS

The following section describes a clinical program that has been used to teach self-awareness skills. It is based on the four-part model presented in Chapter 1 that includes Instruction, Supervised Practice, Feedback, and Independent Practice. The following material is detailed enough to be used as a guide for the clinician and may be followed section by section. Although the information in this chapter is intended for use in a group therapy format, the resourceful practitioner can adapt these materials for other applications. It is suggested that the material be divided and presented in two or three meetings, not all at once. The instruction section describing thoughts, feelings, and behaviors should be followed by the exercise that includes the Thought-Feeling-Behavior Crossword Puzzle. The remaining material that focuses on the four basic feelings and their interrelationships should be presented in a separate lesson accompanied by the FLASH Bingo exercise and independent practice.

Instruction

Skills training begins with an explanation of the skills to be learned. Since this is the first in a series of skills training sessions, the information is intended to establish a positive orientation to skills training and to the potential for behavioral change. The first part of the presentation basically informs the participants (a) what skills they will be learning and (b) how they can benefit. Next, the expectation is established that all people are *capable* of changing their pattern of communication if they so desire. This expectation is developed through presentation of the following logical argument: (a) a person's typical pattern of communication is part of his or her "personality"; (b) "personality" consists of the sum total of the person's behaviors, and the associated underlying thoughts and feelings; (c) thoughts, feelings, and behaviors are learned; (d) human beings are always capable of learning; (e) therefore, just as the person learned to relate to others in the past by learning to think, feel, and behave in a particular way, he or she can learn new, more effective, ways to communicate.

Following this presentation, the other skill concepts are discussed. The following outline provides an overview of the material to be presented here.

1. Explain how self-awareness is based on understanding thoughts, feelings, and behaviors.
2. Define the concept of a thought and give examples of the five types:
   a. Explain emphasis on wants and expectations.
   b. Provide examples to illustrate.
3. Define feeling including physical and cognitive components.
   a. Explain focus on four basic feelings and why:
      i. Simplification.
      ii. Many feelings are combinations of the basic four.
      iii. Many feelings are variations of intensity of basic four.
   b. Explain pairing of thoughts and feelings (Table 2–2).
   c. Explain how feelings are created (Figures 2–1 and 2–2).
4. Define concept of behavior with emphasis on four basic behaviors.
5. Explain interrelationship of thoughts, feelings, and behaviors (Figure 2–1):
   a. Present example of man anticipating interaction with street petitioner.
   b. Use Figure 2–3 to explain how information about either thought, feeling, or behavior provides awareness of all three.
6. Explain how change in either thought, feeling, or behavior can change other two (use Figure 2–3).

Supervised Practice

As indicated in Chapter 1, the client or group of clients should be provided with structured activities that will facilitate practice of the skill concepts presented in the Instruction section. The following activities were developed for use in a group format, although they can be adapted for use with individual clients and couples.

Each of the two exercises should be conducted in a different session. Each session, which includes a lecture on the relevant skill concepts and a supervised practice exercise, takes 90 minutes for a group of 8 to 10 people. Thus, the two sessions dealing with thoughts, feelings, and behaviors and the four basic feelings will take about three hours. The independent practice and review would involve additional time.

Exercise 1. Understanding Thoughts, Feelings, and Behaviors

This exercise is entitled "The Thought-Feeling-Behavior Crossword Puzzle."

1. Give clients a handout with the definitions of thought, feeling, and behavior on it (Table 2–3). Also, hand out TFB Crossword Puzzle (Figure 2–4).

2. Provide the following instruction for completing the puzzle: "This puzzle is completed like any other crossword puzzle, with a few differences. Like other crossword puzzles, words are filled in the grid going either across or down. There is a number in one of the boxes of the grid that corresponds to a statement with the same number. The word that you use to fill in the blank space in the statement is written in the grid.

   "When reading the statements, select the word from the choices listed below it. Select the choice that is either a thought, feeling, or behavior as indicated by the word written to the left. The under-lined portion of the phrase is the part that is written in the grid. Just like a regular crossword puzzle, words that cross in the grid must share a common letter at that point." It usually takes clients 20 minutes to complete the crossword puzzle.

TABLE 2–3
Definitions of Thoughts, Feelings, and Behaviors

Thought	A message from the brain that expresses a wish, want, expectation, evaluation, comparison, or description.
Feeling	An internal state that often results from our thoughts. Feelings can motivate behavior. Feelings may be either pleasant or unpleasant.
	Four basic feelings and the thoughts most often associated with them:
	Fear You experience this feeling when you expect something to happen that you don't want.
	Anger You experience this feeling when you want something and don't get it (and you still want it).
	Sadness You experience this feeling when you want something, don't get it, and give up hope of ever getting it.
	Happiness You experience this feeling when you want something and you get it.
Behavior	An action that can be seen or heard.

3. Discuss the responses to the crossword puzzle. Go through each across and down item. Ask clients in turn to indicate what response they choose and why. It is helpful to ask why other responses were not chosen. For example, number 1 across calls for a behavior. The correct answer is "coughed." Why was this correct? Also, why were "felt sad" and "dreamed" incorrect answers? The objective of this exercise is to review the concepts of thought, feeling, and behavior until all group members understand them and can differentiate among them. This game is quite enjoyable and patients review the concepts many times without becoming bored.

Exercise 2. Learning to Identify the Four Basic Feelings

Conduct the FLASH Bingo game. The definitions of the four basic thought-feeling pairs should be in full view for all to use as reference. Copies of Table 2–3 may be distributed for this purpose. A sample bingo card is shown in Figure 2–5. Additional cards should be made so that each player has a unique one. Present the following instructions to the group: "FLASH Bingo is very similar to regular Bingo, with a few exceptions. Each of you has a different bingo card and you win if you mark out all the numbers in a row, a column, or diagonally across the grid. If you do this, yell 'Bingo!'

"To determine what square to mark out on your bingo card, we follow this procedure: I will read a statement to each of you in turn, starting with the first person on the right, and proceeding around the group. You are to tell me which of the four basic feelings is described by the sentence I read. The box you will mark will be in the column under the first letter of that feeling word (F-A-S-H). If the feeling word expressed in the statement is overly general and therefore impossible to translate into a basic feeling, it will be called a 'Lousy' feeling word and a mark will be made under the 'L' column.

"Next, you will roll this die to see what number in the column should be marked off. If you have the number in that column, you can mark it out." (Demonstrate the task as you give the instructions, using the first example on the bingo stimulus item sheet (Figure 2–5). When a statement is read and a group member identifies it as one of the basic feelings, he or she should be asked to explain this choice. That is, how did the content of the statement match the definition of one of the basic feelings, or why was it a "lousy" feeling word?

Across

Behavior   4. Mike _____ in group today.
        a. <u>felt sad</u>
        b. <u>coughed</u>
        c. <u>dreamed</u>

Behavior   5. Jan said she likes to _____ .
        a. <u>be happy</u>
        b. <u>go dancing</u>
        c. <u>daydream</u>

Thought   6. Patrick _____ that he might not go to the movies.
        a. <u>mumbled</u>
        b. <u>felt sad</u>
        c. <u>guessed</u>

Feeling   9. Tom will _____ the snake.
        a. <u>fear</u>
        b. <u>feed</u>
        c. have an <u>idea</u> about

Feeling   10. Sam _____ about going on an airplane.
        a. feels <u>fear</u>
        b. will <u>talk</u>
        c. has an <u>idea</u>

Thought   13. Pete _____ wanting the promotion.
        a. <u>talked</u> about
        b. had a <u>reason</u> for
        c. feels <u>happy</u>

Figure 2–4.   Thought-feeling-behavior crossword puzzle.

Thought   15. Steve ———— about his trip.
              a. <u>laughed</u>
              b. <u>felt</u> angry
              c. had a <u>fantasy</u>
Feeling   17. Maggie ———— she passed her test.
              a. <u>thinks</u>
              b. <u>smiled</u> when
              c. felt <u>happy</u> when

Down

Thought   1. Patty will ———— if more money is needed for the party.
              a. <u>judge</u>
              b. feel <u>angry</u>
              c. <u>frown</u>
Behavior   2. Nick ———— when his team won the game.
              a. had <u>an idea</u>
              b. felt <u>happy</u>
              c. gave a <u>cheer</u>
Behavior   3. Tom ———— the baby.
              a. <u>loves</u>
               b. <u>wants</u>
              c. <u>kissed</u>
Behavior   4. David ———— at the end of the concert.
              a. <u>felt sad</u>
              b. <u>clapped</u>
              c. expressed his <u>opinion</u>
Behavior   7. Lisa ———— about the girl at the party.
              a. had <u>an idea</u>
              b. <u>smiles</u>
              c. felt <u>angry</u>
Thought   8. Fran will ———— about her new boss.
              a. be <u>talking</u>
              b. feel <u>happy</u>
              c. <u>decide</u>
Feeling   11. Jim ———— about losing his job.
              a. <u>felt sad</u>
              b. <u>wonders</u>
              c. <u>frowned</u>
Feeling   12. Cynthia ———— computers.
              a. <u>ponders</u>
              b. <u>works</u> with
              c. <u>loves</u>
Feeling   14. Marty ———— about the letter.
              a. felt <u>anger</u>
              b. <u>joked</u>
              c. will <u>worry</u>
Thought   16. Arlene ———— about the new group leader.
              a. <u>asked</u>
              b. has an <u>idea</u>
              c. feels <u>fear</u>

Figure 2–4. *(Continued)*

F	L	A	S	H
B	I	N	G	O
5	6	1	1	2
3	3	4	2	4
1	2	3	4	5
2	1	6	6	1
4	5	2	5	3

1. Mary expected her mother to send her some money but she has not received it. Mary is angry.
2. A student is going to have an exam. He thinks he will do poorly on it. He is feeling fear.
3. The student wanted to make a good grade and he did. He was happy.
4. Mary wanted to visit her friend and now she knows she will not be able to visit. She is sad.
5. Joan said "I'm insecure about riding a motorcycle." Joan feels lousy fit.
6. Could it be true that he is late again, even after I had a long talk with him about being on time? I'm really angry.
7. When I talk to Peter, he seems unconcerned. I feel lousy fit.
8. I'm happy when I win at Bingo.
9. When I meet a new person I don't know I sometimes think they won't like me. This causes me to be fearful.
10. When I think about the game coming up, I feel lousy fit.
11. I wanted to win the game but didn't think I could. I'm happy that I did win.
12. I really get angry when I want to get home on time and traffic holds me up.
13. Sometimes I rush to get home early and when I get home early, I'm happy.
14. All I ever wanted from you was to have you as a friend, but you keep avoiding me. Now I'm feeling angry.

Figure 2–5.   Stimulus items for FLASH Bingo game and sample Bingo cards.

15. If I take a guess and am wrong people will think I'm stupid. I'm <u>afraid</u> to take a guess.
16. I wanted to have a girlfriend but I never seem to meet any friendly girls. I'll never have a girlfriend. <u>Sad.</u>
17. When I saw what time it was, I was upset. I feel <u>lousy fit.</u>
18. I called my friend and she was home when I called. This made me <u>happy.</u>
19. I have been craving for that new dress for a long time. Every time I have enough money, I have to spend some on something else, like the electric bill. I'll never get that dress. I feel <u>sad.</u>
20. If I tell John that I want my tape recorder back, he might get mad at me. <u>Fear.</u>
21. John should have given my tape recorder back to me without my asking. I have to ask for it. <u>Angry.</u>
22. You really make me <u>angry.</u> You never do what you say you will do.
23. I've tried so many times to work things out, I don't think it will ever work. <u>Sad.</u>
24. Every time I go to a party, I feel this way. You never know who is going to be there. <u>Fear.</u>
25. Boy, I feel good this morning. A good night's sleep really pays off. <u>Happy.</u>
26. What if we don't have enough money for the electric bill? What will we do then? <u>Fear.</u>
27. The bus is on time. I'll make it to work without being late. <u>Happy.</u>
28. I'm OK with my promotion to office manager. I feel <u>lousy fit.</u>
29. I'm not perfect. Why can't you give me a break? <u>Anger.</u>
30. My girlfriend broke up with me. I feel <u>sad.</u>
31. I'm frustrated today. I haven't gotten anything done. <u>Anger.</u>
32. I'm depressed. I don't think I'll ever make another friend. <u>Sad.</u>
33. I'm delighted to have you visit. I've been trying to arrange this for a long time. <u>Happy.</u>
34. I'm feeling tense. I guess it is because I'm going to talk to Betty today. <u>Fear.</u>
35. How many people am I going to have to talk to today? I thought this would be quick and easy. <u>Anger.</u>
36. I feel inadequate talking to you. I feel <u>lousy fit.</u>
37. The trip to Mary's house worked out just the way we planned it. I'm glad we went. <u>Happy.</u>
38. I had everything planned and nothing worked out. I'm <u>angry.</u>
39. Every time I plan something it never works out. I'm not planning anything else again, ever. <u>Sad.</u>
40. What if my plans don't work out? Mary would probably say "I told you so." I feel <u>fear.</u>

Figure 2–5. *(Continued)*

There will be differences of opinion regarding the correct answer. When this occurs, encourage discussion and ask each person to provide information to support his or her choice. In many cases, more than one answer is correct, depending on different reasonable interpretations of the stimulus item. Stimulus items were not written with sufficient detail to rule out multiple interpretations in some cases. Difference of opinion regarding the basic feeling described is not a problem since clients, in supporting their judgment, will better learn the concepts. One answer will ultimately be determined to be correct and the column and row to be marked will be determined using the procedure described previously. The therapist should keep in mind that the goal of this exercise is to stimulate practice in applying the skill concepts relating to the four basic feelings. *Note:* Use of a large fuzzy die like those sometimes hung from automobile rear view mirrors adds some fun to this exercise.

Proceed with the FLASH Bingo game until someone gets five squares in a row and yells "Bingo."

Feedback

Feedback can be provided as described in Chapter 1. In general, responses that match the skill concepts being practiced in the exercises are desired. Feedback should comment on ways behavior matched the skill concepts and ways that performance could be improved to better match them. In some cases, feedback may involve not only verbal but also motor behavior. For example, facial expressions (smiling and frowning) and body movements (approaching and leaning forward or walking away) are nonverbal forms of feedback. Nonverbal forms of feedback are not specific and therefore are of value as supplements to verbal feedback.

Independent Practice

The client is instructed initially to begin to attend to thoughts, feelings, and behaviors that are experienced outside the group. "Homework" assignments can be made that instruct clients to record one thought, feeling, and behavior experienced each day. This information will be discussed at the beginning of subsequent group therapy sessions to see if the client is able to apply the concepts and skills outside the group.

Following this initial practice in real-life situations, the client should develop a plan to use these self-awareness skills that is consistent with his or her treatment plan. This training program does not emphasize self-awareness as an independent skill. Rather, self-awareness is embedded into the communication, problem-solving, and coping skills in the following chapters. Nonetheless the client may benefit from applying these self-awareness skills to daily experiences.

3

Awareness of Others
A Fundamental Communication and Problem-Solving Skill

In the previous chapter, the discussion focused on learning how to recognize and differentiate thoughts and feelings. Also, four basic "thought-feeling-behavior triads" were identified and arranged into a circular configuration to illustrate the interaction of these phenomena. Learning these concepts provided a schema for *self-awareness*. In this chapter, many of the same concepts and procedures will be applied to the development of *awareness of others*.

Understanding others involves more than intuition or "gut" feelings. Such an unstructured and subjective approach to understanding others is not sufficiently rigorous or reliable to be useful. In the present program, many of the practical concepts of self-awareness presented in Chapter 2 will be applied to others.

One of the primary factors that impedes the understanding of another's thoughts and feelings is that these internal, private events cannot be directly observed by another person. Only behavior, and the situation in which the thoughts and feelings occur, are directly observable. Therefore, these factors serve as the foundation to understanding the other's thoughts and feelings. How a person progresses from the observation of objective, observable behaviors and situations to understanding private events going on inside someone is the primary focus of this chapter.

THE CONCEPT OF EMPATHY

In this book, skills related to understanding the thoughts, feelings, and behaviors of others are referred to as empathy skills. There are a number of different ways to conceptualize empathy, which is a construct used to describe an abstract and theoretical variable. It is something scientists or practitioners devise from their own imagination to describe observations (Nunnally, 1967).

Thus, different therapists have developed different views of the concept of empathy. Carl Rogers provided some of the preeminent theories and descriptions of the nature of empathy based on his psychotherapy research (e.g., Rogers, 1951). Although empathy is viewed here as an element of everyday interpersonal communication, the research of Rogers is still relevant.

According to Rogers and Sanford (1989), empathy involves entering the private, perceptual world of another person without making judgments. It is an attempt to "assume the internal frame of reference" (Rogers, 1951, p. 29) of another person and to perceive the world in the same way that person perceives it. Similarly, Truax and Carkhuff (1967) indicated that an empathic therapist must be able to "be with, grasp the meaning of, or accurately and empathically understand the client on a moment-by-moment basis" (p. 1).

Certainly, the ability to enter the private world of another person in a nonjudgmental way is essential to our use of the concept of empathy. However, when empathy is applied to psychotherapy, there is an implied depth and intensity of experience that goes beyond that which is reasonable for everyday use. Full immersion in the perceptual world of another and the suspension of boundaries as desired in some forms of psychotherapy are unnecessary in the present application. Therefore, the construct of empathy, as used here, is defined as the vicarious nonjudgmental understanding of the wants, expectations, and feelings of another person.

It is also important to differentiate between empathy and sympathy. The former, as previously defined, is a person's attempt to understand and express the thoughts and feelings of another person. Sympathy, in contrast, is an expression of how one feels about another. Thus, "You must be sad" or "You sound angry" are empathic statements while "I feel sorry for you" and "I would be angry too if that happened to me" are statements of sympathy.

THE COMMUNICATION OF EMPATHY

To be maximally useful, empathy must go beyond the simple cognitive understanding of the thoughts and feelings of another person. It is essential that the person *communicate* his or her empathic understanding. This communication, naturally, contains both verbal and nonverbal components, with the former known as an *empathic statement* and defined as "a statement a person makes to another that expresses his or her understanding of the other's wants, expectations, and feelings." The sources of information for empathy are the other person's behavior and characteristics of the situation. The nonverbal components of empathy include all behaviors accompanying the words spoken that demonstrate caring and concern for the other person. Voice tone, facial expression, posture, and body movements are some of the behaviors that would be expected to support the empathic statement in communicating an understanding of the other's thoughts and feelings (or at least an attempt at understanding).

SOURCES OF EMPATHIC INFORMATION

Behavior

As indicated, empathy is acquired primarily by assessing behaviors and characteristics of the situation. The primary *behaviors* of interest are the other person's verbal statements of wants, expectations, and feelings. Other verbal information will be less helpful in establishing empathy. Also, observation of the "four basic behaviors" (positive approach, negative approach, avoidance, and slowed or "down" behaviors) provides important information relevant to the empathic statement, especially when considered as part of a TFB triad.

Situation

There are four sources of information available about any situation that may be used to develop empathic understanding. These four observable elements are (a) *who* is present, (b) *what* activities are occurring, (c) the time *when* the situation is occurring, and (d) *where* the activity occurred. These components of the situation are helpful in providing clues to the internal state of another person. For example, observing a woman at a birthday party with her young daughter in the middle of the day suggests feelings of happiness. An interaction with a noisy neighbor at 3:00 A.M. would suggest anger. A situation involving the loss of a good friend might indicate sadness. Interpretations of mood based on the situation require additional corroborating information. Situations do not unfailingly reveal the mood of a person.

Similarly, an empathic statement is not always accurate. There is no method of indirect observation of the private thoughts and feelings of another person that provides foolproof and infallible information. Therefore, it is important to understand that a skilled attempt at empathy will minimize the margin of error, but cannot be accurate on all occasions. Nonetheless, as observed by Rogers (1951), an incorrect yet genuine attempt at expressing empathy may foster improved communication.

HOW TO MAKE AN EMPATHIC STATEMENT

As discussed, the empathic statement is based on the observation of another's behavior and the context in which it occurs (the situation). From an information-processing and skills-training perspective, this requires at least three sets of skills. First, the person must be able to *attend* to certain relevant information and filter out, or ignore, the rest. Second, to make sense relatively quickly of the relevant data, the person must acquire a reliable and time-efficient way of organizing and *processing* it. This skill enables the person to choose the appropriate empathic statement. Finally, he or she must be able to *express* the empathic statement in a clear and understandable way. These three skills, attending, processing, and expressing, are interdependent and sequentially related in that the development of one ability requires the presence of those preceding it. We will discuss each of these three aspects of empathy.

Attending to Relevant Information

Verbal Expressions of Wants

Social situations produce an immense amount of information. Assimilating all of it is neither possible nor desirable. It is natural and adaptive to narrow the range and scope of this information. As proposed earlier, the behavior of the other person is a primary source of information leading to empathy. An important group of behaviors to attend to is the other person's *verbal statements about wants, expectations, and feelings.* Listening specifically for information about these three phenomena, as defined in Chapter 2, will be more helpful in developing empathy than acquiring verbal information about other areas.

For example, a friend may present a situation that developed with a roommate. In the midst of explaining a problematic social interaction, he might say ". . . and all I *wanted* to do was finish one thing before I began another instead of jumping from one thing to the next." This statement should be selected as significant and worthy of attention because it expresses a want. Information communicated that was not relevant to either the friend's wants or expectation in the situation under discussion is of secondary importance.

The friend's statement would have been equally important if he had expressed his want more indirectly without using the word "want." Wants may be stated as wishes, desires, ambitions, aspirations, longings, yearnings, and likes. Use of any of these words indicates expression of a want. For example, the person might have said, "I *like* finishing one thing before beginning another," "I *don't like* trying to do two things at once," or "I *hate it* when my roommate keeps moving from one job to another before I can get done." When hearing comments like these, it is often helpful to translate them into statements that are indicative of wants. Thus, the preceding statements could be transformed into one in which the person states his want to finish one task to completion before embarking on another.

Expressions of Expectations

Expectations are also the subject of empathy. A woman may indicate that she expects a job interview to go poorly by stating "I have an interview for a promotion tomorrow but I don't *expect* to get it. I have been late to work too much." Expectations, like wants, may be expressed more indirectly, or may be implied. For example, the woman in this example might express an expectation by saying "I'll never get that job, I've been late too much." Expectations may also be expressed in the form of "If I do x, y will happen." That is, the person expects y to follow x but does not state this belief using the word "expectation." For example, "If I improve my punctuality, I'll get that job next time."

A person may imply an expectation by referring to a characteristic or trait he or she attributes to another person. Reference to a characteristic implies an expectation that the individual will act in a predictable way determined by the trait. For example, someone may state, "I can't discuss that subject with Joe, he has a fiery temper." Thus, the person expects an angry response because Joe has a "fiery temper."

Expressions of Feelings

It is also important to listen for expressions of *feelings*. Attention to statements containing the four basic feelings or their synonyms is useful. The person attempting to be empathic should listen for words like fear, happiness, anger, and sadness.

Rather than stating these basic feelings, people often use general descriptors such as "upset," "bad," or "negative." These words should be attended to because they express feelings. They are more informative, however, if translated into one of the four basic feelings. For example, a person may say "I get upset when I have to stop what I am doing in the middle." The word "upset" is a probable statement of a feeling, but because it may express anger, anxiety, or sadness, it is not discriminating and, therefore, not very informative. To develop accurate empathy, it is necessary to obtain sufficient information to determine which of the four basic feelings "upset" refers to. Words like "bad" or "negative" similarly need to be translated into basic feelings to be useful. More will be said about *eliciting* information about wants, expectations, and feelings in the next section of this chapter.

Thus, what at first appeared to be a simple task—listening to the statements of others and picking out words expressing wants, expectations, and the four basic feelings (fear, anger, sadness, and happiness)—has proved to require some sophistication. People can keep the task manageable by restricting their focus to the four "basic" feelings and the wants and expectations of the other.

Eliciting Additional Verbal Information

Making Direct Requests

It would be naive to think that others will always express their wants, expectations, and feelings clearly and spontaneously. Therefore, it is often helpful to directly ask for additional verbal information from the other person. It will be most beneficial if the information elicited helps build a TFB triad, as will be explained later. The desired information is obtained by asking questions such as "What you want?" "What do you expect to happen?" and "How are you feeling?" Although these are not the only questions that can be used, they are the most direct. Most importantly, the questions focus on wants, expectations, and feelings.

Indirect Methods of Obtaining Information

Some indirect methods can augment or substitute for direct behavioral observations of a person when attempting to assess wants, expectations, and feelings.

Prior Knowledge of Other Person.   If the observer knows another person well, it is helpful to use *prior knowledge* about his or her wants, expectations, and feelings. That is, judgments may be based partially on knowing the person's wants or feelings in similar past situations. If it is known from past experience that a person likes to finish a task before starting a new one, it would be reasonable to assume that the same want exists in the present situation.

Shared Experience.   Sometimes empathic understanding of other people's wants and feelings can be facilitated by "stepping into their shoes." This technique involves the *application of knowledge about ourselves* to others. In this case, having observed the other person's situation, an observer thinks, "What would I want if I were in this situation?" "What would I expect if I were in that situation?" or "What feeling would I have if I were in that situation?" To the extent that we share reactions to life experiences with others, we are able to accurately guess their wants, expectations, or feelings.

Observation of Nonverbal Behaviors.   Verbal statements of another person are not the sole source of information about his or her inner state. Motor ("body language") and paralinguistic (nonverbal sounds such as, voice inflection) behaviors also provide such information. Although much has been written about body language (e.g., Fast, 1970), primary attention should be paid to the four "basic behaviors" (avoidance, positive approach, negative approach, and "down behavior"). When used as part of a TFB triad, basic behaviors give information about the wants, expectations, and feelings of the other. A presentation of the nonverbal aspects of communication may be found in Chapter 6 and will not be repeated here. The use of the TFB circle to facilitate empathy will be discussed in another section of this chapter.

Organizing and Processing Information

Once information about wants, expectations, and feelings is acquired, it needs to be organized and understood. The next section describes how to process information that will facilitate empathic understanding.

Use of TFB Triads

Organizing and processing information leading to empathy is aided by the concept of the thought-feeling-behavior triad. When only some of the information relevant to the empathic statement is obtained (e.g., the want or expectation is known but not the feeling, or vice versa), the TFB triad can supplement the missing component(s). Behavioral observations can also be fit into a TFB triad from which the user can discern a variety of information about wants and feelings.

A person attempting to be empathic is alert to two kinds of information: (a) verbal reports of feelings, wants, or expectations and (b) observations of the four basic behaviors (avoidance, positive approach, negative approach, and slowed behaviors). Applying this information to the TFB circle makes it more useful. For example, if someone states he is feeling angry, it can be assumed (by reference to the TFB triad) that he has an unmet want that is still desired and is engaging in "negative approach" behaviors. If he says he is feeling anxious, it is likely he is expecting something "bad" to happen and is engaging in avoidance behaviors. A statement of sadness would imply that something was wanted, but hope is gone of ever obtaining it. Here, slowed or "down" behavior would be expected. Finally, hearing statements of happiness would suggest that the person has obtained a want and is exhibiting positive approach behaviors.

Similarly, if the want or expectation is stated, the feeling can be determined by completing the "TFB triad." If the person indicates he expects his roommate to be angry at him for not doing the grocery shopping, it can be assumed that he also expects something "bad" to happen, which is accompanied by a feeling of fear.

As illustrated, when attempting to determine a feeling on the basis of information about wants and expectations, it is necessary to determine (a) whether the want or expectation was fulfilled, (b) whether it is still desired, or (c) whether the hope of obtaining it is gone. This information helps determine which of the four "TFB triads" applies to the present want or expectation, and allows the feeling to be identified.

Observation of nonverbal behavior can also be organized using the TFB circle. For example, seeing that a person is engaged in behavior classifiable as "avoidance" (e.g., not going to school, staying home when invited to a party, avoiding interaction with a roommate), it can be inferred that the person *expects* something bad (unwanted) to happen and is *feeling* fear, anxiety, or some feeling in that family. Similarly, if the person is engaged in "positive-approach" *behaviors* (e.g., walking toward another waving her arm and smiling), it may be assumed that she has had, or expects to have, a *want* satisfied and is *feeling* happy. "Negative approach" behaviors may be assumed to be related to anger and slow or "down" behaviors signify sadness.

When using the TFB circle, only general information about wants and expectations is initially obtained. That is, the TFB circle indicates that there is a want or expectation and it was either obtained or not and it is either still wanted or not. It does not initially specify the want or expectation. Detailed and situation-specific information must be obtained by inquiry. The information from the circle helps guide the inquirer, who can ask "What is it you want that you have not gotten [angry person]?" "What is it that you wanted but have given up hope on [sad person]?" "What did you want that you got [happy person]?" "What do you expect to happen that will be bad [anxious person]?" Such inquiry can result in accurate and meaningful information about the other person.

Deciding When to Use an Empathic Statement

Empathic understanding and the communication of awareness of another's wants, expectations, and feelings is a common and positive part of human interaction. However, constant expression of empathy is seldom desirable. Empathic statements should be reserved for specific occasions for which they are most useful and appropriate.

The ability to communicate empathically allows a person to relate to someone else in a way that encourages sharing of personal experiences. Empathy shows caring and concern, which is likely to create a social bond between people. An empathic statement is appropriate when such a bonding is desired.

An empathic statement can also soften an otherwise harsh or conflict-engendering message through the demonstration of concern for the other. Knowing he or she has been considered helps a person accept negative information. For example, a person may understand that his roommate does not like (want) to start a second task before completing the first. If it becomes necessary to ask the roommate to start a new task before the first is completed, the expression of empathy will soften the request. An empathic request, such as "I know you don't like to stop what you are doing in the middle and I usually avoid asking you to do so, but since the dinner guests will arrive in five minutes would you drop what you are doing and set the table?" would likely be better received than a flat statement of wants that did not show concern for the other.

In addition, the empathic statement is appropriate (a) when a person wants to show that he or she is actively listening and concerned about another person, (b) it is expected that the other person will react negatively to a request that is going to be made, and (c) when refusing another person's request. The latter two applications will be the subjects of Chapters 4 and 5.

Expressing an Empathic Statement (Information Sending)

Three Kinds of Empathic Statements

Having taken in relevant information and organized it using the TFB circle, the next step is to express an empathic statement. People can express empathy by making one of three different types of comments. They can make a statement that reflects: (a) only the wants and/or expectations of another, (b) only the feeling(s) that the other person is experiencing, or (c) the wants, expectations, *and* feelings of another.

The Structure of an Empathic Statement

The empathic statement consists of two parts: a lead-in phrase and a statement of a want, expectation, and/or feeling. The lead-in-phrase should be a brief statement such as "It seems like you are . . . ," "It sounds like you . . . ," "You look . . . ," "You seem to be . . . ," "I know you are . . . ," "I get the feeling that you are . . . ." An effective empathic statement is composed simply by combining one of these "lead-in phrases" with a statement of the expectation, want, or feeling. For example, "Steve, it sounds like you really wanted that job."

The empathic statement is always a statement of the wants, expectations, and feelings of *another person* (e.g., "It seems like you are angry"). It is not a statement of the feelings of *the speaker*. Statements such as "Steve, I am so sorry you didn't get that job," "I am disappointed that you didn't get the job," or "That was so unfair, it makes me sick!" reflect the *feeling or beliefs of the speaker and are not empathic*. Statements that express the wants, feelings, and beliefs of the speaker are best characterized as *sympathetic* statements. It is a common error to confuse empathy and sympathy. Sympathetic statements have their place in interpersonal communication, but they do not express understanding or awareness of the other person.

Example of an Empathic Statement

As indicated in the definition of the empathic statement, it expresses one person's understanding of another's wants, expectations, and/or feelings. For example, assume Steve sighs deeply as he looks down and says: "I had two interviews for that great job I told you about, but they gave it to someone else." The first step to understanding Steve's wants, expectations, and feelings is to note the relevant behaviors. Those described as "sighing and looking down" are relevant and may be classified as belonging to the "basic behavior" group of *"inaction—slowed action" or "down" behaviors.* Next, the information about the observed behaviors is processed by placing them in a TFB triad. Down behaviors are part of the TFB triad that includes the feeling of *sadness* and *unmet wants for which hope has been abandoned.* Thus, based on the observation of down, slowed-action behaviors, it is hypothesized that Steve has given up hope of getting what he wanted (the job) and he is feeling sad.

In addition to focusing on Steve's motor behavior (sighing and looking down), one could also focus on his verbal behavior. In this case, Steve indicated that he had gone to two interviews and had failed to be given a job he desired. Steve did not use the word "want" or "expectation." However, it would be reasonable to assume that since Steve went on two interviews to try to obtain a job that he described as "great," he *wants* the job. If the company has given it to another person, Steve's want has not been satisfied. Furthermore, since the job was apparently available to only one person and it has been awarded to someone else, Steve is no longer a candidate for the job. Therefore, there is no possibility that his desire will be satisfied. In this case, he most likely has given up hope of obtaining this job. Finding the TFB triad that is consistent with this information leads to the one that contains the feeling of sadness. Thus, based on an evaluation of what Steve said, we would hypothesize that Steve is feeling sad.

Given the observations and conclusions about Steve's wants and feelings, three different empathic statements would be appropriate:

1. *Empathic Response to Wants and Desires.* "It sounds like you really wanted that job."
2. *Empathic Response to Feelings.* "You must be sad."
3. *Empathic Response to Wants and Feelings.* "It sounds like you really wanted that job and are sad because you did not get it."

This example demonstrates that considerable mental effort and processing may yield an empathic statement consisting of as few as four words. Empathic statements are frequently brief and are focused on reflecting the want, expectation, and/or feeling. Accurate empathy, not brevity, is the primary goal when it comes to the empathic statement, but accuracy and brevity frequently occur together.

In the preceding example, Steve's problem was not solved by the empathic statement. In fact, a problem-solving statement such as "Why don't you call the company and see if they have any other jobs" would not have been empathic. Many people have difficulty simply being empathic and want to give the person suggestions about how to get his or her wants met, or how to change feelings. In the latter case, one might say "Don't be sad, you'll get another job." There is nothing wrong with taking a problem-solving or supportive orientation, but it does not serve the same purpose as empathy. Being empathic is a specific skill that attempts to show an understanding of another's wants, expectations, and feeling. Individuals must learn the value of such a statement.

TRAINING PROGRAM TO TEACH THE EMPATHIC STATEMENT

The following information is provided as a guide to the practitioner interested in the clinical use of the material presented in this chapter. It is organized according to the model of skills training presented in Chapter 1 and includes four components: Instruction, Supervised Practice, Feedback, and Independent Practice.

Instruction

The key "skill concepts" in this chapter should be presented to the clients in the form of a brief lecture or discussion. This information may be used in a group therapy format or it can be adapted for use with individual clients or families. It can be presented informally or as a structured lecture.

As may be recalled from Chapter 1, the purpose of the Instruction phase of skills training is to describe the concepts and skills that are to be learned. In Chapter 3, these skill concepts are designed to define the empathic statement, organize the individual's thinking about the empathic statement, and provide a cognitive guide for performance. The skill concepts are the basis of subsequent learning about the empathic statement. In the Feedback section, they are the basis for evaluation of performance. In the Supervised Practice and Independent Practice sections of training, the skill concepts describe the target behaviors that clients attempt to match with their own performance.

The following is an outline of topics to cover in the Instruction phase:

1. Describe relationship of empathy to self-awareness (refer to Chapter 2).
2. Define an empathic statement and describe three kinds.
3. Describe ways to understand wants, expectations, and feelings of others:
   a. Verbal statements.
   b. Nonverbal statements.
   c. Characteristics of the situation.
   d. Prior knowledge of other person.
   e. "How would I feel, what would I want?"
4. Describe how to process and organize information relevant to the empathic statement through use of TFB triads.
5. Provide examples of empathic statements.

Supervised Practice

Empathy Demonstration and Role-Play Exercise

The process of making an empathic statement is practiced using a group exercise. The exercise includes (a) observing behavioral and situational cues, (b) processing this information and deciding the content of the statement, and (c) performing an empathic statement. The empathic statement should be demonstrated (modeled) for the clients by the therapist. If there are two staff present, they should model the exercise first. If there is only one staff, a group member can read the sample statements and the staff person will model empathic responses. One or more of the statements in Table 3–1 can be used for demonstration. This table provides examples of four simple and four complex statements/vignettes that can be used in this exercise. Following the demonstration by the therapist, the exercise is conducted as follows:

1. One statement from those listed in Table 3–1 is given to each client on a slip of paper. Clients are instructed to read it and write down the feeling, want, or expectation expressed by the statement.

2. Dyads are formed among the persons present. A staff member can be used to complete a dyad if there is not an even number of clients.

3. One member of each dyad (the sender) reads his or her statement to the other (the recipient), who listens to the statement, composes an empathic statement, and replies to the sender.

4. Sender informs recipient whether or not the empathic response matched the feeling and/or want he tried to portray and recorded in Step 1. Participants discuss the process used to make empathic statements including information used, how it was processed using the TFB triad, and how the response was composed.

5. Members of dyad switch roles and use the same procedure as before, following Steps 1–4.

6. When this part of the exercise is completed, the large group is reassembled and pair(s) of volunteers are asked to demonstrate the task before the entire group. This includes Steps 3 and 4 above.

TABLE 3–1
Empathy Demonstration and Role-Play Stimulus Items

1. I lost my wallet.
2. I finally managed to pay my rent on time this month.
3. I lost my keys to my house.
4. I have a job interview tomorrow.
5. I wanted to do something nice for my mother so I asked her if there was anything that I could do for her. She said, "Nothing, I can take care of myself, thank you."
6. Man 65 years old: My wife died last year, and this year my youngest son moved out of the house. My other son lives in Albuquerque. Now I just spend a lot of time rambling around this old house that is really too big for me.
7. Student to adviser: I have a term paper due tomorrow. I'm giving a report in class today. My wife has the flu. And now I just got a letter stating that a special committee wants to meet with me to review my progress in the program.
8. I wanted Tom to start coming home on time so I spoke to him about it. Do you know what? He was on time for supper every day last week!

7. The exercise is repeated using additional items of the type shown in Table 3–1 until the clients demonstrate the ability to make an empathic statement.

Feedback

The general guidelines for the Feedback phase are provided in Chapter 2. It is best to emphasize the use of a model of feedback that comments on ways the behavior *matched and did not match* the skill concepts. There is often a tendency to comment only on the negative or deficit aspects of performance. We recommend commenting first on a positive aspect of performance (a way it matched or approximated the skill concept) and then providing a specific recommendation that would improve performance (a way to better match the skill concept).

A client might make a sympathetic response instead of an empathic one, saying "Bob, you have so many problems, I feel sorry for you." Appropriate feedback would be "I liked the way you took a minute to think about the statement before you spoke, and your voice was supportive. However, since you stated how you felt, you made a sympathetic statement. Your statement would have been empathic if you expressed your understanding of how Bob was feeling, not how you were feeling about Bob." The feedback should reinforce the degree to which behavior matched the "skill concepts" presented in the instruction section of training.

Independent Practice

Each client identifies several persons with whom he or she will interact during the week and to whom he or she can make an empathic statement. Clients select persons with whom they will share personal experiences, and/or with whom they want to create a social bond. The target person could be someone for whom the client wants to show a sensitivity and concern. Perhaps the client will want to "soften" an otherwise harsh message, show that the client is actively listening and concerned about another person, increase the receptivity of someone to a request the person might otherwise refuse, or show consideration for another whose request the client is refusing.

The therapist should discuss and rehearse what the clients anticipate doing in interactions and how they would make an empathic statement.

The therapist instructs clients to engage in these interactions during the week. The interactions are to be discussed during subsequent therapy sessions to determine which skills were performed well and which could be improved.

The client and therapist should develop a plan to use the empathic statement that is consistent with his or her overall treatment plan. This training program does not emphasize the use of the empathic statement as an independent skill. Rather, empathy is embedded into the request statements that are presented in the following chapters. Nonetheless, the client may target personal relationships such as those that occur in important everyday life situations where empathy is appropriate and adaptive.

4

Communicating Requests

The self-awareness and empathy skills that have been presented lay the foundation for learning how to communicate requests. Request making is emphasized in this book because it is one of the most direct ways of getting wants met. Wants are considered to be the cognitive representation of something that, once obtained, provides positive reinforcement to the individual. Thus, making requests is a direct way to elicit positive reinforcement from the environment. Developing skill in the acquisition of reinforcement helps create self-efficacy. This chapter focuses on requests appropriate in three kinds of situations:

1. Where there is *no conflict* between what the requester and the recipient of the request want.
2. Where there *is conflict* between the wants of the two parties regarding the request.
3. Where the requester wants another person to *change an undesired behavior.*

Nearly all requests in everyday life fit one of these three situations. Because making requests when there is a basic conflict in wants, and asking a person to change his or her behavior can be difficult, at least at times, it is adaptive to develop skill in the performance of such requests.

The ideas and procedures in this chapter have been influenced by our research and clinical experience as well as that of other practitioners (see Chapter 1). Skills training programs that teach people how to use language to influence others and get what they want from the environment have been shown to produce better functioning and reduced psychological symptoms (Archer, Bedell, & Amuso, 1980; Bedell & Ward, 1989; Hogarty et al., 1986; Wallace & Liberman, 1985). As indicated by Bandura (1969), persons who have the skills to exercise control over the environment and influence the reinforcements they receive in life function better interpersonally. This is the goal of the present program.

UNDERSTANDING THE PROBLEM
OF MAKING REQUESTS

The desire to make a request implies that someone wants something from another person. How does one go about getting things from others? An exercise entitled "You Have It, I Want It" illustrates some common ways to accomplish this. In it, individuals form pairs and one member of the pair pretends that he or she has something and wants to keep it. The other person uses verbal means to persuade the first person to give "it" to him or her.

Repeated experience with this exercise reveals that there are a few common approaches to get something from another person. Often the requester begins with statements providing information (e.g., why the requester needs "it"), logically arguing why "it" should be given over and making polite pleas for generosity. When these methods fail, the requester generally resorts to various forms of threat, bribe, demand, or guilt induction. The latter methods usually create negative feelings (fear, anger) and a desire to terminate the interaction on the part of the recipient of the request.

This exercise demonstrates that most people have a relatively limited repertoire of "request-making" behaviors. And, many of the methods used to get something from another are harmful to future relations between the parties. It is desirable to learn communication skills that are effective in getting what is wanted and, at the same time, help build and maintain the relationship, rather than tear it down. The specific skills needed to accomplish this objective will be described in this chapter.

GENERAL FEATURES OF REQUESTS

There are two features of a request that increase its potential for effectiveness. First, it should express what is wanted in a clear and direct way. Second, the requester should include a statement that communicates sensitivity to the wants and feelings of the recipient of the request.

A clear and direct request unambiguously states what is wanted from the other person. An example of a direct request would be, "I understand that you like to rest on weekends, but if you would go shopping with me next Saturday morning to help me pick out the new couch, I'd appreciate it." This statement indicates precisely what is wanted (help on Saturday to pick out a new couch). In contrast, an indirect expression of wants usually involves hinting, suggesting, implying, or providing incomplete information about what is wanted, such as, "If you are not busy next week maybe we could get the new couch." This statement does not make it clear that the speaker wants the other person to accompany him to the store on Saturday to pick out the couch. This statement hints or suggests what is wanted but provides incomplete information.

Expressing what is wanted in behavioral terms helps to make the request clear and direct. This involves a statement of the behaviors that are desired of the other person. In the preceding example, a behavioral statement could be, "I understand you like to rest on the weekend, but if you *walk around the stores with me* on Saturday morning and *point out* the couches you like, I'd feel more comfortable about making such a large purchase."

Behavioral language also helps to clarify requests involving complex or vague concepts. Rather than telling someone "I want you to be a *better roommate*," or "I want you to *shape up* around the house," a person making a behavioral statement would indicate the actions desired. For example, "being a better roommate" could mean "I want you to do the grocery shopping on alternate weeks, wash the dishes every other night, and say hello to me when I come home in the evening."

Sometimes, people want seemingly intangible things such as friendship, affection, and respect from others. These broad concepts may mean different things to different people and are often difficult to put into words. In addition, how is the other person to know what the requester means when he or she asks for something with many meanings? Relying on the other person's interpretation may result in the requester's failing to get what he or she wants. Therefore, it is imperative to transform the ostensibly intangible items into specific behaviors that will fulfill the want. Requesters can ask themselves, "What behaviors would show friendship (or affection or respect)?" "How would I know if he was being friendly (or affectionate or respectful)?" The answers to these questions should be made clear in the request.

Some people object to requesting specific behaviors related to phenomena like friendship, love, and affection. They ask, "If the person is just performing the behaviors requested, how genuine can he or she be?" or, "If he is really a friend, he would know how to show me." Notwithstanding the possible validity of these comments, the philosophy of the present program is that, if a person wants something, it is usually adaptive to ask for it in a clear and direct manner. Providing behavioral specificity is especially helpful when the other person is not skilled at expressing complex feelings (such as friendship, love, and affection).

The second feature of a request involves taking into consideration the wants and feelings of the other person. This process is based on the concepts of empathy (Chapter 3) and assertiveness (Chapter 6). The individual who is empathic when making a request of another demonstrates sensitivity and caring. When this is done skillfully, it is likely that the other person will recognize this expression of caring. A request recognized as being empathic is likely to be better received as it satisfies one of the most basic desires of a human being—to be appreciated (James, 1987). Feeling appreciated facilitates communication and is an important element of a request.

Interestingly, expressing oneself clearly and directly and maintaining an attitude of empathy also positively affects the person *making* the request. Communicating in this way results in a higher level of self-awareness than a person can attain when offering vague information. Also, when maintaining awareness of the wants and feelings of another person, the requester may elect to modify wants to accommodate the other person. Thus, people become more likely to make appropriate compromises and to modify unreasonable, unrealistic, or exorbitant wants. For example, a woman named Betty was going to ask a friend at work to drive her to the garage where her car had been repaired. Before making the request, she asked herself what her friend would want to do after work and how she would feel if asked to drive her to the garage. Betty remembered her friend had the responsibility to pick up her little boy at day care promptly after work each day. Betty thought her friend would not want to go to the garage due to the time pressure. So, Betty decided to ask her friend if she was available at lunchtime to pick up the car, or if after picking up her child she could take her to the garage. In this case, Betty *expressed* her consideration of her friend by saying, "My car is in the shop and I need a ride to get it. I know you have to pick up your son after work, so could you give me a ride at lunchtime to get my car or maybe after you go to day care this afternoon?" The essential point is that, once an individual begins to consider the wants of the self and other, changes in requests will occur, reflecting interpersonal sensitivity.

Making requests that are (a) clear and direct and (b) sensitive to the wants and feelings of others will provide several benefits, including an increased likelihood of the request being granted and the relationship between the maker and recipient of the request being well maintained (whether or not the request is granted). Although we cannot guarantee that requests will be granted or that any benefits will occur, even when people follow the rules of communication suggested in this chapter, developing skills in the methods presented maximizes the likelihood of positive outcomes.

MATCHING REQUESTS TO THE SITUATION

A request generally focuses on asking another person to perform some task, provide some service, or act in a certain way. A request may also ask another person to think or feel in a desired way or to express appreciation, respect, loyalty, or love. The nature of what is requested can be trivial or significant, concrete, or abstract. Requests also vary in the amount of time and effort needed to grant them.

Just deciding what kind of request is appropriate for a given situation can become a complex and bewildering task. Therefore, a simplified method of decision making has been developed for matching a request to the situation. The appropriate request can be determined by using self-awareness and empathy skills to assess (a) the wants of the requester and (b) the wants of the recipient of the request. If the requester's wants do not conflict with the wants of the recipient, a simple unelaborated request will do. However, if there is a conflict between the wants of the requester and recipient, a more elaborate request is required.

An evaluation of the wants of others may involve consideration of the time and effort required to grant the request. Asking a person to perform a task that requires little time or effort (e.g., passing the salt at mealtime), is unlikely to create conflict. Passing the salt does not significantly delay the enjoyment of the meal, and this behavior may, in fact, be consistent with the person's desire to be polite and to behave in a socially acceptable way. However, asking a friend to take time off work to help move furniture may conflict with that person's desire to save vacation days for leisure use. Moreover, he may not want to move furniture at any time, finding it overly strenuous, tiresome, and tedious. Obviously, different kinds of request would be appropriate in these two situations. The ability to decide what type is appropriate for the situation is an important skill to learn.

Three Basic Request Situations

Consistent with the approach used throughout this book, we have identified three "basic request situations" that encompass a wide variety of everyday interactions. The following brief overview describes three types of request situations; they are primarily determined by the degree of agreement (or conflict) between the wants of the requester and those of the recipient of the request. The procedures for making the appropriate request for each of these situations will be described later.

Request Situation 1. Compatible Wants, No Conflict

In all request situations, the wants of the self and other are assessed and compared. When there are no significant conflicts between the wants of the person making the request and the wants of the recipient of the request, a "no conflict in wants" situation exists. As indicated previously, my want for you to pass the salt at mealtime is probably not in conflict with yours to do so, thus exemplifying this type of situation. Similarly, if two roommates want the house clean for company tonight, then each one's desire to have the other perform specified cleaning tasks would likely constitute a "no-conflict in wants" situation.

We should reiterate that another's wants are internal events to which an outsider does not have direct access. Therefore, unless a person expressly informs another about such wants, they can only be hypothesized. To increase the likelihood of accurate hypothesis, we presented strategies for understanding others' wants in Chapter 3.

The no-conflict situation is relatively congenial. A high degree of social skill is not needed to get wants met in such a situation. The other person is already disposed to grant the request. While trivial in many ways, the no-conflict situation is important because people must be able to differentiate it from one in which conflict between wants exists, and the skills used here are also used in other types of request situations.

Request Situation 2. Incompatible Wants, Conflict

This situation exists when, after the wants of the person making the request are compared with those of the recipient, a conflict is judged to exist. Wants are in conflict when they cannot both be satisfied at the same time; the conflict, however, does *not* entail the requester's want for the other to change an undesirable behavior. For example, a person may want his roommate to go shopping every two weeks. The roommate may dislike grocery shopping and want someone else to perform that task. The wants of these two roommates are in conflict since they cannot both be met at the same time. Similarly, when two people are engaged in conversation, a conflict exists if one wants to continue and the other wishes to leave and go to work.

This type of conflict situation arises frequently and is often the basis of a difficult interpersonal interaction. How does a person make a request that is in conflict with what the other person wants? Although one option is to avoid making such requests, the person then would satisfy only those wants that were consistent with those of others, leaving many wants unfulfilled. Also, as indicated in Chapter 2, unmet wants lead to feelings in the anger and sadness families. Frequent experience of these feelings over a long time is dysfunctional.

Rather than avoid making requests that conflict with the desires of others, the individual might use power, guilt, coercion, and other types of maladaptive methods to overcome the desires of the other person. This approach, however, is also undesirable since it might be destructive to the maintenance and growth of interpersonal relationships.

Making requests when there is a conflict in wants is an inevitable part of everyday life. It is natural for people to want things that conflict with the wants of others. Most people benefit from learning skilled ways of addressing these situations. Making requests in "conflict situations" will be discussed later.

Request Situation 3. Desire for Behavior Change

This situation arises when someone wants another person to change an undesired behavior. A conflict in wants results because the individual making the request wants the other person to behave in a certain way, whereas the other person wants to continue the former behavior. While this interaction is similar to that of Request Situation 2, this conflict involves only those instances in which the request arises directly from the wish to have the recipient change an undesired behavior.

For example, perhaps someone objects to the way another person interrupts him when he is speaking. This situation gives rise to a request specifically because of the *interrupting behavior.* Or, consider the person who consistently leaves the shower adjustment in the position that causes the water to spray on his roommate's head when he turns it on. The desire to change the *behavior of the roommate* regarding the shower adjustment is the focus of this situation. Or, suppose someone is habitually late for the Friday card game, requiring others to delay beginning the game until he arrives. *The behavior of being late* is the focus of this request situation. In all these examples, the behavior of the other person is judged undesirable by the person making the request.

It may be reasoned that any type of request asks for a change in behavior. Even a trivial request, such as asking another person to pass the salt shaker, requires a change in behavior. To comply with such a request, the recipient must stop eating, pick up the salt shaker, and hand it to the requester. However, the difference between Request Situation 3 and Situations 1 and 2 is that the request in the latter types of situation is not prompted by the behavior of the other person. There is no disapproval of the other's behavior and the behavior is not aggravating or annoying to the requester. The change in behavior that occurs in Situations 1 and 2 is incidental and secondary to the request. The fact that a dinner partner stops eating for a moment to pass the salt is not the desired outcome of this no-conflict request.

Three Basic Kinds of Requests

Since there are three "basic request situations," there also are three kinds of requests, one for each type of situation: the "No-Conflict Request," the "Conflict Request," and the "Request for Behavior Change." The no-conflict request is the simplest type of request and has the fewest components. The conflict request is somewhat more complicated. The request for behavior change is the most complex and has the greatest number of components.

In progressing from the simplest to the most complex request, the requester keeps adding components. The components of the no-conflict request are included in all the requests. The conflict request requires the addition of one component, while the request for behavior change entails the addition of another two. Because each request builds on another, knowledge of four basic components enables a person to make all three types of request.

We will present these four components first, followed by the method used to combine them into the different types of request.

FOUR BASIC COMPONENTS OF REQUESTS

Component 1. Statement of One's Own Wants

The first component of any request involves understanding what one wants from the other person. It is surprising how much the quality of a request improves when the requester takes the time to understand what he or she wants. A useful procedure is to first label an unmet want and then determine how another person may be instrumental in satisfying it. The person should be able to answer the question, "What do I want from the other person in this situation?"

This process is usually helped by distinguishing between general and specific wants. This distinction is important because, although they are related, what an individual wants in a given situation (general want) may be somewhat different from what is wanted from the other person (specific want). For example, when going to the movie, a man may want to sit with his uncle and watch the movie (general want). If two adjacent seats are not available, a more focused and specific want develops regarding what someone else can do to help get the general want met. A response to the question, "What do I want from the other person in this situation?", may be "I want someone who is sitting next to a vacant seat to move over so that I can sit next to my uncle and watch the movie." In this example, what started out as a general want ("I want to sit next to my uncle and watch the movie") was transformed into a specific want ("I want this man to move over one seat"). The desire to have someone move over one seat is the way to use communication to get the general want met.

Component 2. Statement of the Consequences If the Want Is Granted

The second component of the request is a statement of the beneficial consequences expected if the want is fulfilled. The communication of this information demonstrates respect for the recipient of the request and may increase the probability of his granting it.

There is always a consequence if the want is fulfilled. In our example, if the stranger fulfills the nephew's want for him to move over one seat, the nephew will be able to sit with his uncle. If I ask my friend to spend the evening at my house, the consequence is that "we could watch a movie together" or "we could have a quiet evening."

Experience with this model has shown that expression of consequences sometimes sounds silly, awkward, or stilted, when the consequences are either trivial or completely obvious. For example, in a no-conflict situation, an individual may want to read a magazine that is out of reach and, therefore, ask another person to hand it to him. The consequence, which is obvious, is that the requester can read the magazine. In such cases, it is appropriate to indicate a general consequence, such as a feeling of appreciation. So, the person might say, "If you would hand me the magazine, I would appreciate it."

Although it is sometimes unnecessary to state a specific consequence, it is generally helpful to do so. For example, if someone in a movie theater is asked to move over one seat, it may be obvious that the consequence will be that someone can sit down. However, if adding "so I can sit with my uncle" provides helpful information and shows consideration to the recipient of the request, it may aid in securing compliance.

Understanding the consequences of having another fulfill your want also helps the *initiator* of the request to better understand his action. Determining the consequence if a want is fulfilled sometimes leads to a modification of the request, and subsequently to more skilled social interaction. For example, a person may consider asking his roommate to go shopping to get some food for dinner. When he considers the consequences associated with the roommate fulfilling his want, he may realize that the primary result is that he does not have to go to the store. That is, if the roommate went shopping, the requester would not have to go. In this case, the requester may decide that there is no particular reason he cannot go himself and, therefore, modify the request or refrain from making it.

Component 3. Statement of Other's Wants

An important element of any request involves understanding the wants of the other person in relation to what the requester wants. This understanding should answer the question, "What does the other person want with regard to what I want from that person?"

How does the requester determine what another person wants? After all, the request has not yet been made. To answer this question refer to the information provided on empathy in Chapter 3, which explained that information about the wants of others can be obtained by (a) their verbal statements of wants, (b) characteristics of the situation, (c) knowledge of their wants in prior situations, and (d) by asking, "What would I want if the request were made of me?" Among other things factored into the answer to this last question are the amount of time and effort involved in fulfilling the other's want.

If we consider the movie example in which the nephew wanted to ask a stranger to move over one seat so he could sit next to his uncle, what would the stranger want in relation to what the nephew is going to request? The nephew might reason as follows: "In a movie theater, no one is assigned a seat or guaranteed an empty one on either side. Therefore, this stranger would most likely want to behave in a way consistent with this social norm. Also, what I want from him, that is, to move one seat, requires minimal effort. If I were him, I'd just want to have a seat with a good view of the screen and, if moving a little didn't affect this, I'd be happy to do it." This logical thought process suggests that the stranger would *want* to cooperate and provide the opportunity for two people to sit together if they so desire.

As indicated in the discussion of the empathic statement, one's *judgment* of what the other person wants may not be accurate. However, the procedures that lead to empathic understanding maximize the degree to which the user can accurately gauge the wants of the other person. Awareness of the wants of the other may cause the requester to modify wants, compromise, or defer to the wants of the other if the requester determines that such changes may promote a positive response. Modifying one's wants is not recommended, nor is it discouraged. It is simply a natural and inevitable outcome of being sensitive to the wants of others.

Component 4. Feedback

Feedback is used only when making a request for behavioral change. Feedback focuses on describing the *undesired* behavior and indicating how this undesired behavior *affects the requester.*

The undesired behavior is described clearly, preferably in behavioral terms. If the undesired behavior is interrupting when one is talking, it should be described as "interrupting me when I am speaking" or "starting to speak before I have finished." It should not be described as "being rude" or "hogging the conversation" or any similar description that involves a value judgment or is pejorative. If someone is not fulfilling her share of the housekeeping duties, the specific chores not being done should be named. For example, "leaving the sink full of dirty dishes overnight" or "failing to go grocery shopping resulting in us running out of milk" would be appropriate behavioral descriptions of undesired behavior. Describing the other person as "lazy," "sloppy," or "inconsiderate" is not a behavioral description and is not a useful part of the feedback statement.

The second part of the feedback statement is a description of the requester's reaction to the undesired behavior. The reaction is how the requester thinks, feels, and/or acts in response to the behavior that he or she wants changed. In a situation in which someone is "starting to speak before I have finished," the individual may *want* to stop socializing with the other person (a thought), feel *annoyed* (a feeling), and/or plan to *avoid* having conversations with the other person (a behavior). Any or all of these three reactions to the undesired behavior may be included in the feedback component.

The two elements of the feedback statement are usually spoken sequentially, with the behavior to be changed stated first followed by the requester's reaction to the behavior. In the preceding examples, the feedback statements could be, "When you start speaking before I have finished, I feel annoyed," and "When you leave the sink full of dirty dishes overnight, I think you are not interested in doing your share of the apartment chores."

HOW TO MAKE A REQUEST

In the preceding sections, we have identified the three types of request, and differentiated them according to both (a) the presence of a conflict between the wants of the requester and request recipient (no conflict vs. conflict) and (b) the type of conflict present (conflict between the wants of the requester and the recipient of the request—the conflict request; or wanting another to change an undesired behavior—request for behavior change). The composition of each request has been provided as well, consisting of the following two, three, or four components:

No-Conflict Request

1. Statement of what I want from other.
2. Statement of the consequences if want fulfilled.

Conflict Request

1. Statement of what I want from other.
2. Statement of the consequences if want fulfilled.

3. Statement of (my perception of) other's want in relation to my want.

Request for Behavior Change

1. Statement of what I want from other.
2. Statement of consequences if want fulfilled.
3. Statement of (my perception of) other's want in relation to my want.
4. Feedback statement.

Figure 4–1 is a flowchart designed to guide a person through the process of making a request. It shows the person:

1. Information needed for the request.
2. How to decide on the appropriate request.
3. How to assemble the statement.

As shown in the chart, three stages of information are related to determining which request to make. At the top of the figure is the *information-gathering* stage. After identifying this information, the person processes it and decides on both the types of request to make and the ways in which to make it. This is the *information-processing stage*. The *information-sending stage* is the execution of the specific request. Thus, the individual verbalizes the statements at the bottom of the chart in the row of boxes corresponding to the particular request selected for use.

The following section demonstrates the use of Figure 4–1 for each of the three types of request.

No-Conflict Request

We will refer back to the example in which a young man and his uncle are attending a movie and they want to sit next to each other but two adjacent seats are not available. There is a man, however, sitting in between two vacant seats. If he moves over one seat, then two adjacent ones would be available. The nephew decided to make a request of this man.

To make this request, the nephew has to gather the information indicated in the top section of the chart.

1. *Information Gathering*
    a. *What does nephew want from the other person?*
       He wants him to move over one seat.

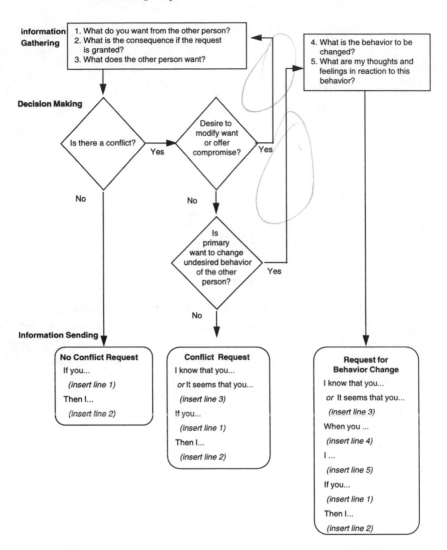

Figure 4–1. How to make a request.

b. *Consequences if want is fulfilled.*

The nephew would be able to sit next to his uncle during the movie.

c. *What does the other person want?*

He probably wants to sit in a seat that enables him to see the movie. He probably wants to be polite. What nephew is asking requires little effort on his part.

Once gathered, the information is used first to determine whether there is a conflict between the wants of the requester and those of the intended request recipient. Determination of the presence of a conflict is the first task in the information-processing stage.

2. *Information Processing and Decision Making*

a. *Is there a conflict between nephew's wants and those of other?*

The answer to this question is made in the first decision diamond using information from the Information Gathering section.

b. *Decision.*

There is no conflict.

This decision requires the requester to follow the solid vertical line down from "no" to the box in the information-sending stage with the title "No-Conflict Request." Thus, a *no-conflict request* would be appropriate in this situation.

c. *Organizing the no-conflict request to be stated.*

First, the nephew thinks of the statement that expresses what he wants from the other person (see line 1a of Information Gathering), introducing it with the words "If you":

If you would move over one seat . . .

Next, the nephew thinks of the statement that identifies the consequences if the request is granted, prefacing it with "then I" (see line 1b of Information Gathering):

then I would be able to sit with my uncle and watch the movie.

3. *Information Sending*

    a. The nephew makes the request he has composed in the previous stage following the order shown in the box at the bottom of the flowchart in Figure 4–1.

As may be seen in this description of the "no-conflict request," both parties are expected to be in agreement about the targeted want. All that is really necessary to make the request is to state what is wanted in a clear and direct way. The addition of the "consequences" component facilitates communication (Kagan, 1975; Truax & Carkhuff, 1967). Thus, in this example the nephew would make the request saying "If you would move over one seat, then I would be able to sit with my uncle and watch the movie."

Conflict Request

The following vignette depicts a situation in which the conflict request is most appropriate.

Walking to the Store

I am walking to the grocery store with Betty. We are both looking forward to some leisurely time together, but Betty is especially concerned that we complete the shopping and get home before it starts to rain. She doesn't want to get her new shoes wet. Halfway to the grocery, I remember that I have to mail my rent check at the post office, which is a couple of blocks out of the way. I rarely get to see Betty anymore and today is the only opportunity I'll have all week. If she goes ahead to the grocery store while I go to the post office, we'll hardly have any time to speak with each other. I want to make a request of Betty.

As with all requests, I must first gather information that will enable me to determine the type of request to make and the content of the various components.

1. *Information Gathering*

    a. *What do I want from the other person?*

        I want her to accompany me to the post office.

b. *Consequences if my want is fulfilled.*

I will be able to mail my letters and spend time with Betty.

c. *What does the other person want?*

She wants to get home before it starts raining and keep her shoes dry. She also wants to spend time with me.

After answering these three questions, the requester exits Information Gathering following the arrow leading to the first decision diamond in the Information Processing section. Here the person decides whether or not a conflict in wants exists.

2. *Information Processing and Decision Making*

a. *Is there a conflict in wants?*

It appears that we might get rained on if we make the side trip to the post office. If that happened, I would get what I wanted (to mail the letters) but she would not get what she wanted (to keep her new shoes dry). Yes, there is a conflict in wants.

The "yes" arrow leads to the second decision diamond.

b. *Desire to modify want or offer compromise?*

Since there is a conflict between what I want and what Betty wants, I am prompted to think of a way to compromise or modify my want. In this case I cannot think of a compromise.

Following the "no" arrow I am prompted to determine whether my interest in making a request is primarily a response to Betty's undesired behavior.

c. *Is the primary want to change an undesired behavior of other?*

This is not the case; I want her to go to the post office with me.

This "no" decision leads to the Conflict Request box indicating that I will make this kind of request. The next task is to assemble the three components of the conflict request.

d. *Organizing the three components of the conflict request:*

i. Make an empathic statement that shows I am considering the other's wants regarding my request, "*I know you* want to get home before it starts raining, but . . ."

ii. Make a positive statement of what I want from the other person, "*if you* would come with me to the post office . . . ,

iii. State the consequences if the request is granted, "*then I* can mail these letters and we can have more time to talk."

3. *Information Sending*

I make the conflict request that I assembled in the information processing stage: "*I know you* want to get home before it starts raining, but *if you* would come with me to the post office, *then I* can mail these letters and we can have more time to talk."

As may be seen in this example, a conflict request is actually a combination of two skills that have already been discussed: the empathic statement and the no-conflict request. Combined in this manner, the empathic statement softens the request. The purpose of this type of request is to let the other person know that the requester is attempting to be sensitive to the other's wants at the same time that he or she is asking for something.

Changing a Conflict Request Situation to a No-Conflict Request Situation

When making a request, the person must determine the wants of both parties and compare them to see if a conflict exists. The act of going through this process may cause the requester to become more sensitive to the wants of the other person and to assess their validity more favorably. As a result, the requester may decide to modify his or her own want or offer a compromise so that both parties can get their wants met.

In a conflict situation, the requester may modify a want or offer a compromise to eliminate or minimize the conflict. If so, it may be appropriate to make a no-conflict request. In the preceding example I might decide to modify my request about going to the post office by offering to pay for a taxi for the trip home from the grocery store, after going to the post office. This way, instead of making a request that would satisfy only my want, (to go to post office with Betty), I would also be attempting to satisfy her desire to get home before it rains and she gets her shoes wet. If I am successful, our wants will no longer be in conflict. Therefore, a no-conflict request could be made as follows: "*If you* walk with me to the post office, I will pay for a cab to ride us home from the grocery store. *Then I* can mail my letters and you can be sure to stay dry."

The method of converting a request from one that has conflict to one that does not is illustrated in the flowchart shown in Figure 4–1. In this figure, the decision to attempt a compromise is made in the second decision diamond. The arrow line leading from the "yes" decision of that diamond leads back to the beginning of the Information Gathering box. The requester's want will be modified, and it is likely that the consequences and wants of the other in relation to the revised want will also be modified. When the final product of this revision is evaluated to determine the presence of a conflict, the answer the second time around may be "no" leading to a no-conflict request.

The Request for Behavior Change

Figure 4–1 shows that the request for behavior change involves the same information gathering and information processing as the conflict request. However, if the answer to the third decision diamond is "yes" because the reason for the request is an undesired behavior of the other person, more information must be collected. Therefore, following the arrowed "yes" line, the requestor resumes information gathering and collects additional information to provide the feedback component of the request for behavior change.

After identifying the target behavior and his or her reaction to it, the requester proceeds to the Information Sending section of the flowchart (see Figure 4–1), which guides the user as follows: First make an empathic statement that starts with a "lead in" phrase such as "I know that you . . ." or " It seems that you . . ."; next, provide feedback using two statements starting with the words "When you . . . , I . . . ; then state the behavior change wanted and the anticipated consequences, following the "if you . . . , then I . . ." format.

An example of a Request for Behavior Change would be: "*I know you* prefer that I do the shopping because you have confidence that I'll get the best buys, but *when you* consistently ask me to do all the shopping, *I think* it's unfair and I get angry. *If you* would offer to pick up the groceries even once every two or three weeks, *then I* would be satisfied because it would mean you were sharing this task with me."

This is one of the clearest and most effective requests that can be made. It combines the components of both *an empathic statement and a conflict request,* with a new component identified as *feedback.* The following example illustrates the process of making a request for behavior change.

The Interruption

Group therapy meets every Wednesday at 9:00 P.M. at Dr. Jones's office. Janet and I are members of this group, which meets to discuss problems and learn effective communication skills. Janet frequently interrupts me when it is my turn to talk. Although I have already spoken to her about this problem, she has not changed her behavior. It is one week after my discussion with Janet, and I have decided to follow up on my initial request the next time she interrupts me in group. I have something important to discuss today and, sure enough, shortly after I begin to talk, Janet starts talking right in the middle of my sentence. I respond with a Request for Behavior Change.

---

1. *Information Gathering*

   a. *What do I want from the other person?*

      I want Janet to wait until I am finished talking before she starts to talk.

   b. *Consequences if want is granted.*

      I would be able to get my point across to the group and feel happy that Janet was treating me with consideration and respect.

   c. *What does the other person want?*

      Judging from her behavior (interrupting me to talk about something else) and the situation in which it occurs (therapy group, where problems are discussed), my guess is that Janet wants very much to talk about things that bother her.

2. *Information Processing and Decision Making*

   a. *Is there a conflict? Do I want to make a compromise? Do I want to change the behavior of the other?*

      There is a conflict because she and I cannot talk at the same time. There is no compromise that I can think of that would eliminate the conflict. Primarily I want Janet to change an undesirable behavior. Therefore I will make a Request for Behavior Change. This decision requires that I think about the feedback statement.

b. *Feedback:*

    i. Specify the other's undesirable behavior that I want changed. "She is interrupting me."

    ii. How do I think, feel, or behave in response to this behavior? "I think she's not acting considerately and I feel angry. I also lose my train of thought."

c. *Organizing the components into the request for behavior change:*

    i. Make an empathic statement that shows I am considering the wants of the other person: "Janet, *I know you* want to have the group help you with your problems, but . . ."

    ii. Describe the undesirable behavior of the other person: "*When you* interrupt me when I am speaking in group . . ."

    iii. Describe how I think, feel, or behave in response to this undesirable behavior. "*I* get angry because it tells me you're not interested in what I'm saying. And, I also lose my train of thought . . ."

    iv. Make a positive statement of what I want from the other person. "*If you* would wait until I'm finished before you start to speak . . ."

    v. State the consequences if the request is granted. "(Then) I'd be able to think more clearly and feel like I was getting more out of the group."

3. *Information Sending*

The requester makes the following Request for Behavior Change as assembled in the previous stages: "Janet, *I know you* want to have the group help you with your problems, but *when you* interrupt me when I am speaking in group, *I* get angry because it tells me you're not interested in what I'm saying. And, sometimes I lose my train of thought. *If you* would wait until I'm finished before you start to speak *then I*'d be able to think more clearly and feel like I was getting more out of the group."

Use of These Communication Skills

This concludes the presentation of basic information about request making. The practitioner using this approach will find that it is an extremely flexible guide to the cognitive and behavioral processes involved in making requests. It is important to use this model as a guide and not as a rigid set of rules for making requests. The practitioner should not think that it is expected that clients will only utter those statements included in the Information Sending component of the request statements. It is suggested that this information be the core of any request, but these statements can certainly be elaborated. Use of these communication procedures has shown that clients benefit greatly from the relative simplicity, clarity, and structure of this approach, especially when first learning the procedures. In general, it is useful to adhere closely to the statements during the early stages of learning and then begin to elaborate on them as skill develops.

Most people find comfort in falling back on the exact processes and procedures suggested in this chapter when difficult interpersonal communication situations arise. Practitioners may suggest to clients that they follow the schema shown in Figure 4–1 until they have thoroughly mastered these skills.

TRAINING PROGRAM TO TEACH
THREE KINDS OF REQUESTS

This section will provide a series of practical examples for teaching an individual or group to make a no-conflict request, a conflict request, and a request for behavior change. The material will follow the four-part model of skill training that was presented earlier in Chapter 1: Instruction, Supervised Practice, Feedback, and Independent Practice. Each of the three different types of requests will be presented in turn, starting with the no-conflict request.

THE NO-CONFLICT REQUEST

Instruction

The following is an outline of the material to be presented to clients.

1. Provide rationale for learning requests (to get reinforcers and maintain relationships).

2. Describe two features of all requests:

   a. Clear and direct.

   b. Take wants of other into consideration.

3. Describe three basic request situations:
    a. Compatible wants, no conflict.
    b. Incompatible wants, conflict.
    c. Wish to change undesired behavior of other.
4. Describe three kinds of requests.
5. Explain four components to requests:
    a. Statement of one's own wants.
    b. Statement of consequences if the want is granted.
    c. Statement of other's wants.
    d. Feedback.
        i. Description of undesired behavior.
        ii. Thoughts, feelings, and behavior response.
6. Introduce flowchart in Figure 4–1.
7. Provide example of no-conflict request using Figure 4–1.

Supervised Practice

The next phase of training is to allow the individual to practice the skill concepts described in the Instruction section in an environment supervised by the therapist.

The supervised practice component of this lesson involves a series of role-plays of no-conflict requests. The therapist, after handing out copies of Figure 4–1 and also the vignettes shown in Table 4–1, provides the following instructions: "The flowchart in Figure 4–1 describes the process for making a no-conflict request. I want you to practice with a couple of made-up situations. Start with the vignette entitled 'Dirty Dishes.' Be sure to perform the necessary information-gathering and decision-making steps before making the no-conflict request. The no-conflict request statement should follow the 'If you . . . , then I . . .' format."

To complete the worksheet (see Figure 4–1), divide the group into dyads and continue with the following instructions: "Complete the request in writing on the flowchart. Then, I want you to role-play the situation with your partner. Decide which person in the dyad will present (the sender) the request to the other (the recipient), then act out the scene. In other words, role-play (a) the situation that led up to the request as described in the vignette, (b) the actual request, and (c) the response to the

TABLE 4–1
Vignettes for Supervised Practice in No-Conflict Request Training

Dirty Dishes

The friends you invited over to your house are due to arrive in an hour. You and your son are busy dusting the living room. It is now obvious that you don't have time to finish all the cleaning tasks that you wanted to complete. Mostly, however, you want to get the dirty dishes washed and put away. You look at your son and say . . .

"Kool" It in the Disco

You and your friends are at a party. The DJ is great, and everyone is dancing to the disco music he's playing. You haven't gotten on the dance floor yet, but your favorite "Kool and the Gang" song has just come on and you're in a "move and groove" mood. You've been interested in meeting the person across the room, and since you're looking for a partner, you figure this is the perfect opportunity. You observe that s/he is standing alone and snapping his/her fingers to the beat of the music. You start to walk toward him/her and, as you approach, you say . . .

request. When you're finished with this, repeat the process but switch roles; the "sender" should now become the "recipient."

After the dyads have interacted as described, re-form the large group and ask volunteers to act out their requests. Be sure they tell the group about the information-gathering and decision-making components of the process they went through as well as acting out the request they made. Then, discuss the following issues:

1. What was it like to make a request this way? How about the information-gathering and decision-making components?

2. What was it like to receive a request like this? How would the recipient respond to such a request in real life?

3. How is this request statement different from what people might ordinarily have done?

Repeat the preceding process with the second no-conflict request vignette provided in Table 4–1, entitled "Kool It in the Disco." A new blank copy of the flowchart is used for each role-play. Additional vignettes may be developed and used to supplement those provided.

Practice continues until clients have developed sufficient proficiency to begin independent practice of this skill.

Feedback

Feedback for this exercise should follow the guidelines provided in Chapter 2.

Independent Practice

The client should develop a plan to use this and other kinds of requests that is consistent with an overall treatment plan. Keeping that plan in mind, identify several situations in which the client will be involved during the week where a no-conflict request would be appropriate.

Prior to attempting the requests, it is often desirable to discuss and rehearse what the client anticipates happening in these situations and how he or she would carry out a no-conflict request.

Instruct the client to engage in the targeted interactions during the week. The interactions will be discussed during subsequent group (or individual) meetings to determine what skills were performed well and what aspects can be improved.

Sometimes it is helpful to provide a structured format for practicing request skills outside the therapy group that includes the following instructions: "For the next week, make at least one request per day. Pay attention to (a) the thinking parts of the request, (b) your nonverbal and verbal communication, as well as the other person's, and (c) the consequences of your statement; that is, how things worked out."

"The following are suggestions for your requests; however, you are certainly not limited to these:

1. In a restaurant, ask waiter/waitress for refill of coffee/water/soda, etc.

2. Stop someone in the street and ask for directions to the nearest park.

3. Go into the library and ask the librarian how to find a particular book.

4. Go into a video rental store and ask the salesperson for a video recommendation.

5. Ask to return an unused item to either a department store or supermarket.

6. Ask a bus driver for the best route to a particular destination.
7. Go into a store and ask a worker where the closest Italian restaurant is located."

THE CONFLICT REQUEST

Instruction

The basic skill concepts were presented previously in the section on the no-conflict request. Prior to beginning the Supervised Practice section addressing the conflict request, the portion of the instructions dealing with this type of request should be briefly reviewed.

Supervised Practice

The next phase of training is to allow the individual to practice the previously described skills in an environment where the therapist can supervise performance. This supervised practice involves a series of role-play sessions. Hand out the vignette entitled "Four O'clock Meeting" (see Table 4–2) and give the following directions: "Now that you

---

TABLE 4–2
Vignettes for Supervised Practice of Conflict Request

Walking to the Store

I am walking to the grocery store with Betty. We are both looking forward to some leisurely time together, but we're also in a hurry to get home before it starts to rain. Halfway to the grocery, I remember that I also have to mail my rent check at the post office, which is a couple of blocks out of the way. I rarely get to see Betty anymore and today is the only opportunity I'll have all week. If she starts her shopping while I go to the post office, we'll hardly have any time to speak with each other. I turn to Betty and make a conflict request, saying . . .

Four O'clock Meeting

It is 4:00 P.M. and Sharon's meeting with her therapist is just about to end. Sharon's therapist likes to leave precisely at 4:00 because she starts early and sees a lot of people during the day. They have been discussing a new work program Sharon will be starting tomorrow, and Sharon is feeling very anxious about this. She feels she needs a little more help deciding on some things she can do today to deal with her fear. As her therapist is writing out a appointment slip for their next meeting, Sharon turns to her and makes a conflict request, saying . . .

---

have a process for making the conflict request, I want you to practice with a couple of made-up situations. When the exercise begins, read the situation described on the paper, then follow the steps outlined in the flowchart (see Figure 4–1).

When the participants have completed the flowchart and have composed the request, divide the group into dyads and continue with the following instructions: "Now that you have completed the worksheet, I want you to role-play the situation with your partner. Decide which person in the dyad will present his request to the other, then act out the scene. When you're done, switch roles; the person who made the request should now receive it, and the recipient should now make the request."

After the dyads have interacted as described, re-form the large group and ask volunteers to act out their requests. Be sure they tell the group the information-gathering and decision-making components of the process they went through as well as the request they made. Then, discuss the following issues:

1. What was it like to make a request this way? How about the thinking component?

2. What was it like to receive a request like this? How would the recipient respond to such a request?

3. How is this request statement different from what people might ordinarily have done?

The process should be repeated using the other vignette in Table 4–2 and others that may be composed. This process is repeated until clients acquire sufficient skill to warrant independent practice.

Feedback
Same as described for the no-conflict request.

Independent Practice
Same as described for the no-conflict request.

THE REQUEST FOR BEHAVIOR CHANGE

Instruction
The portion of the instructions presented in the no-conflict request section that deals with the request for behavior change should be briefly reviewed.

Supervised Practice

The supervised practice component of this lesson involves essentially the same process as that used for the no-conflict request and the conflict request. The therapist should hand out the vignette entitled "The Interruption" (see Table 4–3). It is suggested that the first vignette be completed as a group exercise, with the responses to the various components written on the blackboard and each part discussed.

Discuss with the group the rationale for responding to Janet's behavior with a request for behavior change. This type of request is justified because (a) what the requestor wanted from Janet was in conflict with what Janet wanted for herself, and (b) the request for behavior change was selected over the conflict request because the requester's want arose in response to Janet's undesired behavior.

The supervised practice can be repeated with the other vignette provided in Table 4–3 entitled "Playing Cards." The directions and discussion could parallel those described in the two prior exercises for the no-conflict request and the conflict request.

If additional practice is warranted, compare other vignettes and repeat the process. If participants are having difficulty with the task as described, the group may be divided into dyads so that two people, in-

---

TABLE 4–3
Vignettes for Supervised Practice: Request for Behavior Change

The Interruption

Group therapy meets every Tuesday at 8:00 at Dr. Brown's office. Janet and I attend the group, which meets to discuss problems and learn effective communication skills. Janet frequently interrupts me when it's my turn to talk. Although I have already spoken to her about this problem, she has not changed her behavior. Today is one week after my discussion with Janet, and I have decided to follow up on my initial request the next time she interrupts me in group. I have something important to discuss today and, sure enough, several minutes after I begin to talk, Janet chimes in right in the middle of a sentence. I respond with a request for behavior change, saying . . .

Playing Cards

You play cards with Raymond every Tuesday at 6:30 P.M. You are always on time, even if you must rush. Raymond is late all the time and this annoys you. You have decided to ask Raymond to be on time in the future so you don't have to wait for him. You make a request for behavior change, saying . . .

stead of one, can work on each worksheet, and thus share the burden of developing the request.

Feedback

Same as described for the no-conflict request.

Independent Practice

Same as described for the no-conflict request.

5

Responding to a Request
from Another Person

In the preceding chapter, we explained how to make requests that increase the likelihood of getting wants met and thus experiencing reinforcement. Now we will consider how to effectively respond to requests from others and, whenever appropriate, avoid doing things that are undesired behaviors.

ASSERTIVE ASSUMPTIONS

The same two critical components of requests should be part of every response: (a) a *clear and direct* statement of the want of the responder, and (b) *consideration of the wants, expectations, and/or feelings* of the requester. When a response to a request comprises these two characteristics, it is considered to be an assertive response. Because an extensive presentation of assertive communication, from a cognitive-behavioral perspective, appears in Chapter 6, we will limit our discussion of assertiveness here. It is important, however, to provide a few basic "assertive assumptions" that apply to responding to a request from another person. These assumptions will encourage a fresh and objective look at how to respond to requests.

120

1. First of all, everyone has the right to consider *his or her own wants and needs* when deciding to grant or refuse a request or to offer a compromise. The wants of the recipient of a request are just as important as those of the requester.

2. Whether the request is granted or refused, or a compromise offered, the choice will be assertive as long as the responder expresses wants and feelings clearly and directly, *and* demonstrates an attempt to take the wants and feelings of the requester into consideration.

3. Knowing an effective method of granting, refusing, and offering compromises is an important part of assertiveness. People who know what to do when confronted with a request will be better able to satisfy their wants and gain desired reinforcements from life while considering the wants of others.

Thus, it should be evident that it is not possible to refuse a request assertively by simply saying "No," or grant a request assertively by simply saying "Yes." Yes and no responses such as these are sometimes advocated by assertiveness skills trainers who want to demonstrate that people have the right to say "no." Responding to a request in this way, however, only expresses the wants of the speaker in a clear and direct manner; it does not consider the wants, expectations, and feelings of the person making the request. As we will see in Chapter 6, this type of response is characterized as aggressive.

Responding to a request so that the wants of the recipient and the requester are both considered will involve the use of the information presented in Chapter 2 (self-awareness) and Chapter 3 (empathy). When attempting to combine self-awareness and empathy, it is natural to begin to think in terms of *compromise*. One of the ways to respond to a request is to offer a compromise. Compromise is consistent with the assertive philosophy since it assures that the *requester* and *responder* both get their needs at least partially met. However, it would be incorrect to assume that compromise is always possible or desirable. Interestingly, however, once people start to think assertively and to consider their own wants and those of others, it is surprising how many opportunities for compromise are discovered that may have previously been overlooked.

Responding to a request as suggested in this book may be one of the more difficult communication skills. When confronted with a request, it is sometimes difficult to decide whether to grant, refuse, or compromise. One reason is that the wants of the self and others may not be habitually evaluated and compared in any systematic way. Another reason for difficulty is the individual may not know how to phrase the response once the type of reply has been selected. Sometimes people experience difficulty responding to requests because they fear a "bad" reaction from the other if they express their wants directly.

In the last case, an individual may grant a request rather than refuse it and risk the negative consequences of a refusal. There may be a concern that the requester will feel angry and respond aggressively (negative approach) because of not getting what was wanted. For similar reasons, a request is sometimes refused indirectly, by offering a legitimate-sounding excuse that will get the person "off the hook" without taking responsibility for refusing the request. In the long run, however, failure to respond directly may not be in the best interest of either the person or the relationship. A pattern of offering excuses may lead to a poor self-image because of denying one's own wants. Assertive responses to requests avoid this problem.

THREE RESPONSES TO REQUESTS: GRANT, REFUSE, OR COMPROMISE

To begin the discussion, it is useful to consider the options available to someone who receives a request from another person. Logically, there are three ways to respond: (a) grant the request, (b) refuse the request, or (c) offer an alternative or compromise. We will describe these options, and the circumstances in which each is appropriate, using the information-processing model introduced earlier.

Compatible Wants—No Conflict: Grant Request

As in all request situations, the wants of the person receiving the request and the person making it are assessed and compared using the procedures described in Chapters 2 and 3. Basically, when the wants of the two parties are compatible, the situation is one of "no conflict." In such a situation, the recipient of a request will usually grant it, thus satisfying a want that is shared with the person making the request. The grantor of the request is, in essence, promoting his or her own wants as well as those of the requester (or, at least, not acting inconsistently with them).

Incompatible Wants—Conflict: Refuse Request or Suggest an Alternative or Compromise

In this situation, the wants of the requester and the recipient are incompatible (cannot occur at the same time). In such a situation, a conflict in wants is judged to exist.

Requests with a conflict in wants occur often and may lead to difficult interpersonal situations. How should people respond to requests that conflict with their own wants? Should they deny their wants and acquiesce to the request to avoid conflict and, as a result, do something they do not want to do? Doing something that is desired by another instead of what is wanted by the self will result in an unmet want. Reference to the TFB triads indicates that unmet wants are associated with feelings of anger or sadness. While it is not reasonable to expect always to do only what one wants, it is also self-defeating to frequently deny one's wants and perform undesired acts that will create feelings of anger and sadness.

On the other hand, should a person just refuse the request? What effect will frequent refusal have on a long-term relationship such as a marriage, kinship, or friendship? Frequent refusal of requests may lead to the use of power, guilt, coercion, and other types of maladaptive and aggressive methods on the part of the requester, who becomes frustrated and angry at the unyielding recipient.

Thus, performing undesired tasks may anger or sadden one party while the other may be angered and frustrated by frequent refusals of requests. At this point, the concept of compromise, in which each party gets part of his or her want met, seems to be appropriate. Chapter 6 provides a detailed discussion of the value of compromise and the consequences of acquiescence and refusal.

It is consistent with the current approach to recommend that when wants are in conflict, the recipient of the request should either *refuse the request* or offer an *alternative or compromise*. Because of the issues previously raised, both of these responses should express consideration of and empathy with the requester. Empathic responding together with consideration of one's own wants will help to moderate angry and sad feelings on the part of both the sender and receiver of requests. The role of compromise is also important in this regard.

In the discussions that follow, much will be said about offering compromises and alternatives to requests. Before proceeding, some discussion of what constitutes an alternative and a compromise may prove helpful. Usually an *alternative* is suggested when the recipient of the request does not want to do what has been asked, but understands the want of the requester and provides a different way to satisfy it. The alternative is better for the recipient of the request because it is more compatible with his wants. When an alternative is offered, the want of the requester may not need to be modified or changed, just satisfied in a different way. For example, when the man in the movie was asked to move over one seat so the other two people could sit together, he might have offered an alternative such as, "I understand your desire to sit with your uncle, however, there are two seats together two rows up, why don't you sit there?"

The decision to offer a *compromise* indicates that the recipient is attempting to develop a plan in which each party gets part of his or her wants met. The attempt is to resolve the conflict in wants between the person making the request and the recipient of the request by a process of *mutual* concessions.

For example, if two roommates are cleaning their apartment, one roommate may say to the other (using the Conflict Request format): "I know you'd prefer to finish dusting before starting anything else, but if you can start on the dishes while I finish up in here, we can get ready for company sooner." If the recipient does not like to stop a task in the middle, he could offer a compromise. He could say, "If you want to get ready for the company sooner, I will work faster at the dusting. Meanwhile, you start the dishes and I will join you shortly when I finish dusting." This compromise requires change from both parties, but both also get part of what they want too. That is, the requester gets the cleanup done more quickly, but has to start the dishes herself. The roommate gets to finish one task before beginning another, but must work more quickly than desired.

When the wants of the two parties are compatible (no conflict), the recipient will usually grant the request. When there is a conflict in wants, the recipient may either (a) refuse the request, or (b) offer either a compromise or alternative. The process for granting, refusing, and compromising is presented next.

A Process for Responding to a Request

The concepts underlying the three types of response to requests are consistent with those of making a request. Moreover, many of the ideas applicable here were originally presented in prior chapters dealing with self-awareness and empathic understanding. So, the response to a request can be understood in terms of the three phases of information processing described earlier: (1) information gathering, (2) information processing and decision making, and (3) information sending. The following section will provide a detailed example of how to respond to a request from another person. The response will be based on a hypothetical situation described in a vignette entitled "Let's Have Some Coffee." Figure 5–1 illustrates the development of this response.

Let's Have Some Coffee

Your name is John and you're on your way to your doctor's office when you meet your good friend Bill. He's wearing a broad grin and, not knowing you have a previous commitment, excitedly asks you to join him for some coffee at a cafe so he can tell you about his new job. You want to keep your appointment with your doctor. How do you respond to Bill's request?

Information Gathering

Two of the three pieces of information relevant to *making* a request are required for *responding* to: (a) what the other person wants from me, and (b) my wants in relation to the requester's. As may be seen in Figure 5–1, the answers to questions 1 and 2 provide this information.

1. What does the other person want from me?

   He wants me:

   a. To go for coffee now.

   b. To listen to his story about his new job.

2. What do I want in relation to Bill's want?

   a. I want to go to my doctor's appointment now.

   b. I want to hear about my friend's new job.

Once the relevant information is gathered, the person evaluates it to determine what type of response to make and how it should be stated. Figure 5–1 shows that the first stage (Information Gathering) is exited by following the black arrow down to the first decision diamond which

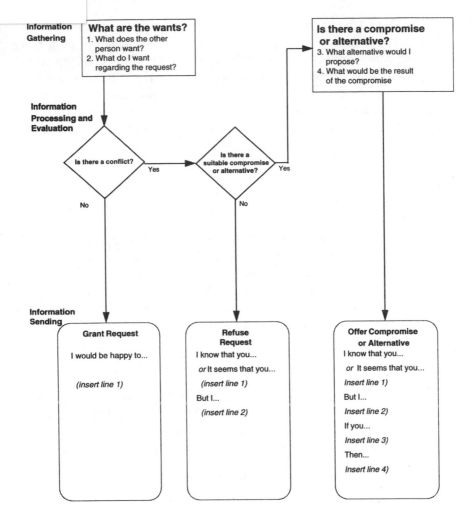

Figure 5–1. How to respond to a request.

asks if there is a conflict between the wants of the requester and recipient of the request.

Information Processing and Decision Making

1. Do wants of self and other conflict?

a. Yes, they conflict. I cannot go to my doctor's appointment (my want) and go for coffee with Bill (Bill's want) at the same time.

Note: At this point, if my wants did *not* conflict with Bill's, I would follow the arrow directed downward to the Information Sending section of the diagram entitled "Grant Request." As indicated in that box, I would start with the "lead in" statement "I would be happy . . ." followed by a clear and direct statement of what I want to do in relation to the request (taken from line 2 under Information Gathering). Thus, to grant the request, I would say: "I'd be happy to have coffee and hear about your job now."

However, as the wants in this example do conflict, the process leaves the first decision diamond moving to the right, following the black arrow to the box that asks "Is there a suitable compromise or alternative?"

If I cannot think of a compromise or alternative and the answer to this question is "no," I follow the arrow leading down to the "Refuse Request" box in the Information Sending section. Here I am prompted to make an empathic statement using the information from line 1 of the flowchart followed by a statement of what I want, from line 2 of the chart.

Thus, to refuse the request, I would say: "I know that you want to have coffee now and tell me about your new job, but I have a doctor's appointment and I want to go to it."

However, if I think of a compromise or alternative, I follow the "yes" arrow out of the second decision diamond. This leads me back to the "Information Gathering" section of the flowchart where I compose the compromise (line 3) and the consequences of it (line 4). In this example (on line 3), I could suggest an alternative in which Bill meets me later this evening. The consequence of this alternative (on line 4) is Bill will be able to tell me about his job and I can go to my doctor's appointment now.

The arrow leaving the "compromise box" leads down to the "Offer Compromise or Alternative" box in the Information Sending section of the flowchart. I start my response with the same two statements that constitute a refusal (an empathic statement of the other's wants, followed by a statement of my wants that are in conflict), then I offer *my alternative* in the form of a *no-conflict request,* (a statement of the alternative or compromise I thought of in line 3 and the consequences from line 4). The latter two pieces of information are stated using the "If you . . . , then I . . ." format. Thus, a response that offers a compromise is:

> *I know that you* want to tell me about your job now (answer to question 1), *but I* have a doctor's appointment now (answer to question 2). *If you* will meet me later this evening (answer to question 3),

then I can find out about your job *and* go to the doctor (answer to question 4).

Information Sending

Once the relevant information has been evaluated and the response formulated, communicate it to Bill, as indicated.

This structured method of composing a response to a request has proven to be very useful in skill development. It should be used as a guide and followed closely until clients have developed a degree of skill. As skill increases, the responses generated by this method can be elaborated and made more conversational. It is important, however, to maintain the core elements in Figure 5–1, even as the response is elaborated.

TRAINING PROGRAM TO TEACH HOW TO RESPOND TO ANOTHER PERSON'S REQUEST

Instruction

The following outline has been prepared as a guide for a lecture describing the skill concepts underlying responding to a request from another person.

1. Explain the two fundamental characteristics of a response to a request:
   a. Clear and direct expression of own wants.
   b. Consideration of wants of other.
2. Review "assertive assumptions":
   a. Right to consider own wants.
   b. Assertive if express own wants and consideration of others.
   c. Importance of knowing what to do.
3. Introduce role of compromise in responding to requests.
4. Explain possible responses to request:
   a. Compatible wants—no conflict: Grant request.
   b. Incompatible wants—conflict: Refuse request or offer compromise.
5. How to respond to a request:
   a. Information gathering:
      i. What does other want?
      ii. Understanding own wants in relation to request.

    b. Decision making:

        i. Is there a conflict?

      ii. Try to suggest alternative or compromise:

           (1) Define a compromise.

           (2) Define an alternative.

     iii. Explain format when grant request.

     iv. Explain format when refuse request.

      v. Explain format when offer compromise or alternative.

    c. Information Sending:

        i. Communicate the response.

6. Apply preceding information to example, "Let's Have Some Coffee."

Supervised Practice

The leader should guide this discussion and write the responses on a chalkboard.

Hand out the flowchart (Figure 5–1) that describes the process of responding to a request. Also hand out a copy of the vignette entitled "Let's Have Some Coffee" (Table 5–1). Read the vignette aloud and ask group members to respond to each of the steps in Figure 5–1. The group leader should record the responses on the board as members record them on their worksheets. Discuss each step of the process and the reasoning behind each decision.

After completing all the steps on the worksheet, members should role-play the vignette using the following procedure:

1. Break group into dyads, then reread the vignette.

2. Participants in each pair should assign themselves roles of requester and responder, then enact the situation described.

3. Next, one dyad will role-play the vignettes in front of the rest of the group. The role-play will be discussed by the rest of the group and feedback provided according to the guidelines in Chapter 1.

4. The process can be repeated with a second dyad acting out the vignette in front of the group and receiving feedback.

After discussion of "Let's Have Some Coffee," distribute the vignette entitled "Sick Friend" (Table 5–1). Read it to the group and ask members to respond aloud to each of the steps on the flowchart. This time,

TABLE 5–1
Vignettes for Supervised Practice Responding to a
Request from Another Person

Let's Have Some Coffee

Your name is John and you're on your way to your doctor's appointment when you meet your good friend Bill. He's wearing a broad grin and, not knowing you have a previous commitment, excitedly asks you to join him for some coffee at the cafe so he can tell you about his new job. You want to keep your appointment with your doctor. How do you respond to Bill's request?

Sick Friend

It's 5:00 P.M. and you (Mike) are leaving work and looking forward to a relaxing evening at home. First, however, you want to go to the store to pick up some items you need for tonight. Then you plan to return home and prepare your favorite pasta for dinner, brew some fresh Colombian coffee, and sit down to watch the football game on your new large screen TV. As you open the door to leave, the phone rings. It's your friend Jim who has been in the hospital for 3 days with a minor ailment. He says that he is bored in the hospital and makes a request of you to visit him tonight. You respond by saying . . .

---

however, go around the room in sequence, having each member respond to one question until the worksheet is finished. As this procedure provides an opportunity for everyone to respond, the group leader can get a better understanding of problematic areas that need to be addressed. Discussion of each person's response is encouraged so the whole group can participate.

After completion of the worksheet, conduct role-play as before. Interaction should begin with (a) the requester making the appropriate type of request, proceed with (b) the other person giving the response recorded on the worksheet, and terminate with (c) the requester's response.

Following discussion of "Sick Friend," the practitioner may compose other vignettes if additional practice is needed. In that case, divide group into dyads and instruct each pair to complete the worksheet in writing, and role-play the interaction.

When conducting the role-plays, group members may repeatedly generate the same type of response (always grant or refuse, or offer compromise). If this happens, have them repeat exercise responding in different way.

The following discussion is suggested to accompany the supervised practice section of the training:

1. What was it like for the responder to communicate this way? Did he or she feel effective? What might the participants have said "normally" in such a situation?

2. What was it like for the requester to receive this assertive response? How did it feel? Was it clear that the requester's wants were considered by the other person? If so, what about the response made it clear? If it was not clear that the requester's wants were considered, what could responder have said to make it clear that the requester's wants were considered?

3. If the responder refused or compromised, what would it have been like if he or she had simply said "no," or offered an excuse to the requester? If the responder granted the request, what would it have been like if he or she had simply said "okay"? (The role-play can be repeated with each of these responses to compare the effect with that of the comparable assertive response.)

Feedback

Feedback should be provided as described in Chapter 1.

Independent Practice

Identify several situations in which clients will likely be asked to do something and will be required to respond to the request.

Discuss and rehearse what the clients would anticipate happening in these situations and how they would respond.

Instruct clients to engage in these interactions during the week. The interactions will be discussed during subsequent meeting to determine what skills were performed well and what can be improved.

Clients should develop a plan of using this skill that is consistent with their overall treatment plan.

6

Introduction to Assertive, Aggressive, and Passive Behaviors

The concepts and procedures in this book are based on a model of assertiveness. Assertiveness promotes interpersonal behavior that simultaneously attempts to maximize the person's satisfaction of wants while considering the wants of other people, thus promoting respect for the self and others. An assertive approach maintains positive interpersonal relations by providing the basis for respectful and constructive conflict resolution. This chapter will further the teaching of social skills by presenting concepts of assertiveness that are fundamental to communication and problem solving.

BRIEF HISTORY OF ASSERTIVENESS TRAINING

Current assertiveness training techniques have their earliest roots in the writings of Wolpe (1958), Wolpe and Lazarus (1966), and Salter (1949). Wolpe, a behavior therapy pioneer, widely known for his work on systematic desensitization, saw assertion training as similar to this procedure in its ability to reciprocally inhibit anxiety. He helped differentiate assertion from aggression, and used behavior rehearsal as the primary training technique. Wolpe and Lazarus (1966) described methods of teaching assertiveness including shaping, autofeedback, modeling, and homework assignments that are still the foundation of training.

Salter described six "excitatory exercises" that his patients practiced. If rehearsed regularly, these exercises were said to increase assertiveness, a skill Salter perceived most everyone to need. The exercises were (a) feeling talk, which involved practice in expressing feelings, (b) practice in expressing contradictory opinions, (c) facial talk (practice in facial expressions that reflect different feelings), (d) practice in making "I" statements (speaking in the first person and taking "ownership" of feelings and behaviors rather than making impersonal reference to the self with phrases such as "one gets angry" or "people get upset"), (e) practice in taking compliments, and (f) practice in improvising responses in interpersonal situations. Many of these practices are still used in assertiveness training.

According to Rimm and Masters (1974), three additional writers contributed to current assertive training techniques. One is Moreno (1946), the developer of psychodrama, which involved dramatizations of actual attitudes and conflicts of participating patients. Although the goals of psychodrama are not those of assertion training, this therapy makes excellent use of a role-playing strategy.

George Kelly (1955), who developed fixed-role therapy, also contributed to assertiveness training. He pioneered an approach in which patient and therapist developed a sketch of a fictitious person free of psychological difficulties whose role the client was to assume. This form of behavior rehearsal was believed to result in actual change of cognition, feelings, and behavior such that the client would eventually no longer be playing a role, but would become the envisioned person.

Finally, Albert Ellis (e.g., Ellis & Harper, 1961), known for rational emotive therapy, has contributed to assertion training strategies. He instructed his patients in the self-defeating nature of nonassertive behavior, then assigned homework to engage in assertive behavior.

As may be seen in these early writings, assertiveness was developed for coping with conflictual interpersonal situations. It was geared toward helping people effectively handle situations in which their wants were incompatible with another's. Assertiveness recognizes the adaptive role of standing up for one's right to have wants met while simultaneously respecting the wants of others. All variations and refinements of assertiveness training have been built on this core concept. This book is no exception, and in Chapter 6, we will define assertiveness and demonstrate its benefits compared with alternative ways of behaving.

CONTEMPORARY APPROACHES
TO ASSERTIVENESS

Contemporary approaches to assertiveness do not consider it to be a single, unitary concept (e.g., Gottman, Notarius, Gonso, & Markman, 1976; Jakubowski & Lange, 1978; Lange & Jakubowski, 1976). Rather, it consists of three types of behavior: assertive, aggressive, and passive. These three behaviors lie on a continuum relevant to coping with interpersonal conflict. Although we frequently refer to each as a discrete entity, it is important to recognize the dimensional nature of these relationships. Each of these ways of behaving has unique but related verbal and nonverbal behaviors and consequences. The lack of assertive communication typically produces many negative effects on interpersonal relationships, especially close relations of long duration. In contrast, assertive communication is associated with the highest probability of positive personal and interpersonal consequences. We recommend assertive behavior because of the functional benefits, not because of moral or ethical standards.

To present the central features of assertive, aggressive, and passive behavior, we have divided this chapter into three sections: (a) verbal defining characteristics, (b) nonverbal defining characteristics, and (c) consequences of each of the three communication styles.

VERBAL ASPECTS OF ASSERTIVE, AGGRESSIVE,
AND PASSIVE BEHAVIOR

Assertiveness, aggressiveness, and passivity represent three different approaches to interpersonal relations, each of which has a corresponding set of verbal and nonverbal behaviors. The following descriptions of the verbal aspects of these three styles of interpersonal behavior will illustrate their similarities and differences.

Assertive Verbal Behavior

Assertiveness is generally considered to be the most effective way of resolving interpersonal differences. Assertiveness is characterized by:

- Verbal behavior that reflects a choice to consider the wants of others while attempting to get one's own wants met. Because assertiveness considers both one's own wants and the wants of others, it often results in the statement of a *compromise*. Discussion by both parties results in an agreement to modify one or both of their wants so that each will get at least part of what is desired, and neither may get everything desired.

- Verbal behavior that involves *direct expression* of what is wanted and the associated feelings. Direct expression means that a clear and unambiguous statement of what is wanted will be made whenever possible.

- Verbal behaviors that are considered socially acceptable.

The following example illustrates the use of assertive verbal skills.

John and Judy are discussing what movie they will rent for viewing this evening. John states his desire to see *Terminator*. However, Judy says that she wants to see *Casablanca* because it is a classic. She states that she does not want to see *Terminator* because of the violence. John expresses his understanding of Judy's dislike of violence and agrees that *Terminator* is a very violent movie. He has a moderate interest in seeing *Casablanca* and agrees to do so if he can choose the movie next time (a nonviolent one). Judy readily agrees and they go to rent the movie together.

In this example, John and Judy have conflicting wants that cannot be satisfied at the same time (they cannot rent a movie that is simultaneously violent and nonviolent). They have chosen to settle this conflict through compromise. John has agreed to forgo his preferred movie for one he is less interested in. Judy gets to see her preferred movie at this time, but has agreed to give up her choice of what movie they will see at a future date. Both parties have achieved at least two wants: to watch a movie and to have each other's company.

Aggressive Verbal Behavior

Aggressive verbal behavior is the second style of dealing with interpersonal disagreements. It may be as effective as assertiveness in obtaining the wants of the aggressive person, at least in the short run. However, it frequently results in long-term negative consequences, which will be presented later. Aggressiveness consists of:

- Verbal behavior that reflects a choice to disregard the wants of others while attempting to get one's own wants met. It does not entail compromise but rather involves continued expression of what the aggressive person wants and an attempt to get others to give up their wants.

- Verbal behavior that may or may not involve the *direct* expression of what is wanted and associated feelings.
- Verbal behavior that is frequently socially inappropriate.

The following example illustrates what could have happened if John behaved aggressively to the movie "conflict" between him and Judy. The new scenario would, perhaps, be as follows:

John and Judy are discussing what movie they will rent this evening. John states his desire to see *Terminator.* However, Judy wants to see *Casablanca* because it is a classic film. She states that she does not want to see *Terminator* because of the violence. John does not acknowledge Judy's concern about the violence and instead tries to focus the discussion on how popular the movie was in the theaters and the quality of the special effects in the *Terminator.* He also states that she can close her eyes during the violent scenes, and anyway, she should not be such a "big baby." Judy suggests an alternative movie that might be of interest to him, but John is not interested. He tells her that if she wants to see a movie with him, she will have to see *Terminator.* Judy finally agrees to see *Terminator,* and they leave for the rental store with John saying, "This is a great movie, you are going to love it."

Here John is obviously considering his own wants *only* and tries to get Judy to give up what she wants. He is direct in his expression of what he wants. He is also behaving in a socially inappropriate manner when he belittles Judy saying she should not act like a "big baby."

Passive Verbal Behavior

Passive verbal behavior is less effective than assertiveness in obtaining one's wants, although it can at times be successful. However, it is ineffective in sustaining satisfactory long-term relationships, as will be shown later. It is characterized as:

- Verbal behavior that reflects the choice to disregard or subordinate one's own wants while allowing others to get their wants met.

- Statements that either (a) fail to express one's wants (and related feelings) or (b) indirectly express wants and feelings. The latter might involve conveying them in an apologetic, obsequious, self-effacing manner, or minimizing their importance.

So, in our example, if Judy decided to see the movie preferred by John simply because they always did what he wanted to do, then Judy would have been disregarding her wants and desires. She would also be passive if she either (a) failed to express her desire to see *Casablanca* or another nonviolent movie, or (b) stated, "Well, reviewers say *Casablanca* is good, but it is getting old and out of date" when, in fact, she wanted to see the movie and thought it would be more enjoyable than *Terminator*.

Table 6–1 summarizes the verbal components of assertive, aggressive, and passive behavior.

TABLE 6–1
Verbal Aspects of Assertive, Aggressive, and Passive Behavior

Assertive Behavior

- Verbal behavior that reflects a choice to consider the wants of others while attempting to get one's own wants met. May involve compromise, a decision by a party to sacrifice part of his/her wants so that both parties will benefit in some way.
- Verbal behavior that directly expresses wants, expectations, and feelings.
- Verbal behavior that is socially appropriate.

Aggressive Behavior

- Verbal behavior that reflects a choice to disregard the wants of others while attempting to get one's own wants met. It does not entail compromise.
- Frequently does not involve direct expression of wants, expectations, and feelings.
- Verbal behavior that is frequently socially inappropriate.

Passive Behavior

- Verbal behavior that reflects the choice to disregard one's own wants while allowing others to get their wants met.
- Involves either (a) failure to express wants, expectations, and feelings, or (b) indirect expression of wants, expectations, and feelings, which may involve conveying them in apologetic, self-effacing manner, or minimizing their importance.

NONVERBAL COMPONENTS OF ASSERTIVE, AGGRESSIVE, AND PASSIVE BEHAVIOR

The previous section described the verbal components of assertive, aggressive, and passive styles of interaction. Social interactions, however, entail verbal and nonverbal aspects, with the latter being considered by some to be more important (see Lange & Jakubowski, 1976; Mehrabian, 1972; Sacks, 1985). When transmitting information in social interactions, *how* things are said adds significantly to *what* is said.

The primary nonverbal components of behavior that supplement the verbal content include eye contact, distance between the parties, body posture, hand gestures, facial expressions, head movements, and qualities of voice such as tone, volume, or inflection (e.g., Alberti & Emmons, 1975; Lange & Jakubowski, 1976; Whitely & Flowers, 1978). Each nonverbal behavior can be performed to support and help clarify the verbal content of the message. In other words, assertive, aggressive, and passive communication are each defined by specific verbal and nonverbal content. Table 6–2 illustrates the nonverbal components associated with each of these three types of behavior.

Assertive Nonverbal Behavior

Assertive statements take the wants of both speaker and recipient into consideration. The assertive nonverbal behaviors have the same effect. By facing and looking (without staring) at the other person, one demonstrates interest without minimizing one's own importance. When speaking, relaxed, smooth hand movements emphasize and punctuate what is said, and speech should occur at a hospitable conversational rate at a volume that makes it easy for the other to comprehend what is said. Voice should be well modulated and firm. Voice modulation is important in transmitting affect and should match the message expressed verbally to seem sincere. Flowers and Booraem (1975) reported that coaching in voice modulation actually helped to increase emotional feeling. It is possible that facial expression, which should also match the content of the verbal message, can serve the same function. Flowers and Booraem claim that many clients who display little nonverbal affect admit they experience little emotion in assertion situations. A greater nonverbal display of affect, moreover, can enhance the experienced emotion.

In assertive communication, the response to a verbal message from the other person should occur promptly without hesitation or undue

TABLE 6–2
Nonverbal Aspects of Assertive, Aggressive, and Passive Behavior

Assertive Behavior

Eye Contact	Direct eye contact without staring.
Posture	a. Faces person.
	b. Faces or sits straight while holding asymmetrical posture; arms and legs relaxed, not rigidly held in same position on each side.
	c. Might lean a bit toward person.
Gesture	Relaxed, smooth motions that accentuate verbal expressions.
Distance	Maintains appropriate conversation distance, approximately 1.5 to 3 feet between person and other.
Latency	Response made without hesitation once speaker completes statement or question, interrupts when goal is to terminate interaction.
Voice	Firm; sufficient volume without being loud; well-modulated; normal speed.

Aggressive Behavior

Eye Contact	Expressionless, narrowed, cold, staring.
Posture	Rigid, tight, body tensed, feet apart, symmetrical stance.
Gesture	Hands clenched or on hips; abrupt or large gestures, especially over the shoulders; directive gestures.
Distance	Closer than 1.5 feet.
Latency	Very short latencies, frequent interruptions.
Voice	Very loud; fast rate of speech.

Passive Behavior

Eye Contact	Looks down or away.
Posture	Does not face person; rigid, symmetrical, or stooped; shrunken, "sagging."
Gesture	Fidgety hands; shuffling, restless motions; small gestures close to body.
Distance	Farther than 3 feet.
Latency	Leaves long latencies between termination of speaker's statement and response.
Voice	Very low volume; monotone; slow rate of speech.

delay. On the other hand, the response should not come too quickly and pressure the other person. To demonstrate that one is listening to the other's statement and, therefore, values that person's desire to be heard, it is important to wait until the other is finished before responding. Other assertive behaviors that convey interest and active listening include "minimal urges to talk," such as head nods and general animation (see Egan, 1990).

Finally, with regard to proximity, or the physical distance between two people, 1.5 feet to 3 feet seems to represent the comfort zone, at least in the American culture. Closer proximity promotes distancing, and greater separation prompts closure.

Aggressive Nonverbal Behavior

Aggressive statements take only the speaker's wants into consideration and attempt to reject the other person's wants. This intent is reflected in the nonverbal behaviors that accompany them. Eye contact is in the form of fixed, hard staring, and posture is tense and rigid. A forward-leaning posture may appear aggressive or threatening. Hands may form fists, with movements generally consisting of large symmetrical gestures with intermittent finger pointing. All these behaviors serve to intimidate, to imply that the speaker is dominant and the other's wants must yield to a stronger power.

The voice is overmodulated, demonstrating intense affect. The voice volume is loud and the rate of speech fast. Typically, no respect is demonstrated for the other, who is frequently interrupted and not allowed to complete statements.

Aggressive facial expressions are rigid and tense. Teeth may be clenched, lips pursed. As indicated previously, a distance between people less than approximately 1.5 feet is generally perceived as uncomfortable. A person exhibiting aggressive nonverbal behavior generally decreases distance below this point. By doing so, the aggressor creates discomfort in the other and communicates that he or she does not care about invading the other's personal space.

Passive Nonverbal Behaviors

Finally, passive statements subordinate the speaker's wants to those of the other person. Passive nonverbals reflect this lack of self-concern and include looking away from the other, with body facing away, and posture stooped. Hand gestures, if present, are small and close to the body, feet shuffle and movements are typically restless.

Speech is at a slow rate, and its volume is low. It is as if the person is saying, "You don't need to hear me, what I have to say is not important anyway." There are long delays in response, again demonstrating that the other's verbal communication is more important than that of the passive individual. Finally, physical distance is maintained beyond the three feet generally considered to be the outer limit for interacting with comfort.

Other Considerations

Several points should be made here. First, given the complexity of communication, the information provided here should be used as *guidelines* for characterizing assertive, aggressive, and passive behaviors rather than applied as a set of inflexible rules. The nonverbal behaviors discussed in this chapter are *generally,* but not always, associated with their verbal counterparts in the ways described.

Since verbal statements and nonverbal behaviors may be brought under voluntary control, people can manipulate their presentation of self. Aggressive people may lower the voice, rather than raise it. Passive people may take a position three feet from another person and maintain a rapid rate of speech. Nonetheless, the verbal and nonverbal behaviors of assertive, aggressive, and passive communication styles will tend to follow the descriptions provided. And, when the verbal and nonverbal messages are consistent, communication of assertive, aggressive, or passive intent is more apparent to the recipient of the message. On the other hand, when the verbal and nonverbal messages are inconsistent, the communication is more confusing and responding is more difficult. For example, an assertive statement delivered with downcast eyes, shuffling feet, and low voice volume would be more difficult to interpret than one given with direct eye contact, at a normal volume, and a firm confident stance.

It is also important to interpret nonverbal (and verbal, to a lesser extent) behavior in its cultural context. What has been described as assertive in this chapter is true for the main culture in the United States, not necessarily for other cultures. The anthropologist Hall (1959) writes about the cultural diversity of nonverbal communication. In reference to conversational distance, he speaks of the frequency with which he has observed two people from different countries engaged in conversation, with one always backing up to increase his or her comfort, perceiving the other as "pushy" because of proximity, the latter in constant pursuit to decrease distance, perceiving the "retreater" as unfriendly.

An example would be an interaction between a Latin American and a U.S. citizen. As the conversational distance in Latin America is much less than it is in the United States, the comfort zone for discussion differs between them. The Latin American may speak at a distance that the U.S. citizen perceives as hostile or sexually evocative (a distance that has been classified here as aggressive). Since no aggressive intent may be present, the approach of the Latin American may be misinterpreted by someone who is not culturally sensitive.

Finally, as indicated earlier, nonverbal communication can be of paramount importance because of its presence in all phases of communication. Verbalizations are intermittent, but nonverbal communication is omnipresent. We are *always* transmitting information this way. Moreover, ontogenetically and evolutionarily, nonverbal communication is primary. It precedes spoken language and has been essential to the survival of the species.

The early appearance of nonverbal communication probably also accounts, at least partially, for its transmission being frequently out of awareness. Hall (1959) attributes our lack of awareness to the cultural determination of nonverbal learning; it is conditioned from the outset and learned so well that it is automatic, nearly reflexive.

The nonverbal aspects of communication form an integral part of assertive, aggressive, and passive behavior. They define *how* a message is transmitted, and are possibly more important than *what* is said. They constitute the more primitive forms of communication, are automatic and always in use, and to some degree at least, are culturally based. For these reasons, we are largely unaware of the nonverbal information we transmit, do not use it much to dissemble and, therefore, place more faith in it representing the true feelings and wants of the communicator.

CONSEQUENCES OF ASSERTIVE, AGGRESSIVE, AND PASSIVE BEHAVIOR

As we are advocating the use of assertive behavior, it is important to demonstrate that the consequences of such actions are generally beneficial, and those of aggressive and passive behavior typically are not. Aggressive or passive behaviors may be effective in attaining some wants, especially in the short run, and are therefore reinforced. However, the overall, long-term probability that wants will be fulfilled is greatest with assertive behavior.

More important than the immediate attainment of concrete wants are the social consequences of each of the three communication styles. The consequences of the communication styles impact on the communicators' wants and expectations (their thinking), their feelings, and their future behavior as well as those of the recipients. Further discussion and clarification of the social, cognitive, affective, and behavioral consequences follows, and is also summarized in Table 6–3.

Assertive, aggressive, and passive behaviors do not *guarantee* that the consequences specified will always occur. However, they are the most likely consequences.

It is also important to explain why maladaptive aggressive and passive forms of behavior are developed and maintained. After all, if the positive consequences of assertiveness and the negative consequences of aggression and passivity were experienced, wouldn't everyone learn to be assertive?

First, let us assume that "average" people want to be in two-sided or reciprocal relationships where they can get things they want from the other and give things to the other person. When such people interact with an aggressive or passive person, they will be only partly satisfied (rewarded) since they cannot get these two wants met. If they interact with an aggressive person, for example, they will have difficulty getting what they want, although they will be able to give to the other. Interactions with a passive person are just the opposite. Average people can get what they want but will be frustrated when trying to give to the passive person.

On the other hand, when interacting with the average person, aggressive or passive people get their wants completely met. In each interaction with another person, aggressive people get their wants met while giving little, and passive people take care of others, and take nothing in return. Interactions that turn out this way are reinforcing to the aggressive and passive person. Consequently, these styles of behavior are strengthened and future interactions with the average person are desired.

So, we see that in an individual interaction, the average person is at best partly rewarded and the aggressive or passive person is completely rewarded. However, what happens when there are multiple interactions over time? The average person—who is not rewarded or is only partially rewarded for interacting with the aggressive or passive individual—will seek other more satisfying relationships. And, because of expecting future interactions with the aggressive or passive individual to be unrewarding or aversive, the average person will avoid future interactions.

TABLE 6–3
Consequences of Assertive, Aggressive, and Passive Behavior

Assertive	Aggressive	Passive
Social Consequences		
Others are pleased that their wants are considered.	Others are angry that their wants are not considered.	Others are pleased that their wants are considered.
Others view me with respect.	Others view me with fear.	Others lack respect for me.
Others are motivated to treat me in a similar way.	Others are motivated to treat me in a similar way.	Others do not trust me to be truthful.
Others seek out my company.	Others avoid my company.	Others treat me as a doormat.
Thinking Consequences		
I expect the world to be friendly.	I expect the world to be hostile and uncaring.	I expect the world to be hostile and uncaring.
I expect others to be helpful with regard to my wants.	I expect others will thwart my wants or take advantage.	I expect others to be uninterested in my wants.
I expect that my wants will be fulfilled.	I expect that my wants will be fulfilled.	I expect that my wants will not be fulfilled.
I think that I have some control over my environment.	I think that I have to control my environment.	I think that others control my environment.
I expect to achieve my goals.	I expect to achieve my goals.	I do not expect to achieve my goals.
Feeling Consequences		
Happiness	Anger Fear	Fear Sadness Anger
Behavioral Consequences		
Positive approach	Negative approach	Avoidance Episodes of negative approach

Thus, the aggressive individual experiences social isolation and a loss of reinforcement that causes the person to step up the frequency and intensity of these modes of behavior. This effort to meet wants only makes the interactions more negative for others and increases their avoidance.

In some circumstances, however, people can maintain unbalanced relationships. A person may be involved in a kinship, employment, or marriage relationship in which external circumstances, not the reinforcement of the relationship, keep the people together. It is also possible that a pair consisting of one aggressive and one passive person can maintain a relationship because their styles are complementary. This type of relationship would, however, be void of mutual respect and would be problematic, especially if the passive person develops a stronger desire for self-satisfaction of wants.

Thus, aggressive and passive behaviors can be developed and maintained by their short-term rewards. In the long run, however, they drive away people who desire a mutually reinforcing, two-sided relationship. This process leaves the aggressive and passive person isolated or involved in dysfunctional relationships maintained by external factors such as marriage and kinship but lacking in mutual respect.

Assertive Behavior

Social Consequences

In a conflict situation, behaving assertively to another pleases the other party, who sees that his or her wants and feelings are important and have been considered. The recipient of an assertive message will tend to evaluate the communicator positively and with respect, as this person has demonstrated a positive *self*-evaluation by asserting his or her own wants. The empathy and self-respect exhibited through assertive communication generate a desire in the recipient to treat the assertive person in kind. With repeated demonstrations of assertive behavior, others develop the expectation that the person will behave cooperatively, sensitively, sincerely, and self-respectfully. Attracted to these qualities and motivated to treat in kind, others develop reciprocally cooperative, honest relationships with the assertive communicator.

Effects on Wants and Expectations

Given assertive treatment from others, plus their positive evaluation and friendship, an expectation that the world is "friendly" develops. The expectation is that others will facilitate, not thwart, the person's attainment of wants. Assertiveness thus leads to the belief that wants *can* be fulfilled, and that there is some control over outcomes. The expectation of control is a phenomenon that apparently has great impact on a person's well-being, with lack of control associated with depression and other problems (e.g., Alloy, Peterson, Abramson, & Seligman, 1984; Bandura, 1969; Taylor, Wayment, Heidi, & Collins, 1993).

Becoming more effective in attaining wants and dealing with others boosts self-esteem as well. The increase in perception of one's ability to achieve goals is associated with a generalized positive expectation of the self and others.

Feeling Consequences

The expectations of cooperation from others and the ability to get wants fulfilled help the individual acquire feelings of happiness. The desire to have good social relationships, to be able to exert influence over one's life, to view oneself as worthwhile are each fulfilled, adding to feelings of happiness.

Behavioral Consequences

Because good social relationships develop, wants are fulfilled more frequently, and a feeling of happiness results, people are likely to repeat assertive behavior, and will positively approach social relations. These positive consequences of behaving assertively therefore increase the probability of future assertive behavior. Assertiveness is maintained, or *reinforced,* by the effects it produces.

Aggressive Behavior

Social Consequences

Since one goal of aggressive behavior is to focus on one's own wants and deny others what they want, feelings of competition and anger develop in recipients. Because their wants are not taken into account, they will reciprocate by choosing not to consider the aggressor's wants. With repetition of such episodes, others come to expect this bullying behavior, view the aggressor with mistrust, and look for opportunities to retaliate or to avoid social interactions. Aggressive behavior, therefore, leads to social isolation.

Effects on Wants and Expectations

As aggression engenders anger and promotes aggression in others, aggressive people expect the world to be hostile and dangerous. They expect others to take advantage of them and therefore remain vigilant. They expect to fight for things that are rightfully theirs because they expect others to be competitive and selfish. In fact, aggressive people perceive the reality they have created. Others act selfishly and with hostility in response to the selfishness and hostility with which they have been treated.

Feeling Consequences

Expecting to have to fight for everything they want, with others avoiding them, aggressive people may begin to feel angry. Their desire for closeness and meaningful relationships is not fulfilled, and they learn to anticipate that they never will be. This unmet want may increase feelings of anger. If hope is lost, it may lead to sadness and depression. With every new social interaction, they expect—and frequently find—a conflict, thus, fear invades their social interactions.

Behavioral Consequences

Because aggressive people are alienated, they learn to expect that others will resist fulfilling their wants. The consequent anger and fear increase the frequency and intensity of negative approach and avoidant behaviors.

Passive Behavior

Social Consequences

When people act as though their wants are unimportant relative to another's, they are showing lack of self-respect, which others are then likely to reciprocate. Others learn to be unconcerned with the wants of passive people, thus treating them aggressively or withdrawing from contact due to lack of interest. Their input is devalued or perceived as unimportant. Because the primary aim of passive people is to please others, they are not trusted to express their real wants and feelings, so meaningful relationships are hard to develop. Others may initially feel sorry for passive people or may give them things they guess are wanted without being asked. In the long run, others come to view the passive person with contempt and disgust and avoid interaction.

Effects on Wants and Expectations

As passive behavior involves the disregard of one's own wants and the relinquishment of decision-making power, it minimizes expected control over outcomes. The person who habitually behaves passively may develop an expectation of no control.

Associated with the devaluation of wants by self and others are perceptions of the self as inadequate and the world as hostile or uncaring. The person *acts* as though others are more capable of making decisions, and thus develops the expectation that this is true. Passive people expect to be unable to make decisions independently.

As their wants are ignored, they are always anticipating negative outcomes. The world is unpredictable and threatening as the attainment of wants is determined by others, and the expectation is that it will continue to be that way.

Feeling Consequences

As people ignore their own wants and allow others to do so, wants go unsatisfied leading to feelings of anger and sadness. A generalized expectation also develops that wants will not be fulfilled and, that negative outcomes will occur, resulting in a state of persistent fear and anxiety in social situations. At times, passive behavior is associated with depression, when the person loses hope of ever attaining positive social outcomes.

Behavioral Consequences

Given the person's belief in his or her inadequacy and inability to control outcomes, passive behavior tends to persist for awhile. With repeated passive behavior, the person's anger intensifies due to the ongoing failure to obtain personal wants. At some point, the intensity of the anger is greater than that of fear and depression, and an aggressive outburst is likely to occur. Once the aggression has been exhibited, the anger dissipates and the fear and depression peak as the person perceives him- or herself to have committed an irrevocable wrong with inherent social loss, and expects more negative responses from others.

So, we see the sad plight of aggressive and passive people, trapped by a cycle of intermittent short-term reinforcement coupled with long-term alienation of others. The scenarios presented do not occur invariably as described because human behavior and social interactions are too complex and sophisticated to be so predictable. Many of these consequences do occur, however, and the likelihood of some of them happening is great. Consequences for assertive behavior are far more favorable than those for either aggressive or passive behavior. Thus, it *pays* to act assertively and to use the social skills described in this book. Learning these skills may require substantial effort, but the long-term compensation should offset the cost many times over.

TEACHING ASSERTIVENESS SKILLS

As described in earlier chapters, the format for skills training used in this book consists of four components: Instruction, Supervised Practice, Feedback, and Independent Practice. The training uses many exercises involving behavior rehearsal and modeling. In the Supervised Practice section of assertiveness training, it is often necessary for the instructor to model the assertive behavior required in the interaction. Following this, the clients in the group are frequently divided into dyads (or triads), with one group member enacting the assertive behavior, and the other enacting the recipient (with possibly a third individual observing the interaction to provide feedback). Typically, the client enacting the assertive role assesses his or her performance first, initially stating what he or she liked, then providing suggestions for improvement. The observer, if present, follows with feedback, the requirements for which are the same (stating those aspects of performance that matched the skill concepts first, then change recommendations). If the recipient has anything to add, he or she does so. Feedback is provided in specific behavioral terms. What is labeled feedback here comprises assertiveness training techniques that are otherwise referred to as reinforcement and coaching. Reinforcement is the first phase of feedback, where specific behavior performed well is praised; coaching is the second phase, in which recommendations for change are made.

Following feedback, the role-play is reenacted, with feedback again provided at its completion. This sequence might continue until performance fulfills criteria. Alternatively, if one of the clients is having difficulty, either the instructor or another client might model the assertive behavior, while the client having difficulty enacts the role of the recipient. In other words, a role-reversal procedure may facilitate skill acquisition.

Once performance fulfills criteria, the dyads switch roles, with the former recipient now assigned a task requiring assertive behavior, and the client formerly enacting the assertive behavior now serving as the recipient. The sequence proceeds as described. If there was an observer, the three individuals switch roles. To ensure that all three group members have an opportunity to function in all roles, assertiveness tasks must be assigned in multiples of three, not two.

It is a well-established rule of behavior therapy to reward *improvement* in performance, and not wait until perfection is achieved. Rewarding *successive approximations* to *criterion* performance, known as *shaping or exposure,* is an extremely effective teaching strategy. Learning is also optimal when clients practice *short* segments of assertive behavior at any given time, *then* piece them together.

The final phase of training is Independent Practice, in which clients generalize their skills to actual life situations. So, depending on the Instruction and Supervised Practice on a given day, clients might be asked to engage in an assertive interaction every day, or respond to a request by assertively offering an alternative. Performance is evaluated each session. If all goes well, another assignment is given to practice the skill. Clients are encouraged to generate their own assertiveness tasks to increase their meaningfulness and relevance to their lives.

ASSERTIVENESS TRAINING PROGRAM

Training in assertiveness is divided into three sections focusing on verbal and nonverbal components and the consequences of behaving assertively. The training includes Instruction, Supervised Practice, Feedback, and Independent Practice segments.

Lesson 1. Verbal Aspects of Assertiveness

Instruction

The Instruction section of this lesson of assertiveness training consists entirely of explaining and differentiating the verbal aspects of assertive, aggressive, and passive behavior. Table 6–1 can be used as a guide for this presentation.

Supervised Practice

Having presented the skill concepts associated with the verbal aspects of assertive behavior, the group leader progresses to an exercise entitled the "Assertion Crossword Puzzle" (Figure 6–1) that will facilitate practice in differentiating assertiveness, aggression, and passive behavior. The therapist distributes the puzzle saying: "Okay, this is the Assertion Crossword Puzzle, which is completed like any other crossword puzzle, with a few changes":

1. Look at the statements listed in Figure 6–1. Read each item and choose the response (a, b, c, or d) that depicts the type of behavior underlined to the left.

2. Record your answer in the place on the puzzle corresponding to the (a) number of the question and (b) its direction, ACROSS or DOWN.

3. Note that you only put the underlined letters in the crossword puzzle grid."

It is recommended that the first item be completed by the group as an example. If there is still difficulty understanding, individual help can be provided.

Most people complete this task in about 20 minutes. On completion of the crossword puzzle, the facilitator says to the group: "Now we'll review the responses by going around the room, each person answering one question. Please (a) indicate which choice you selected to place in the grid, (b) specify why you selected it, and (c) state your reasons for not selecting each of the other three responses by identifying the type of behavior (assertive, aggressive, or passive) each reflects.

"After a response is given, I'll ask for feedback from other members of the group. If you agree with all the parts of the response, state this. If you disagree with all parts of the response, give the ones you believe would be more accurate. If you agree with part of the response, specify the part(s) with which you agree, then indicate those parts with which you disagree." The therapist then guides the group through the discussion of the items. On some items, there may be disputes about which is the most correct answer because so little information is provided for each stimulus item. Moreover, if two different responses can be justified, neither may be incorrect. But, only one item will correctly fit into the crossword puzzle.

The goal of this exercise is to stimulate discussion that compares and contrasts assertive, aggressive, and passive verbal behavior according to the criteria used to describe these components. The more discussion and dispute that takes place, the better the concepts will be learned.

Lesson 2. Nonverbal Aspects of Assertiveness

Instruction

The Instruction section of this component of training consists of defining and differentiating the nonverbal aspects of assertive, aggressive, and passive behavior. It is suggested that the therapist draw a three-column (assertive, aggressive, passive) by seven-row (eye contact, distance, posture, hand gestures, facial expression, voice inflection,

Across

Passive   1. After you overspend your budget, your husband _____
   a. <u>reviews</u> the budget with you.
   b. <u>takes over</u> all the spending.
   c. says <u>nothing</u> about the extra money you spent.
   d. none of <u>the above</u>.

Assertive   3. You are sensitive about your weight and your friend just criticized you for gaining a few pounds. You _____
   a. <u>thank her</u> for the feedback.
   b. tell her your <u>reaction</u> to her comment.
   c. tell her <u>she is ugly</u>.
   d. tell her it is not right to say <u>anything</u>.

Assertive   5. When he asked his boss for a raise, John looked _____
   a. <u>at his feet</u>.
   b. <u>at his boss</u>.
   c. <u>very angry</u>.
   d. <u>none of the</u> above.

Passive   9. John wanted to go to the movies with Sue. Sue wanted to stay home because she felt ill. Sue _____
   a. <u>demanded</u> her way.
   b. <u>went when</u> John said he would go alone.
   c. said she would go <u>with John</u> when she felt well.
   d. <u>told John</u> to enjoy the movie when he left.

Figure 6–1.   Assertion crossword puzzle.

Assertive 11. Mike who was on his way home, wanted John to stop talking so he _____
    a. said, "<u>Please</u> be silent."
    b. tried to <u>ignore</u> John.
    c. said, "<u>Excuse</u> me, I've got class."
    d. <u>none of</u> the above.

Assertive 12. Harry is assertive at work because he always _____ what others request that he do.
    a. <u>considers</u>   c. <u>neglects</u>
    b. <u>does what</u>   d. <u>none of</u> the above

Aggressive 13. Oscar spilled his coffee accidentally on John's suit jacket. Oscar _____
    a. <u>laughed</u> and said "oops."
    b. said "<u>I'm sorry</u>."
    c. <u>cringed</u> and begged forgiveness.
    d. <u>none of the above</u>.

Assertive 14. Three friends were together watching the Super Bowl on TV. Sam and Rickey were smoking, and Mike was having trouble breathing. Mike _____
    a. <u>put out</u> their cigarettes in the ashtray.
    b. kept <u>moving</u> away from them and the TV, little by little, so they wouldn't notice and be hurt.
    c. cleared his <u>throat</u> several times to give them the message.
    d. <u>none of</u> the above.

Down

Assertive 2. Alice & Carla are meeting their friends to go out for the afternoon. Alice says to Carla, "Let's _____ what we will do this afternoon."
    a. <u>find out</u>   c. <u>ask them</u>
    b. <u>demand</u>   d. <u>none of</u> the above

Aggressive 4. Tim noticed he was given 25 cents less change than he was supposed to. He _____ , and walked away.
    a. told the cashier, "Please pay <u>attention</u> to what you're doing."
    b. <u>went to the</u> cashier to point out the error, got the quarter.
    c. <u>hesitated</u>, put the money in his pocket.
    d. <u>none of the</u> above.

Aggressive 6. Mary _____ when she spoke with Bill about his gambling debts.
    a. <u>reasoned</u>   c. <u>screamed</u>
    b. <u>groveled</u>

Passive 7. Sam went to the front of the line and June _____
    a. <u>stepped aside</u>.
    b. <u>cussed him out</u>.
    c. <u>politely told</u> him to take his turn.
    d. <u>frowned at him</u>.

Passive 8. Mary's waiter, who was very busy, brought her a burnt steak. Mary decided _
    a. <u>to complain to</u> the waiter.
    b. to <u>eat the steak</u>.
    c. to <u>request a new</u> steak.
    d. <u>not to bother</u> the waiter, and not to pay for the steak.

Assertive 10. Mary did not understand her teacher's remark so she raised her hand and __
    a. <u>blushed</u>.
    b. asked the teacher to <u>explain</u> the remark again because she did not fully understand it.
    c. asked the teacher to <u>express</u> herself more clearly because her remarks were not easily understood.
    d. smiled, and politely <u>asked to</u> see her teacher's notes.

Figure 6–1. *(Continued)*

response latency) table on the chalkboard that, during group instruction, will gradually be filled in. This information is shown in Table 6–2, which is to be distributed to participants when instruction is finished.

The therapist starts the presentation and discussion by asking participants to give the definition of assertive verbal behavior provided in the previous lesson. Table 6–1 can be used to augment clients' memories. Participants are then asked to describe the kind of *eye contact* that would be associated with the verbal aspects of assertiveness. The various suggestions are discussed and when an acceptable description is developed, the facilitator fills in the appropriate cell in the table on the board. For assertive eye contact, the information placed in the table would be "direct eye contact without staring." Then, either the therapist or a participant demonstrates the behavior to the group.

Next, the therapist asks for the definition of aggressive behavior provided in the previous lesson. Once given, the therapist asks participants to define the type of eye contact associated with aggressive behavior. Again, the description of aggressive eye contact is placed in the appropriate cell on the table, and this behavior is demonstrated (expressionless, narrowed, cold, staring).

The lesson proceeds in this orderly fashion, moving from one cell of the table to the next. We have found it most instructive to proceed as follows. Start with a nonverbal behavior (e.g., eye contact) and define it assertively and write this information in the appropriate cell of the table, which is on the chalkboard. Next, define the same nonverbal behavior aggressively, and finally passively, placing these definitions in the table. The three styles of the nonverbal behavior being discussed (eye contact) are compared and contrasted. Then the discussion proceeds to the next nonverbal behavior (e.g., distance between parties) until the table is completely filled in. Every opportunity should be used to compare and contrast the three different ways each nonverbal behavior can be exhibited. For example, regarding eye contact, the direct contact of assertiveness should be compared with the stare of aggressiveness and both contrasted with the passive failure to give eye contact (looking down and away).

Also, it is important to point out that the nonverbal behaviors being discussed are *generally, but not always,* associated in the way described with the assertive, aggressive, and passive verbal components. A second point is that communication is much clearer when the verbal and nonverbal behaviors *do* match up as described. When they do not, the message is confusing to the other person. That is, matching verbal and nonverbal components helps make the communication *clear and direct.* This can be further explained and demonstrated if necessary.

Supervised Practice

Conduct the "Assert Bingo" game, as shown in Figure 6–2 to provide supervised practice in assertiveness skills. Participants should have the handouts defining assertive, passive, and aggressive verbal behavior, and the nonverbal aspects of these behaviors (Tables 6–1 and 6–2). Assert Bingo is similar to regular bingo in that the goal is to get all the squares filled in to complete a row, column, or diagonal on the grid. To decide which square to mark out on each turn, the following procedure is followed.

Each participant is given an "Assert Bingo" card (see Figure 6–2). The instructor reads a statement from the list in this figure to each participant, in turn. He or she decides if it is Assertive, Passive, or Aggressive and the other members of the group decide if they agree. After discussion, agreement about the stimulus statement should be reached.

If the situation is anything other than assertive, a group member should be prompted to indicate how it could be changed to be assertive. Group members should also be encouraged to verbalize the thinking and decision-making process that goes into changing the situation to an assertive one.

After participants decide on an assertive response, a square on the bingo card is selected, a process that takes two steps. First the group member whose turn it is (the person who was read the statement and decided how to classify it) selects a card from a stack of 15 cards that have been prepared having the letters A, S, E, R, and T written on them (three cards for each letter, shuffled). This will determine the column (A, S, E, R, or T). Next, a group member rolls the die to select the number in that column. Use of a large die like the ones hung from car rearview mirrors adds an element of fun to this exercise.

The group leader should try to emphasize the nonverbal aspects of the communication. What happens when one of the aggressive statements is presented with aggressive verbal content and passive body language? Have a group member role-play some of the "mixed" messages and have the others respond and comment on their reaction.

A	S	E	R	T
B	**I**	**N**	**G**	**O**
1	6	1	2	3
6	2	4	5	5
3	4	3	5	1
1	2	5	2	3
5	1	4	6	2

1. Bill leaned forward, stared at Sam and interrupted his sentence as he spoke. Bill is acting _____ .

2. Pete looked at his feet, stood back from his boss and spoke very slowly as he asked for his salary increase. Pete is acting _____ .

3. Larry borrowed money from Fred three times and hasn't paid it back yet. Fred is expecting Larry to ask for more money so he is rehearsing what he will say. He wants to say "Larry, I know that you are broke and want money for the subway, but when you borrow money I can't count on you paying it back and I feel angry. If you pay me back the money you have already borrowed, then I will consider loaning you some more money." This response would be _____ .

4. As usual, Janet was playing the radio at a high volume when her husband came home from work. Although he has never complained about it before, tonight he turned it off because he had a headache.

5. Mike says that, since we always do what I want to do, today we are going to do what he wants to do. Mike is acting _____ .

6. Sherry wanted to go to the movies if I would drive. I wanted to go shopping. She suggested that we go shopping and I drive. Sherry is acting _____ .

Figure 6-2. Assert Bingo game.

7. Sarah borrowed money from Laura three times this week, and Laura gave it to her without a word. Sarah has just asked for more money, and Laura refused her request. Then she said "You're really irresponsible, Sarah, and I am not giving you the money. If you'd be a little considerate, you'd realize that I have to take care of my own needs once in awhile." Laura is behaving in what way?

8. Billy walked up to his mother, stood 3 feet away, looked her directly in the eye and in a firm, well modulated voice said "if you don't give me the new bicycle I want for my birthday, I am going to hold my breath until I turn blue."

9. "Please take me to the zoo, pretty please!"

10. "I wanted to spend time alone with you tonight but since you haven't seen your aunt for a while, let's do what you suggest and visit her."

11. Arlene wants to end a long phone conversation with Eric, so she tells him her mother has to use the phone. Arlene is being ———— .

12. "I know that you are angry because I said you were lazy, but if we can talk about it, then I think we can resolve things."

13. Bill looked at his brother Tad and said, "Anything you say is fine with me, whatever you want." He is acting ———— .

14. Fred was really inconsiderate of you yesterday. You would like to give him some feedback on his behavior but you know that he will be sweet as pie the next time you see him so you decide not to mention it. You are acting ———— .

15. Fred was really inconsiderate of you yesterday and today when you saw him you said, "Fred, I know you are interested in baseball, but when you change the channel on the TV when I am watching another show, I feel angry at you. If you would discuss it with me before changing the channel, then I would not get angry at you." I am acting ———— .

16. "I know you have to go shopping this afternoon, but if you would go to the beach with me then we could have a nice swim and you could do your shopping later."

17. Michael looked away from his friend, shuffled his feet and stated in a low voice, "You know Jim, I really don't have a preference, we can do whatever you want."

18. Jan asked her friend Kathy to go shopping with her to pick out some new clothes. Jan remembers some negative experiences from past shopping trips so she said to Kathy, "I know you want to be helpful to me when we go shopping, but if you would tell me when you are tired of shopping, then we can stop and I won't feel like I am taking advantage of you."

19. "Well, since I have been waiting for you all day, you can just ride with me and not say a word."

20. "Are you kidding? You want a green one? I hate green, everybody with any taste hates green. Are you sure you want green?"

21. "I like doing things that you suggest. Don't worry about me, I'm sure I'll have fun."

22. Sid walked up to the counter and slammed the package down, waving his hands and blasting, "Where is the store manager? I want to speak to the store manager."

23. Sharon is the only woman at a meeting of ten people. When one of the men asks her to make some coffee for the group, she responds saying, "I'm not your servant, get someone else to make your coffee."

24. "I don't know what to say to you about that. Maybe we should start off by figuring out what we want."

Figure 6–2. *(Continued)*

Lesson 3. The Consequences of Assertive, Aggressive, and Passive Behavior

Instruction

The following is an outline of the concepts to be presented. Table 6–3 is useful as a guide.

1. Assertive behavior:
   a. Social consequences.
   b. Effects on wants and expectations of self and others.
   c. Feeling consequences: self and others.
   d. Behavioral consequences: self and others.
2. Aggressive behavior:
   a. Social consequences.
   b. Effects on wants and expectations of self and others.
   c. Feeling consequences: self and others.
   d. Behavioral consequences: self and others.
3. Passive behavior:
   a. Social consequences.
   b. Effects on wants and expectations of self and others.
   c. Feeling consequences: self and others.
   d. Behavioral consequences: self and others.

Supervised Practice

The facilitator distributes the two vignettes, "Last Night's Party," and "Cleaning the Yard" (Table 6–4), and accepts volunteers or selects two participants to enact the first situation. The participants are instructed as follows: "Each vignette depicts a conflict situation in which assertive communication would be helpful. One participant (the "sender") is to initiate an assertive solution using one of the three assertive requests, (no-conflict request, conflict request, or request for behavior change), or an assertive response to a request, wherever appropriate, and the other (the "recipient") should respond in a way that seems appropriate." It is important that the therapist set up the scene in the vignette as realistically as possible.

   After the group members role-play the situation, the remainder of the group should give feedback to the sender (person who initiated the

TABLE 6–4
Vignettes for Practice of Assertiveness

Last Night's Party

You run into your downstairs neighbor in the hallway outside your apartment. S(he) had a party last night and the music was so loud that it kept you awake. What do you say to your neighbor?

Cleaning the Yard

Your mother (father) asks you to come over to her (his) house Saturday and work in the yard with her (him), cleaning it up. You planned to watch the baseball game on television this Saturday. What do you say when your mother (father) calls and makes this request of you?

---

assertive "solution"). The feedback should focus on how well the response fulfilled the definition of assertiveness. The facilitator should have the definition of assertive communication on the board throughout the session so it can be used to guide the feedback. Relevant feedback might consist of the following:

- *Specific Statement of What Was Done Well.* "I think you expressed your wants clearly, and I liked your choice of a conflict request."

- *Recommendation for Improvement.* "You could make your request even better by starting your empathic statement with a phrase such as 'I know that you . . . '."

After all the feedback is given and discussed, the role-play should be reenacted, incorporating the feedback. A group discussion should ensue regarding the short-term and long-term *consequences* of the sender's behavior. For example, did the other person fulfill the requester's wants? What was each party thinking and feeling before and after the interaction? What was the likely effect of the sender's assertive behavior on the relationship of the two people portrayed in the role-play situation? What expectations were created for future interactions?

The preceding role-play develops competence in the most desirable method of resolving social conflict, assertiveness. It is generally believed that it is best to practice and develop competence in the desired skill and not to practice inappropriate behaviors. In the present case, however, it is desirable also to practice the "inappropriate" behaviors of aggression and passivity. The juxtaposition of all three styles of interaction helps demonstrate the different reactions and the potential short-term and long-term consequences of behaving in these different ways.

Therefore, the situations described in Table 6–4 can be reenacted using aggressive and passive styles. When the aggressive and passive behaviors are exhibited, the recipient should respond as assertively as possible. Follow the same procedures as described earlier for discussion and feedback.

Feedback

Feedback should be provided as described in Chapter 1.

Independent Practice

The concepts and procedures of assertiveness should be incorporated into the independent practice experiences developed to generalize request making and responses to requests presented in Chapters 4 and 5. They will prove to be an important component of problem-solving (Chapter 7), as well. Also, as applications of self-awareness and awareness of others (as shown in Chapters 2 and 3) are implemented, attention to the assertiveness principles described in this chapter are appropriate.

7

Problem-Solving
Basic Principles and
Cognitive-Behavioral Strategies

Previous chapters on communication skills training have focused on developing competency in making and responding to requests so that the individual is better able to obtain rewards from the environment. This chapter focuses on problem-solving skills. These cognitive-behavioral skills enable people to identify effective ways of coping with problems of everyday living (Bellack, Morrison, & Mueser, 1989; D'Zurilla & Nezu, 1990).

Clinical practice in problem-solving continues to be strongly influenced by the original work of D'Zurilla and Goldfried (1971). These researchers identified what continues to be the core process of an effective problem-solving model. D'Zurilla and others (e.g., Bedell et al., 1980; Bedell & Michael, 1985; Bellack & Mueser, 1986; D'Zurilla, 1986; Nezu & D'Zurilla, 1989; Nezu, Nezu, & Perri 1989) have continued to develop and refine the original problem-solving model. It has been found that the utilization of a cognitive-behavioral approach to problem-solving facilitates the process.

161

DEFINITIONS OF BASIC CONCEPTS

What Is a Problem?

Although various definitions are used in the literature, most indicate that a problem exists when a person wants something and does not know how to get it. A problem, then, may be conceptualized as an unmet want, the way to fulfill it yet to be determined.

This broad definition enables the concept to encompass problems that are *specific* or *general, positive* or *negative,* and *major* or *minor* in importance or scope. The following examples will illustrate these points:

Specificity

Specific	General
Mike owes me $10 from three weeks ago and I can't reach him.	I need more money.

Negativity

Negative	Positive
I lost the $500 I got out of the bank this morning to pay my bills.	I got a $500 bonus at work; what am I going to do with it?

Importance

Minor	Major
I don't know what to make for dinner tonight.	I love my wife but she wants to leave me.

Generally, the problem-solving model described in this chapter will work equally well with problems that are major and minor, positive and negative, and general and specific. We emphasize this broad conceptualization as problems are typically viewed in a bad light such as "major," "negative," "aversive," and "bad." Such a narrow understanding unduly restricts the application of the adaptive social skills described in this chapter. The resolution of positive problems is as important as that of negative problems. Practically speaking, most people can recognize the value of focusing on positive problems such as planning the use of leisure time, planning a social event, deciding how to spend money and how to reciprocate a positive gesture from a friend.

Additionally, understanding that problems can be positive helps to eliminate the stigma often associated with having a problem. Elimination of negative value judgments may help a person be more open to admitting the existence of a problem since guilt and shame may be reduced along with the defensiveness and denial these feelings engender. Being receptive to the existence of problems is an important precursor to effective problem-solving. The nonjudgmental and objective definition of a problem suggested here facilitates adaptive problem-solving.

What Is Problem-Solving?

Problem-solving is a process that can help a person find out both what he or she wants and how to get what is wanted in the most effective way.

Why Have a Problem-Solving Skills Training Program?

As having and solving problems is such a natural and common part of everyday life, some clients may question why this skill should be the focus of therapy. After all, don't we all solve problems all our lives? There are, however, advantages to participating in a problem-solving skills training program.

First of all, since problems are a natural and inevitable part of life, it is in everyone's best interest to learn better ways of solving them. Ineffective strategies create or contribute to the continuation of personal and interpersonal difficulties. Alternatively, effective problem-solving skills strengthen self-efficiency expectations and enhance interpersonal relationships.

In addition, learning problem-solving skills in a supervised setting where new ways of thinking and acting are encouraged and practiced greatly facilitates skill development. The group therapy format provides a safe and secure environment for learning from other people's strategies and experiences and getting feedback on one's own skill performance.

BASICS OF PROBLEM-SOLVING

D'Zurilla and Goldfried (1971) described a basic component of problem-solving to be "general orientation." In this component, individuals are counseled to develop a positive "set" or attitude toward problem-solving. This positive attitude is intended to provide interest and motivation to engage in problem-solving activities. While the development of positive expectations and motivation is an important component of all psychotherapy and skills training, these authors proposed to make it a specific area of training.

The present program attempts to operationalize the "general orientation" component of training into a set of discrete procedures. Borrowing concepts and procedures from the family therapy literature (Anderson, Hogarty, & Reiss, 1980; Anderson, Reiss, & Hogarty, 1986), we developed "Seven Guiding Principles of Problem-Solving." The principles are provided to clients in written form, and are discussed in the therapy sessions as well. We even suggest that the list of the guiding principles be posted in the home, perhaps on the door of the refrigerator. Experience has shown that studying this readily accessible list fosters a positive attitude toward problem-solving and helps clients avoid common pitfalls associated with these skills. Participants learn that if they are ineffective in their attempts at problem-solving, it is often because they have violated one of these seven principles.

It is useful to explain to clients that the guiding principles will help establish a practical philosophy of problem-solving. This philosophy will guide them when they are confronted with a problem and are involved in its resolution. Adherence to the guiding principles increases the probability of successful problem-solving and prevents the use of self-defeating strategies.

The Seven Guiding Principles

1. *Problems Are Natural.* It is important to accept problems as a natural part of life. It is not "bad" to have problems, nor does their presence imply weakness. Accepting problems helps people to be more open and less "defensive" about them. Problems that are seen as "bad" are not freely discussed, and feelings of anxiety, guilt, and shame will hamper effective problem-solving.

2. *Think before Jumping to a Solution.* Frequently, once an individual recognizes that a problem exists, he or she will act on the first solution that comes to mind. But, it is more adaptive to do some thinking about the problem before attempting a solution. First, it is important to verify that a problem truly exists. Then it is necessary to define the problem, clearly, formulate several possible solutions, evaluate each solution, and then select the best course of action.

3. *Most Problems Can Be Solved.* Another behavioral pattern of many individuals, especially those who do not have effective problem-solving skills, is the tendency to give up on a problem before trying to solve it. People sometimes assume they are helpless to solve the problems that

arise. This is obviously self-defeating as problem-solving can be effective only if one engages in the process. Willingness to expend the effort required, however, depends on self-efficacy expectations. Principle 3 asserts that positive change be effected with most problems through the application of problem-solving skills. While it is unreasonable to expect all wants to be fulfilled completely, there is usually a way to have wants at least partially fulfilled.

4. *Take Responsibility for Problems.* A person can only solve those aspects of a problem for which he or she is able to take responsibility. Taking responsibility for a problem does not mean blaming or criticizing oneself and engendering guilt. Rather, it emphasizes the importance of recognizing both our contribution to life events and reactions experienced, and that we are capable agents of change. Generally, something can be done about a problem whose existence (at least in past) we attribute to ourselves, but we have little control over ones attributed entirely to an external agent.

5. *State What You Can Do, Not What You Can't Do.* Sometimes people decide to solve a problem by stopping certain behaviors. For example, if someone argues with another family member, he or she might decide to solve the problem by "not arguing any more" or not talking about certain topics. Such an approach may lead to a lot of uncomfortable and unnecessary silence in a relationship as the two participants seek to avoid various topics. Taken to the extreme, the repeated use of this type of solution results in there being few topics to discuss. A more adaptive solution to the problem of how to deal with differences of opinion is to specify a substitute positive behavior(s) for arguing in which the family members could engage. This could entail agreement to take a 10-minute relaxation break at the first sign of increasing voice volume, then to return and talk about the issue calmly, with each member making at least one empathic statement. Having a goal, or a positive alternative, provides direction and incentive, while merely avoiding areas of conflict leads to inhibition and stagnation.

6. *Behavior Must Be Legal and Socially Acceptable.* When trying to solve problems, individuals often extend themselves in new ways. Sometimes, these new behaviors push the limits of what is legal and socially acceptable. For example, someone with a problem with neighbors may decide to "stand up for his rights." If this translates into "telling them off" by being rude and discourteous, the person is exhibiting socially unacceptable behaviors. A more assertive and socially acceptable way

to stand up for one's rights would prove to be more adaptive in the long run.

7. *Solutions Must Be within Our Power and Ability.* People sometimes try to solve problems and implement solutions that are beyond their ability and power. Such solutions are obviously doomed to failure. The most common error is that people forget they can control only their own behavior and attempt to control the behavior of others. A person usually cannot make others behave in a certain way. The most that usually can be done is to attempt to influence someone to behave in a certain way by making requests, providing information, and making bargains. If the other person responds positively to the influence, further help can be provided in the form of feedback, guidance, and support. For example, a parent may want his or her son to get a job. The parent can explain the benefits, encourage, and even establish contingencies based on progress toward finding work. But ultimately, the son is the only one with the power to get himself employed.

Once this principle is accepted, frustration is reduced as individuals learn to appropriately define problems and establish realistic expectations about changing other's behavior. It should be noted, too, that this principle can be applied to our own problems, solutions to which must be within our capacity to execute.

So, this group of guidelines is designed to establish a positive problem-solving set. Some of the "guiding principles" are also used as standards for evaluating various parts of the problem-solving process. This is specifically the case when determining whether the problem has been defined in a solvable form and in evaluating alternative solutions to the problem before deciding which one to implement. Thus, the principles are used to guide and evaluate problem-solving.

THE PROBLEM-SOLVING PROCESS

Since there are many steps to the problem-solving process, an overview will be helpful. Each of the components will then be presented in detail. There are seven steps in the entire process:

1. Problem Recognition.
2. Problem Definition.

3. Generation of Alternative Solutions.
4. Evaluation of Alternative Solutions.
5. Making a Decision.
6. Implementation of the Solution.
7. Verification of the Solution's Effect.

Problem Recognition is the process of identifying a problem, preferably when it is of manageable proportions. Problem Definition is the process of defining the problem in a solvable form. Once the problem has been defined, the next step is to generate a number of alternative solutions. Because the first solution considered is not always the best, it is important to think of a number of potential ways to solve the problem. Various methods for developing alternative solutions will be presented subsequently in the chapter. In the next step, Evaluation of Alternative Solutions, each possible solution is evaluated for its appropriateness and potential effectiveness in satisfying the unmet want that is the basis of the problem. This evaluation results in making a decision to implement one or more of the alternatives. In the final steps of problem-solving, Implementation of the Solution and Verification of the Solution's Effect, the alternative selected is implemented, then evaluated to determine its effectiveness.

A "Problem-Solving Worksheet" (Figure 7–1) has been developed to guide clients through the first five steps of the process with a problem currently experienced. The implementation and verification steps are conducted separately from this worksheet. As may be noted in the figure, there is space to write information regarding each of the various components.

In the following sections of this chapter, we will present each of the problem-solving steps. It may be helpful to use Figure 7–1 as a guide for this discussion.

Step 1. Problem Recognition

Problem recognition was not originally considered by D'Zurilla and Goldfried (1971) to be a step in the problem-solving process, but the experience of Bedell and his co-workers (Bedell et al., 1980; Bedell & Michael, 1985) demonstrated that it was an essential component. The ability to recognize the existence of a problem is fundamental to all

Problem recognition: What cues (thoughts, feelings, or behaviors) helped you to identify this problem?

Problem definition:

Describe the problem situation:
  Who?
  What?
  When?
  Where?
What do you want? (Identify your primary want.)

What are the wants of others?

Make a "How to" statement.

Evaluate the "How to" statement:
  Is is positive?
  Is there another goal that has to be achieved first?
  Is it legal and socially acceptable?
  Is it within your power and ability?

Generate alternatives: Think of 3 to 5 alternative ways to resolve the "How to" statement.

1. _____

2. _____

3. _____

4. _____

5. _____

Evaluate alternatives:
  Does it satisfy your want from the "How to" statement?
  Is it sensitive to the wants of others?
  Is it legal and socially acceptable?
  Is it within your power and ability?

Choose the alternative most likely to succeed.

Figure 7–1. Problem-solving worksheet.

other aspects of problem-solving. Application of the self-awareness skills in Chapter 2 will facilitate the Problem Recognition step of problem-solving.

There are several reasons for considering Problem Recognition a critical step in the problem-solving process. First of all, identification of the thoughts, feelings, and behaviors that signal the existence of a problem provides information that is used in subsequent steps of the problem-solving process. Second, it is possible to learn skills to improve awareness of the existence of problems so they can be identified early in their development.

This early identification enables the person to become aware of a problem when it is potentially more manageable, before it becomes extreme and overwhelming (e.g., recognizing a conflict with one's work supervisor and solving it before being disciplined or fired). It is the sign of a socially skilled person to be able to recognize and act to solve a problem before it is obvious to everyone. It takes little talent to recognize a problem once an argument has ensued or people are calling each other names. Also, it is much more difficult to solve a problem once it reaches this level of intensity and heated emotion. In contrast, recognition of early cognitive, affective, and behavioral signs that signal unmet wants identifies them at a manageable level when they are more easily solved. This early intervention may also prevent the development of severe problems and the accompanying high intensity and destructiveness of emotion.

Problem recognition refers to the identification of an unfulfilled *want* that the individual does not know how to fulfill. Consistent with the model in this book, the best way to develop this awareness is to learn to use thoughts, feelings, and behaviors as guides to the existence of a problem. In other words, an individual can recognize that a problem exists by paying attention to various "personal cues" that signal its presence. There are systematic ways to use thoughts, feelings, and behaviors as "personal cues" and these will be discussed in the following sections.

Thinking Cues

Thoughts can provide cues to the existence of a problem. As defined in Chapter 2, a thought is a "message from the brain that expresses a wish, want, desire, expectation, comparison, or description." In the case of problem recognition, the primary focus is on wants. Those unfulfilled wants may be problems. For example, a person may realize that he wants to live in an apartment that is tidy and clean yet be living with a room-mate who leaves papers and clothing scattered on the floor and furniture. An awareness of this sort indicates that the person has an unfulfilled want and is a cue that a problem exists. In fact, our definition implies that every problem has an associated unmet or unfulfilled want. If there is no unfulfilled want, there is no problem. The main task of Problem Recognition is to develop cognitive techniques that enable people to become aware of the unmet want. This may be accomplished by asking, "What do I want in this situation?" or "What do I want from this person?" Such a simple question, because it focuses attention on wants, is a good way to stimulate thoughts leading to problem recognition.

Feeling Cues

Feelings can also signal the presence of a problem. In fact, feelings may be the *first* signal that a problem exists, often coming to awareness before either thoughts or behaviors.

Just about any feeling can be a cue that there is a problem. If the feeling is translated into one of the four basic feelings (fear, anger, sadness, and happiness), the underlying want can be detected by using the thought-feeling-behavior triad (see Figure 2–3) for that feeling. This want can then be evaluated to determine if it is the basis of a problem.

In many cases, however, the feeling a person is first aware of is a vague or general sensation that might be labeled "apprehension," "tenseness," "feeling upset," or "feeling bad." Once the person is aware of the general feeling, it helps to translate it into one of the four basic feelings (fear, anger, sadness, and happiness). This transformation enables the person to use a TFB triad to identify the unmet want.

For example, a client may say he is upset when he feels fear and anger. If the "upset" feeling is determined to be "anger," the TFB triad for anger is examined. It has been determined that the feeling of anger is associated with wanting something, not getting the want fulfilled, and still desiring to have the want fulfilled. The man's next step is to ask, "What do I want that I am not getting in this situation?" The answer helps to identify the unmet want and, therefore, the problem.

It is important to understand that feelings are a normal part of all aspects of life and, therefore, do not necessarily function as cues for problems. There are, however, certain characteristics of feelings that suggest a problem exists. These characteristics are:

1. A feeling that is experienced with strong intensity (e.g., feeling anger at the intensity of "rage") may signal a problem.

2. A feeling that is experienced very frequently (e.g., feeling sad every time you see a car the same model as your old girlfriend's) could signal a problem.

3. A feeling that lasts a long time (e.g., feeling sad for two weeks) may signal a problem. Being annoyed (angry) at one's roommate for three consecutive days may signal a problem.

4. A feeling that is inappropriate to the situation may also signal a problem. An example is sadness or anger at a birthday party.

To help determine whether a feeling is serving as a cue, then, it is important to evaluate it for one or more of these four characteristics.

Behavioral Cues

Finally, behavior can alert an individual to the existence of a problem. As defined previously, a behavior is an action that can be seen or heard. When people recognize a behavioral cue suggesting that a problem exists, they should determine the TFB triad that includes that type of behavior and identify the corresponding want. Thus, a person who is aware of "negative approach" behaviors may infer the presence of a want. In response to the negative approach behaviors and the corresponding wants, the person may ask, "What do I want in this situation that I am not getting, but still want?"

Not all behaviors are indications of a problem. Certain characteristics of behaviors, however, may be cues that a problem exists:

- *Unusual or Uncharacteristic Behaviors.* These kinds of behavior are often the best cues that a problem exists. For example, slamming a car door, being impatient with a friend when you are usually patient, or being late to work when you are usually on time may all indicate a problem. While these behaviors may or may not be directly related to the problem, they are cause to reflect on feelings and unmet wants. As was the case previously, reference to the TFB triad is useful.

- *Illegal or Socially Inappropriate Behavior.* A person who engages in these kinds of behavior (e.g., driving recklessly; yelling at a coworker) should be alert to the possible existence of a problem.

To clarify the concept of Problem Recognition, a vignette entitled "Sloppy Alice" is provided, in which one or more cues are present.

Sloppy Alice

Sherry and Alice are roommates. Sherry is very neat and clean, whereas Alice rarely puts anything away. Sherry cleaned the entire house this morning because her new boyfriend was coming over for dinner. About an hour before her guest is scheduled to arrive, she returns from the supermarket to observe Alice dropping her candy wrappers on the floor as she watches TV. Sherry, feeling very angry, notices that Alice's clothes are strewn all around the living room as well.

Taking the role of Sherry, the first task associated with Problem Recognition is to identify the thought, feeling, and/or behavioral cues that indicate there is a problem in this situation. The process would ideally proceed as follows.

Most likely, Sherry would first become aware of her feeling of anger. Since it was described as a strong feeling, it could be a cue that a problem exists. As we know from the TFB triads, anger is the feeling associated with wanting something and not getting it, but continuing to want it. In response to the awareness of the feeling of anger, Sherry would ask herself, "Since I am feeling angry, what do I want in this situation that I am not getting?" The answer might be, "What I want is a clean house for company."

Thus, Sherry wants the house to be clean for her company tonight and she prepared the house in anticipation of entertaining her boyfriend. But, since Alice has strewn candy wrappers and clothes around, the house is no longer in the condition desired. Her desire for a clean house is unmet. This unmet want constitutes a problem if Sherry is unaware of how to resolve it. In the current example, there was no indication of behavior that would signal the presence of a problem. If, however, Sherry had observed herself slamming the dishes around in the sink or picking up Alice's clothes and forcefully throwing them in the closet, she might have recognized these behaviors as indicating the presence of a problem. Other behaviors indicative of a problem would include a failure to give her roommate the usual friendly "hello" greeting, speaking in a loud aggressive voice, and making critical statements about the roommate.

In response to these behavioral cues, Sherry would ask herself if they were unusual for her or were inappropriate to the situation. If the answer was yes (she usually does not pick up Alice's clothes and throw them in the back of the closet), she would suspect that there is a problem.

Having recognized the possibility of a problem, she would want to identify the unmet want. In practice, it has been found to be useful to review all three classes of cues to help recognize the unmet want. That is, in a given situation (such as the one described in the "Sloppy Alice" vignette), the person reviews the thoughts, feelings, and behaviors that were cues that a problem exists. Thoughts of interest would relate to unmet wants; feelings would be extreme, long-lasting, or inappropriate to the situation; and behaviors would be out of character for the individual, illegal, or socially unacceptable. This process involves considerable mental effort and may take a few moments' time. However, the benefits are significant and, as will be seen later, this information is useful in the subsequent steps of the problem-solving process.

Step 2. Problem Definition

The second major step in the problem-solving process is Problem Definition. Having recognized the presence of a problem, the individual is now ready to define it in such a way that it can be solved. The primary goal of this section is to ensure that the problem is conceived in a solvable form. When a problem is poorly defined, it may resist solution, even though the individual may possess the skills and supports necessary to deal with it.

As may be seen in Figure 7–1, there are five parts to Problem Definition: (a) description of problem situation, (b) identification of own want, (c) identification of other's want, (d) composition of a "how to" statement, and (e) evaluation of the "how to" statement. This is a laborious process taking considerable time and mental effort. Often persons with problems are eager to get to the solution phase and are impatient with problem definition. It is our experience that efforts in the problem definition phase are well rewarded later in the problem-solving process. A well-defined problem will accurately describe the unmet want and will present the problem in a goal-directed manner. It will also prevent clients from pursuing a solution that is off target. The following is a description of the five steps used to define a problem.

Describe the Problem Situation Objectively

Most problems occur in a context or situation. Problems conceived as occurring without a context are often difficult to solve. For example, a problem may be stated as "I want to be happy." This statement indicates a desire to experience a state of being that is characterized by getting wants met. However, the statement is not situation specific; it does not indicate when, where, or with whom the person desires happiness. In this general form, it suggests that the person wants to be happy in every life situation, and it is simply beyond the resources and abilities of most people to simultaneously address such a broad range of problem situations. A more limited focus is desirable. "Wanting to be happy" would be better defined by focusing the desire for happiness on central life situations in which happiness is desired but absent. This might include happiness when interacting with a spouse, during the evenings, and when making plans for the weekend.

For some problems, the description of the situation is not as essential because the problem is focused but occurs in a number of different situations. For example, wanting a job, not having one, and not knowing how to go about finding one, is a focused problem that is not very situation specific. Even in a case such as this, however, it is important to determine whether the employment problems are situation specific, such as during the job interview. The more specificity provided in defining the situation, the more successful the problem-solving is likely to be.

To facilitate the process of focusing problems, the situation in which the problem occurs should be objectively described. This requires identifying *who* is involved, describing *what* happened, and specifying *when* and *where* the situation occurred. In other words, the individual should describe the situation with the *"Four W's,"* leaving out value judgments and feelings.

Information used to describe the situation objectively would be comparable to that available from a "snapshot," or more accurately, an audiovisual segment, of the situation. It would include information about the identities of those present, their behavior and other situational characteristics. Thus, thoughts, feelings, motivations, and attitudes of the persons are not included in the description since they would not be objective and would not appear in a snapshot of the situation. This type of information enters the problem-solving process at a later point.

As an example, an objective description is provided of the scene presented earlier regarding Sloppy Alice.

- Who: Sherry and Alice.
- What: Sherry saw Alice's clothes in the living room and Alice throwing candy wrappers on the living room floor.
- When: When Sherry came home, late in the day, about an hour before her company was scheduled to arrive.
- Where: In Sherry and Alice's apartment.

A summary statement of the problem situation is: "When Sherry came home to her apartment about an hour before her company was scheduled to arrive, she saw Alice's clothes in the living room and Alice throwing candy wrappers on the living room floor." The reader will notice that this description does not include evaluation of Alice's behavior as good, bad, or even "sloppy"; it is objective, public information.

Identify Own Wants

The next step is for the individual to identify what he or she wants. As indicated previously, this task is complicated because there are often a number of competing, overlapping, and contradictory wants in a given situation.

The list of wants in this section of problem-solving may have already been generated in the Problem Recognition phase. In that section, thoughts, feelings, and behaviors that signaled the existence of unmet wants were identified, and these are the focus of Problem Definition. Thus, the information regarding wants is transferred from the Problem Recognition Phase to the current section.

From this list of wants, individuals must be able to identify the *primary want*. Although there may be a number of unmet wants, they cannot all be considered simultaneously. To attempt to do so would defeat the problem-solving process. So, the most important—or primary—want among the several wants is selected. An objective procedure for identifying the primary want has been developed.

List Wants

To start, the "personal cues" identified in the Problem Recognition step are reviewed. Here, the client identified one or more strong feelings, unfulfilled wants, and/or unusual behaviors that signaled the presence of a problem. Now this information is used to help develop a list of the wants that exist.

If one of the personal cues that helped the individual recognize the existence of a problem was a thought (i.e., an unmet want) then this information is directly relevant now. This unmet want(s) would represent a want in this situation. It would be listed as part of those wants now under consideration in the problem definition phase of the process. This is the most direct source of information for developing the list of wants.

However, the individual may have recognized the existence of a problem through identification of a feeling. In this case, information about wants can be derived by utilizing the TFB triads shown in Figure 2–3. For example, if the feeling observed in the Problem Recognition stage was anger, the person would refer to the thought-feeling pair associated with anger and ask, "What did I want that I did not get and still want?" The structure of this question helps the individual focus attention in such a way to facilitate the awareness of wants.

It is also possible that the existence of a problem was originally recognized by behavior that was unusual for the person or inappropriate for the situation. Here again, reference to the TFB triads would yield information about the relevant wants associated with the type of behavior exhibited. For example, the unusual behavior may have been "speaking in a loud aggressive way." This type of behavior would fit under the negative approach category of basic behaviors. Negative approach is associated with the feeling of anger which is associated with wanting something, not getting it, and still wanting it. The individual would be instructed to answer the question, "What do I want that I am not getting?" This answer will provide information to help in the development of a list of wants.

The "Sloppy Alice" example will be used to illustrate the process of identifying wants in a problem situation.

Sherry's personal cue identified in the Problem Recognition stage was anger. The TFB triad that includes anger indicates "Anger is experienced when a person wants something, does not get it, and still wants it." Sherry should refer to this definition of anger and ask herself "What do I want that I am not getting." The answer would likely be "I want the house to be clean for my company tonight," "I want Alice to put her clothes away and to place the candy wrappers in the garbage," and "I want Alice to be more considerate."

Select the primary want. Since most problems involve multiple wants, it is desirable to select the one that is of primary importance. Direct attention to the primary want; do not attempt to focus on multiple over-lapping ones. The following objective method has been developed to identify the primary want from a list of related wants.

First, the person reviews the assembled list of relevant wants. Each statement of a want is evaluated using the question, "If this want was satisfied, would it take care of all the other wants on the list?" If the answer is "no," indicating that other wants on the list would still be unmet, the want being considered is not the primary want. When the answer to this question is "yes," the primary want has been identified. So, the primary want is the one that, when satisfied, also satisfies the other wants on the list.

This evaluation technique is not foolproof but generally is effective in selecting the primary want. At least this method will narrow the choices to two. If more than one want meets this criterion, the final selection can be made on the basis of other criteria so that the most objective, specific, and clearly stated want is chosen. The following is an example of the process of identifying the primary want using "Sloppy Alice."

As indicated, Sherry's wants were:

- "I want to get the house clean for my company tonight."
- "I want Alice to put her clothes away and to place the candy wrappers in the garbage."
- "I want Alice to be more considerate."

Evaluating each statement with the question, "If this want was satisfied, would all the other wants on the list be satisfied as well?," suggests that Statement 3 is not the primary want. First of all, being considerate is a vague term. Second, being considerate would not directly be related to the house being clean or the clothes and wrappers being put in the garbage. However, Statements 1 and 2 seem to be rather equivalent since they both would result in a clean house. Statement 1 is a more general statement of a want and Statement 2 is more specific. In determining the "primary want," it is possible that either statement would lead to a solution. However, the better choice would probably be Statement 1, as the fulfillment of that want, (a clean house), would entail fulfillment of Sherry's want for Alice's things to be picked up. Having Alice pick up her clothes and wrappers is a means of getting Sherry's want met, but represents only one of several ways of achieving a clean house. It better fits the definition of an alternative solution, which will be discussed later. Therefore, Sherry's primary want is "to get the house clean for my company tonight."

Identification of the Wants of Others

The next step in problem definition is to identify the wants of other people in the problem situation. The information presented in Chapter 3 regarding empathy is applied here. Identifying the wants of others as part of a problem-solving process does not involve learning skills different from those already presented, only a new application of skills.

As indicated previously, it is usually not possible to know what another person wants, so it is necessary to make an educated guess. An understanding of the wants of another person may be based on (a) his or her present behavior, (b) past behavior, (c) the context in which the present behavior is exhibited, and (d) knowledge of what we would want if we were in the other person's situation.

Continuing the example of Sloppy Alice, Sherry might use the following procedure to determine Alice's wants:

- *Present Behavior.* She is throwing candy wrappers on the floor and clothes are thrown around. She may want to be carefree and casual.
- *Probable Past Behavior.* She is living up to her nickname, Sloppy Alice, which she acquired because she is frequently in this casual mode regarding house cleanup.
- *What Would I Want If I Were the Other Person?* If I, like Alice, had a free afternoon and night, I would probably want just to relax and be carefree, and not be concerned with being neat.

So, based on these three factors, a reasonable determination of Alice's wants would be the following: Alice wants to relax and watch TV and is satisfied with the living room being sloppy.

Make a "How to" Statement

The next step in problem definition is to compose a "How to" statement, which is the declaration of the primary want in a form that is action-oriented and goal-directed. This statement becomes the focus of the remaining sections of the problem-solving process.

The formulation of the "how to" statement is actually quite simple and involves stating the primary want as a goal. This is done by placing the words *How to* in front of the statement of the primary want. So, continuing with the example:

Place the words "how to" in front of Sherry's primary want:

"*How to* get the house clean for my company tonight."

Evaluation of the "How to" Statement

Since the "How to" statement is the focus of the rest of the problem-solving process, it is important that it be a workable definition of the problem. It is possible to develop a "how to" statement that is not solvable. To attempt to solve such a problem would be a waste of effort; it would be frustrating and end in failure. To prevent this from occurring, we have identified a number of common flaws that would render a "how to" statement unworkable. These common flaws have been converted into questions that serve as evaluation criteria for the "how to" statement. If the "how to" statement fulfills the following four criteria, it is likely to be workable and capable of leading to a sensible decision at the end of the process.

1. *Is There Another Goal That Must Be Accomplished First?* Before a person starts to develop a plan to accomplish the "How to" statement, it is necessary to determine if another goal must be achieved first. If the "How to" statement cannot be solved until another goal is achieved first, attention must be focused on the other goal. For example, if a young man's goal was "How to get a computer job," but he did not know how to operate a computer, he could not achieve the goal. First, the man would have to learn how to operate a computer. Therefore, he would have to address the problem of "How to operate a computer" before attempting "How to get a computer job."

2. *Is the "How to" Statement Positive?* It is best if the "How to" statement is expressed in a positive and action-oriented manner. The "How to" statement should state what the person *is* going to do rather than what the person is *not* going to do or is going to *stop* doing. So, "How to express my feelings to my wife" is better than "How to stop fighting with my wife." If the "How to" is not stated positively, it can be revised and stated in a positive way.

3. *Is It Legal and Socially Acceptable?* The answer to this question may vary according to the social context. But, if the "how to" statement involves illegal or socially unacceptable behavior, it should be rejected as unacceptable. Using the "Sloppy Alice" example, if the "How to"

statement was "How to throw Alice out of the house for the night," it would be rejected as socially inappropriate.

4. *Is It within Your Power?* "How to" statements sometimes set goals that are beyond the power and ability of the problem solver. If the problem solver does not have the power, influence, or skill to accomplish the goal stated in the "How to" statement, it should be rejected. This is not a detailed assessment of what is needed to accomplish the goal—that will come later when the alternative solutions are evaluated. At this point, the "how to" statement is evaluated to determine if it is obvious, with a little reflection, that there is a critical lack of essential power, influence, or skill.

For example, "How to move out of my parents' house by the end of summer," is a goal that probably is beyond the power and ability of someone who is unemployed, has no money, and has no experience establishing residence in an apartment. This person would have to modify the "how to" statement to fit his or her abilities or abandon it. In this case, perhaps the time frame could be lengthened, or each of the major steps needed to move out of the parents' house might become separate problems to be solved. For example, "How to get money for a deposit on an apartment," "How to get money to pay the monthly rent on an apartment," would be more solvable.

Another common error in the development of a "how to" statement is to state a goal that requires another person to fulfill, such as, "How to get my roommate to keep the apartment clean" or "How to get my wife to stop drinking." It is important to recognize that the behavior of these people (roommate and wife) is not under the control of the person trying to solve the problem. Since a person cannot control the behavior of others, any "How to" statement predicated on it is doomed to failure.

When a problem entails the want for another's behavior to change, the most rational goal for the problem solver is to seek to maximize influence on the other. The "how to" statement should emphasize the role of the problem solver, and should be geared toward learning what will increase the problem solver's impact on the other such that the latter will be motivated to make the change desired. The want expressed in the "how to" statement must be capable of being satisfied by the problem solver's own behavior, not by another's. Thus, the previous examples would be better expressed as "How to ask my roommate to keep the apartment clean" and "How to encourage my wife to quit drinking." In both these examples, the "How to" statement calls on the problem solver to do something that is within his power.

The "how to" statement for the "Sloppy Alice" vignette was "How to get the house clean for my [Sherry's] company tonight." In response to the four evaluation questions, (a) there is no other goal that must be achieved first, (b) the "how to" statement is positive, (c) the goal is legal and socially acceptable, and (d) it is within Sherry's power and ability. Based on this assessment of the "how to" statement, the problem has been conceived in a solvable form.

Step 3. Generation of Alternative Solutions

After the problem has been defined in a solvable form, the next logical step is to begin thinking of alternative ways in which the problem, expressed as a "how to" statement, can be solved. As the first solution considered is frequently not the best (Guiding Principle 2), it is generally recommended that a minimum of three alternative solutions be formulated before deciding on any particular one.

Sometimes it is difficult to think of more than one way to solve a problem. In fact, it may be difficult to generate even one solution. This difficulty may be because people learn to think about problem solution in certain ways and frequently forget that there are a number of different ways to attempt to achieve a goal or solve a given problem. So, to help clients become more creative in their thinking, and enable them to be more productive in generating alternative solutions to problems, we suggest three methods for generating alternatives.

Brainstorming

One very effective strategy for generating alternative solutions is known as brainstorming. This method works extremely well in a group setting and is defined by three criteria:

1. Group members contribute as many alternatives as they can think of "off the top of their heads."
2. Ideas should be generated without evaluation (in other words, "critical judgment is suspended" when brainstorming).
3. "Wild" ideas are welcome.

Sometimes effective alternatives can be generated when individuals think creatively (think about doing things in a novel way). Sometimes "wild," not practical, ideas can be modified into good solutions.

As is implied by the name, in brainstorming many ideas are created with great energy. Just as the atmosphere produces spontaneous, untamed, and unpredictable storms in nature, the person's brain produces a "storm of ideas" with this strategy. Although brainstorming was originally developed for group use, it can also be used individually. All it requires is for the person to follow the three criteria outlined.

Brainstorming can be illustrated using the example of Sloppy Alice. Sherry's "how to" statement is "How to get the house clean for my company tonight," and brainstorming produces the following alternatives:

1. Stuff clothes under the couch or the bed.
2. Throw Alice's clothes and candy wrappers in the garbage.
3. Clean up Alice's mess myself.
4. Ask Alice to clean up her clothes and the candy wrappers before company comes (i.e., make a "Conflict Request").
5. Help Alice clean up.
6. Yell at Alice until she cleans up the room.

Changing Your Frame of Reference

Another method of generating alternatives is to "change your frame of reference." This method requires the person to see the problem from someone else's point of view. Essentially, there are two steps in this method.

First, the person should think of someone he or she respects and considers to be good at problem-solving (e.g., a therapist, friend, or relative). It is especially helpful to think of someone who is good at solving the type of problem under consideration. For example, if the problem has to do with getting along with a roommate, the problem solver should think of the person who is effective at getting along with others. If the problem relates to getting a job, the person should think of someone who just got a job. The person imagined does not even have to be known personally. A public figure, famous writer, character in a movie, writer, or any other effective character could be chosen. The object is to see the problem from a fresh vantage point that suggests new and potentially effective alternative solutions. The problem solver tries to imagine how this other person would solve the problem under consideration by asking the question, "If so-and-so were in my shoes, what would he or she do?"

In the Sloppy Alice example, the problem solver might proceed as follows. Sherry could ask herself, "Do I know someone who is a good problem solver, especially when it comes to resolving problems with a roommate and handling anger in a constructive way?" She might decide, "My mother would probably know what to do. She would suggest that I not take any action until I got the other person's side of the story. She might suggest that I consider that Alice also lives in this apartment, and that she is in the middle of a TV program and should be given the opportunity to finish watching it before I ask anything of her."

Therefore, based on consideration of the problem from this frame of reference (Sherry's mother), an additional alternative is generated:

7. Request that Alice clean up after her TV program is over.

Adapting a Solution from a Similar Problem

The third method of generating alternatives is to adapt a solution from a similar problem. This procedure prompts the person to remember and utilize prior successful experiences with solving problems. This method of generating alternatives recognizes that many current problems are not totally new and have been faced before, although perhaps in a slightly different form. Those efforts that were effective in the past are applied to the present situation.

Using the Sloppy Alice example, it is possible that Sherry could adapt a solution from a similar problem. She could try to think of a similar situation(s) she has encountered in the past in which (a) she shared something (either an apartment, an office, a desk, etc.) with someone, (b) the person had "messed up" this shared space after Sherry had cleaned it, and (c) Sherry especially wanted the space clean that day. Sherry might not be able to recall a situation that included all three elements, but she would attempt to include as many of the important elements as possible. Alternatively, she could develop three separate but related solutions, each of which addressed one of the three elements of the present problem.

Perhaps Sherry remembered a time she cleaned the family room of her parents' house because she expected her boyfriend Mark to visit. Before he arrived, however, her brother threw his schoolbooks, papers, and baseball cards all around the room. In that situation, Sherry asked her brother to put away his things because she was expecting Mark later and, because she knew he liked Mark, also invited him to join them in a snack when Mark first arrived. She knew that her brother was in no mood to clean up the room at that time, but she figured he would be more likely to do it graciously if she did something nice for him in return. Since this solution worked out well in the previous situation, she decided to consider doing something similar in response to her present problem. Using the technique of adapting a solution from another situation, she adds another alternative to her list of possible solutions:

8. Ask Alice to clean up her things and invite her to have coffee with me and my company after dinner.

When generating alternatives, it's frequently advantageous to try all three strategies just described. Alternatives may occur to an individual more easily using one method than another but, nonetheless, learning to use all the techniques may assist the problem-solving process. Problem-solving groups frequently like to use the "brainstorming" method. Use of the other techniques may require some encouragement and practice.

Step 4. Evaluation of Alternative Solutions

Once all the alternatives have been generated, it is time to evaluate the potential effectiveness of each of them in solving the problem. Each alternative is evaluated on the following four criteria:

1. *Does It Satisfy the Want Specified in the "How to" Statement?* For an alternative to be effective in solving the problem, it must be able to satisfy the unmet want that was identified. Therefore, when evaluating an alternative, the person must consider its potential for achieving the goal specified in the "How to" statement. Only alternatives that appear to be able to satisfy the unmet want will be considered for implementation. For example, if Sherry were evaluating the alternative "take my company out to dinner" for her problem "How to get the house clean for my company tonight," she would have to reject it for failing to fulfill this criterion.

2. *Is It Sensitive to the Wants of Relevant Others?* To behave assertively, people must consider others' wants as well as their own. Although it's not always possible to fulfill others' wants, an alternative that demonstrates an attempt to be sensitive to people associated with the problem will be more effective in the long run. A solution that does not consider the wants of others would usually not be given further consideration unless modified.

3. *Is It Legal and Socially Acceptable?* This criterion is one of the four previously used to evaluate the "how to" statement and, more generally, is one of Seven Guiding Principles of Problem-Solving. When trying to solve problems, people often extend themselves in new ways and may consider behaviors that are not legal and/or socially acceptable. Deciding to stand up for oneself and "tell someone off," may seem to be an improvement to a person who has consistently acted passively. However, this behavior probably involves being rude or discourteous, or acting out other inappropriate means of ventilating anger. A more socially acceptable solution should be sought. Any alternative solution that violates a formal written law is not acceptable and would not be further considered.

Having alternatives of this type in the list is to be expected and should not be considered wrong or bad. When people are encouraged to brainstorm and to be creative in developing solutions, some alternatives will go beyond acceptable social and legal limits. It is important that they be recognized as inappropriate and not acted on. Sometimes they can be modified into acceptable alternatives. For example, instead of "telling off" a neighbor, the problem solver may decide to make a "request for behavior change."

4. *Is the Solution within Your Power and Ability?* This evaluation criterion is also taken from the list of Seven Guiding Principles of Problem-Solving and was previously used to evaluate the "how to" statement. People sometimes identify solutions that are beyond their ability and power to implement. Such solutions are doomed to failure for the reasons indicated previously.

The various alternatives developed to solve Sherry's problem ("How to get the house clean for my company tonight") will be evaluated using these four criteria.

1. Stuff Alice's clothes under the couch or the bed.
   a. Does it satisfy your want from the "How to"?   yes
   b. Is it sensitive to the wants of others?   no
   c. Is it legal and socially acceptable?   no
   d. Is it within your power and ability?   yes
2. Throw Alice's clothes and candy wrappers in the garbage.
   a. Does it satisfy your want from the "How to"?   yes
   b. Is it sensitive to the wants of others?   no

    c. Is it legal and socially acceptable?   no

    d. Is it within your power and ability?   yes

3. Sherry would clean up Alice's mess herself.

    a. Does it satisfy the want from the "How to"?   yes

    b. Is it sensitive to the wants of others?   yes

    c. Is it legal and socially acceptable?   yes

    d. Is it within your power and ability?   yes

4. Ask Alice to clean up her clothes and the candy wrappers before company comes (make a conflict request).

    a. Does it satisfy your want from the "How to"?   yes

    b. Is it sensitive to the wants of others?   yes

    c. Is it legal and socially acceptable?   yes

    d. Is it within your power and ability?   yes

5. Help Alice clean up.

    a. Does it satisfy your want from the "How to"?   yes

    b. Is it sensitive to the wants of others?   yes

    c. Is it legal and socially acceptable?   yes

    d. Is it within your power and ability?   yes

6. Yell at Alice until she cleans up the room.

    a. Does it satisfy your want from the "How to"?   yes

    b. Is it sensitive to the wants of others?   no

    c. Is it legal and socially acceptable?   no

    d. Is it within your power and ability?   yes

7. Request that Alice clean up after her TV program is over (make a conflict request).

    a. Does it satisfy your want from the "How to"?   yes

    b. Is it sensitive to the wants of others?   yes

    c. Is it legal and socially acceptable?   yes

    d. Is it within your power and ability?   yes

8. Ask Alice to clean up her things and invite her to have coffee with you and your company after dinner.

    a. Does it satisfy your want from the "How to"?   yes

    b. Is it sensitive to the wants of others?   yes

    c. Is it legal and socially acceptable?   yes

    d. Is it within your power and ability?   yes

Step 5. Making a Decision

Once each of the alternative solutions has been evaluated on the four criteria specified, the individual has good objective information for selecting the alternative that has the greatest potential for effectiveness. To do this in a systematic way, the following two steps are recommended:

1. Since any truly effective solution will satisfy *all four* of the criteria used to evaluate alternatives, any one that does not do so should be eliminated.

2. If more than one alternative meets all four criteria, select the one that *best* satisfies them. For example, one of the alternatives may appear to either satisfy everyone's wants more effectively or be easier to implement than another.

Sometimes, it's difficult to choose among several high-quality alternatives. When there is no basis on which to predict the superiority of one of two or three potential choices, the most reasonable decision may be to select them all. The person's task, then, is to determine whether to implement them simultaneously or sequentially.

Referring back to Sloppy Alice, it is possible to select an alternative or two for action. The two steps for selecting an alternative are followed. As may be seen, several of the alternatives do not meet all four criteria. Thus, alternatives 1, 2, and 6 are eliminated from further consideration. The remaining alternatives seem to meet the four evaluation criteria.

After evaluating the remaining alternatives (3, 4, 5, 7, and 8), Sherry decided that the best solution was a combination of 4 and 8. That is, (a) Sherry's wants will be best satisfied if Alice alone cleans up her clothes and candy wrappers, and (b) sensitivity to Alice's wants will be best demonstrated if the request is stated empathically. Moreover, Sherry would like Alice to share coffee with her friends tonight, and she thinks that Alice will feel happy in response to such an invitation. Sherry expects this overture (inviting Alice for coffee) to have a positive effect on her relationship with Alice, with each woman demonstrating a greater likelihood of fulfilling the other's future wants. Use of a conflict request would be an ideal way of making her request.

Therefore, two alternatives are combined. That is, Sherry will ask Alice to clean up her clothes and candy wrappers before company comes (using the conflict request format) and invite her to have coffee with the company after dinner.

Step 6. Implementation of the Solution

Once the solution has been formulated, it is time to carry it out. Since this action may take some planning, this is the point in time that the Supervised Practice phase of skill training is useful. That is, the individual can plan what he or she will say and do, and act it out in front of an expert who can provide feedback. Once the most effective thoughts and actions have been rehearsed and successfully performed, the person will be better able to carry out the desired behaviors in the real-life situation.

In some cases, however, there is no time or opportunity to practice or obtain feedback from others. In this situation, the person must organize his or her behavior and carry it out with little preparation, relying on established skills. It is rare, however, that a person must ever respond "immediately." There is usually at least a brief amount of time to pause, collect, and organize the relevant information and formulate a response. The models and cognitive maps taught in this program may be recalled and used. For example, whenever the problem-solving alternative involves making or responding to a request from another person, extensive models to guide thinking and behavior have been developed and presented in previous chapters. There is almost always time to recall and use these models.

Thus, in the Sloppy Alice example, Sherry would compose a couple of requests using the models presented earlier in this book. First, she would make a conflict request. She might say, "*I know you* want to relax and enjoy your television show, but *if you* would pick up your clothes and candy wrappers before my company arrives, *then I* would be able to have a clean apartment for entertaining." Sherry would also make a no-conflict request in which she would say "And I hope you will be around after dinner because *if you* are, *then I* would like you to join us for coffee and dessert."

Step 7. Verification of the Solution's Effect

After the alternative solution has been carried out, it is important to verify whether or not it was executed according to plan, and whether or not it fulfilled the *four* evaluative criteria as expected.

Following through on Sloppy Alice, verification would include deter-mination of whether or not (a) Sherry actually made the conflict request and no-conflict request as described, (b) the requests resulted in Alice cleaning up her things before the arrival of company, (c) Sherry actually demonstrated sensitivity to Alice's desire for relaxation and to be a wel-come member of Sherry's company, (d) the request was executed in a so-cially appropriate manner, and (e) making such a series of requests was actually within Sherry's ability to accomplish.

PROBLEM-SOLVING SKILLS TRAINING PROGRAM

The following sections of this chapter will present a practical example of a problem-solving skills training program. The sample program follows the four-part sequence described in Chapter 1 (Instruction, Supervised Practice, Feedback, Independent Practice). Because of the many compo-nents of problem-solving, this practical example is divided into three separate lessons. The content areas of the three lessons are:

Lesson 1   Introduction to Problem-Solving Skills and Seven Guid-ing Principles

Lesson 2   Problem Recognition and Problem Definition

Lesson 3   Generating and Evaluating Alternative Solutions and Making a Decision

Each lesson will include an outline of the Instruction components and exercises to be used in the Supervised Practice components of the train-ing. The three lessons are divided so that, when used in a group therapy format with 8 to 10 clients, each one takes about 90 minutes to complete.

Lesson 1. Introduction to Problem-Solving Skills and Seven Guiding Principles

Instruction

1. Define the concept of a problem.

2. Define problem-solving.

3. Present the seven guiding principles of problem-solving.

Supervised Practice

The following exercise is designed to help the group members recognize and differentiate the Seven Guiding Principles of Problem-Solving.

TABLE 7–1
:ven Guiding Principles of Problem Solving

 natural. We all have wants that we do not know how to

2. Think (!) before jumping to a solution. Your first solution may *not* be the best.
3. Most problems can be solved.
4. You can only solve a problem when you take responsibility for it.
5. In solving a problem, state what you *can do, not* what you *can't do.*
6. Behavior must be legal and socially acceptable.
7. Solutions must be within our power and ability.

Exercise: Detecting Violations of the Guiding Principles. Directions for this exercise: Distribute to the group members copies of Table 7–1, which lists the Seven Guiding Principles of Problem-Solving. One at a time, read the stimulus statements listed in Table 7–2 to the group. After each statement, ask: (a) "What is wrong with this statement based on what we have just learned about the seven principles

TABLE 7–2
Stimulus Items for "Detecting Violations of the
Seven Basic Principles of Problem-Solving"

1. If only I was a millionaire, I wouldn't have any problems at all.
2. I tend to "act" first, and ask questions later. For example, when my roommate accused me of stealing his wallet, I punched him.
3. After taking that Assertiveness Training course, I know now that I am passive, and I will probably always be passive. I will never be able to act assertively and get what I want.
4. I have mental problems, so nobody's going to treat me with respect.
5. I don't have friends because people don't like me.
6. The only way I'm going to get along better with my wife is for me to stop yelling at her.
7. The only way for me to save money for a car is for me to stop buying things for the house and stop going out so often.
8. I don't have any money for rent this month, so I will just not pay it, and I will avoid the landlord.
9. When they didn't offer me the job, I threatened them.
10. I was going to run out of medication before I saw my doctor, so I took only one pill each night instead of the recommended two.

of problem-solving? Which principle(s) do(es) the statement violate? (b) How does it violate the principle(s)? (c) Can the statement be modified so it is consistent with the principle(s)?"

It is recommended that the first one or two statements be addressed to the entire group and responses to the questions be taken from the group as a whole. After a few examples, the group leader may choose to go from one client to another and give each a chance to respond individually. Reference to the information in Table 7–1 is recommended.

Many of the statements violate more than one of the principles. The point of this exercise is to review common ways of thinking that are counterproductive to effective problem-solving and begin to substitute more adaptive thinking.

Feedback

Follow the guidelines provided in Chapter 1 and illustrated in Chapter 2.

Independent Practice

Follow the guidelines provided in Chapter 1 and illustrated in Chapter 2.

Lesson 2. Problem Recognition and Problem Definition

Instruction

The following is an outline of skill topics to be presented.

1. Briefly review information presented in the prior lesson.
2. Present overview of problem-solving process using Figure 7–1 as a model.
3. Present detailed discussion of problem recognition.
   a. Thought cues.
   b. Feeling cues.
   c. Behavioral cues.
4. Introduce "Sloppy Alice" vignette and apply problem recognition to it.
5. Present detailed discussion of problem definition.
   a. Objective description of a situation.
   b. Identification of wants of problem solver.
      i. Relationship to problem recognition cues.
      ii. Identifying the primary want.

c. Identification of wants of others.

d. Making a "How to" statement.

    i. Evaluation of "How to" statement.

e. Apply Problem Definition to Sloppy Alice.

Supervised Practice

The following exercise provides supervised practice defining problems in a solvable form. The group leader should first distribute stimulus items for the exercise entitled *Puzzling Problems* (Table 7–3). The exercise consists of two types of stimulus items to which the members respond. The first group of items (1–8) provides four "How to" statements for each item, from which members choose the most correct one. The second group of items (9–17) requires the members to develop a "How to" statement on their own. Thus, a sequence of difficulty is provided,

TABLE 7–3
Stimulus Items for the Exercise "Puzzling Problems"—An Exercise for Problem Identification and Problem Definition

1. You don't have any food in your house and you don't get a check for a week.
   a. How to get your check.
   b. How to feed your household.
   c. How to get food for one week.
   d. How to pay your bills.

2. You have run out of gas in your car and you are due at work.
   a. How to get gas.
   b. How to get to work.
   c. How to get to a phone.
   d. How to get money.

3. You have homework due and you have only one hour before class. Your homework is not done and you need to eat before class.
   a. How to eat.
   b. How to get to class.
   c. How to get transportation.
   d. How to get the homework done and eat.

4. It is raining and you have planned a picnic for this afternoon.
   a. How to stop the rain.
   b. How to plan a picnic.
   c. How to stay dry.
   d. How to have a picnic out of the rain.

TABLE 7-3 *(Continued)*

5. You meet your friends for a game of tennis and you forget your sneakers.
   a. How to play tennis.
   b. How to get sneakers.
   c. How to tell your boyfriend how to play.
   d. How to play barefoot.

6. You planned to go swimming with some friends, but when you arrived at the pool it was closed for cleaning.
   a. How to open the pool.
   b. How to clean the pool.
   c. How to find another place to swim.
   d. How to get to the river.

7. You are on your way downtown and the bus just left without you.
   a. How to find another way to your destination.
   b. How to rent a bus.
   c. How to call the bus back.
   d. How to tell your boss what happened.

8. You made dinner with vegetables and meat, and your guests are vegetarians.
   a. How to get them to eat meat.
   b. How to throw out the meal.
   c. How to substitute for the meat with another vegetable.
   d. How to tell your guests they will have to go home and eat.

9. You locked your car and left the keys inside.

10. You are in the checkout line in the grocery store and realize that you left your wallet at home.

11. The store has no eggs and you need some for the recipe you are preparing for dinner tonight.

12. Although you think you had something important to say, you did not express your opinion this morning because you thought Sharon would be angry.

13. You criticized Bill's work and now you are sorry.

14. George keeps telling you how to design your project even though you are supposed to do it on your own.

15. Sam told you, "Pete, that was a stupid answer. I thought you knew the material."

16. Mike has not returned the tape player he borrowed from you two weeks ago.

17. You are starting to feel nervous and can't sleep well at night.

to" statement on their own. Thus, a sequence of difficulty is provided, the latter requiring more skill defining problems.

The group leader reads the stimulus items to the group and asks members to respond to them in the following ways.

Directions for Part A, items 1–8: Instruct the group members to follow along as the group leader reads the items in Table 7–3. In response to each item, the group members are asked to perform the following tasks.

1. Identify the *primary* want from among the four provided.
2. Describe how they decided it was the primary want.
3. Evaluate the "How to" statement that represents the primary want:
   a. Is there another goal that has to be achieved first?
   b. Is it positive?
   c. Is it socially acceptable and legal?
   d. Is it within the person's power and ability?

Directions for Part B, Items 9–17. Instruct the group members to perform the following processes on these items.

1. List all the relevant wants.
2. Select the *primary* want.
3. Make up a "How to" statement.
4. Evaluate the "How to" statement:
   a. Is there another goal that has to be achieved first?
   b. Is it positive?
   c. Is it legal and socially acceptable?
   d. Is it within your power?

Feedback

This component of the training is individualized according to the performance of the group members. The guidelines for feedback are the same as those indicated in Chapter 1 and illustrated in Chapter 2.

Independent Practice

The same procedures indicated in Chapter 1 and illustrated in Chapter 2 are used for this skill.

Lesson 3. Generation and Evaluation of Alternatives and Making a Decision

Instruction

The following is an outline of the skill concepts to be presented to the clients.

1. Present detailed discussion of methods for generating alternative solutions to problems.
   a. Brainstorming.
   b. Changing your frame of reference.
   c. Adapting a solution from a similar problem.
2. Apply methods for generating alternatives to Sloppy Alice vignette.
3. Present detailed discussion of how to evaluate alternative solutions.
   a. Does it satisfy the want in the "How to" statement?
   b. Is it sensitive to the wants of relevant others?
   c. Is it legal and socially acceptable?
   d. Is it within your power and ability?
4. Apply evaluation of alternative solutions to Sloppy Alice vignette.

Supervised Practice

So far, the group has applied all the problem-solving concepts to the vignette entitled "Sloppy Alice." The group leader has been very active in using this vignette to demonstrate each of the concepts. The following exercise, entitled "The Red Dress," is designed to provide the opportunity for clients to be more active in applying the skill concepts presented. This exercise is used to practice the entire problem-solving process. The suggested method for conducting the exercise follows.

Distribute copies of vignette entitled "The Red Dress" (Table 7–4), and also a Problem-Solving Worksheet (Figure 7–1). Have a group member read the vignette aloud, or the group leader can read it. Depending on group's skill level, this exercise can be conducted in one of several ways:

1. Complete worksheet as a group. Starting with the first line of the Problem-Solving Worksheet, go around the room and have each group member respond aloud by providing the information needed to fill in one line of the worksheet. Group leader can take a more

TABLE 7–4
Vignette for Supervised Practice of
Problem-Solving Process: The Red Dress

One morning Mary went to her closet to get her frilly red dress so she could wear it to school. She was going to make a presentation in English class about the book *Gone With the Wind,* and its heroine Scarlett O'Hara. She wanted to show some creativity in her presentation and thought the red dress would be just the right touch.

She could not find the dress in her closet and started walking into the next room to see if her sister Betty knew where it was. Just then Betty walked into the room wearing the red dress. Mary's mouth dropped open in disbelief. "What are you doing with my dress on? I have to wear it to school today for English class. Take it off." Betty replied "I can't take it off. I don't have anything else to wear and besides we always wear each other's clothes. I'll miss the school bus if I try to change now, wear something else." Mary said, "No way, this is my dress and I want to wear it today." Betty said, "We'll talk about it later," and ran out the front door just as the school bus pulled up. She got onto the bus and rode away. Mary was left standing in the hallway in her slip.

active role in guiding members through each step when following this approach.

2. Have group members divide into minigroups (three or four) to complete worksheet. When worksheet is completed, each minigroup can present responses to entire group.

3. Have group members complete worksheet individually, with class review to follow.

In each case, the process involves completion of the worksheet, discussion of the information used and decisions made to complete it, and role-play of the solution.

Feedback

Feedback should be provided regarding performance of each of the components of the problem-solving process. The guidelines for Feedback are the same as those indicated in Chapter 2.

Independent Practice

The guidelines for Independent Practice are the same as those indicated in Chapter 2.

8

Coping with Factors That Interfere with Learning and Using New Skills

This is a book about how to help people learn new skills and use them in everyday life. It also presents a series of straightforward procedures for learning effective communication and problem-solving. A number of factors interfere with learning and using new skills. Helping the patient overcome these obstacles is an important part of social skills training.

SELF-DEFEATING BELIEFS

The belief system that each patient brings to treatment may create an obstacle to treatment. It is often necessary to modify beliefs that inhibit the learning and utilization of new skills. Some of the common inhibitory beliefs that may be encountered by the social skills trainer will be discussed in this chapter.

Immutable Personality

Certain generalized beliefs may be problematic. For example, many people come to treatment with the belief that they have stable, unchangeable personalities. Because of this belief, they expect to benefit little from therapy, to basically stay the same, or at best, change very little. This kind of thinking can be a powerful deterrent to treatment because it lowers or eliminates motivation for change. It also destroys hope, a major contributor to positive therapy outcome. It is important for the therapist to directly address such beliefs. Dealing directly with a variety of irrational and self-defeating ways of thinking is consistent with the cognitive-behavioral orientation of this book.

There are many reasons people believe they cannot change. Understanding these reasons and how they may have been created is important for practitioners when attempting to devise strategies to alter them. Patients acquire false and self-limiting ideas about themselves from many sources. Often they receive this kind of information from the mental health professionals who are trying to help them. These ideas are also instilled by the society in which we live.

Biological Determination

It is not uncommon for a patient to say that she has been told by a mental health care provider (psychologist, psychiatrist, social worker) that a biological disorder controls her thoughts, feelings, and behaviors. This information is frequently given to people who suffer from various anxiety disorders, depression, and schizophrenia. They are told that, to change, the biological and chemical imbalances in their bodies (usually the brain) must be corrected.

With this information in mind, clients cannot understand how talking about communication and problem-solving skills is going to have any meaningful effect. They are waiting for their errant neurotransmitter to be discovered and treated with medication. For these clients, it is essential to present a biopsychosocial model of mental illness that will prevent this erroneous belief pattern from interfering with motivation to learn.

This is not a minor issue. Without accurate information about the etiology and treatment of mental disorders, clients may not participate in psychosocial treatments from which they can benefit. And, this type of thinking often becomes a self-fulfilling prophecy. A person who thinks this way will use the notion of a biological deficit to explain away any difficulty learning a new skill. The person will give up trying to learn effective communications behaviors because it is difficult or because of experiencing failure during initial attempts to perform new skills. The client loses sight of the fact that the problems experienced are a natural part of life, shared by everyone who tries to learn something new.

Correcting these erroneous attributions is an important part of skills training. It is often necessary to debunk strong dysfunctional beliefs that are reinforced by other people who strongly influence the client. Many professionals and family members share the belief that clients (especially those with severe mental disorders) primarily need medication and will not benefit from psychological treatment such as social skills training. Thus, significant others in the client's network should be targeted for psychoeducation.

Diagnosis and Trait Labels

Beliefs that overemphasize the biological determination of behavior are not the only sources of clients' self-defeating thoughts. Diagnoses such as major depression, panic disorder and schizophrenia (among others) imply, to varying degrees, stable dysfunctional ways of being. Frequently, people begin to view themselves through their labels and to selectively filter in material that is consistent with their diagnosis. For example, persons diagnosed with major depression begin to understand themselves as being unable to feel happy or enjoy positive experiences. The person with panic disorder may view himself as someone who is always nervous and can expect to experience extreme anxiety spontaneously, without any warning or reason. The person with schizophrenia may believe that she cannot hold a job or function as a productive member of society. If so, she will become progressively more dysfunctional as time goes by.

There are hundreds of labels people may be given, each of which creates a sense of disability and dysfunction. Having received such a label, people can use them to explain every thought, feeling, or action they experience. If the depressed person stays at home in his room rather than going to the family picnic, it is because of his depression. If he has difficulty on the job, it is due to his depression. The person with schizophrenia will believe that she cannot learn to balance a checkbook because of her disorder. An alcoholic takes a drink because he is an alcoholic.

Any trait label or formal diagnosis may become the basis of a belief that behavior is fixed and beyond the individual's control. The "shy" person does not initiate a conversation because he is shy. The woman who has been divorced fails in a subsequent relationship with a man because she is "too independent." A man does not apply for a promotion because he is "a failure." By using labels in this way, many people render themselves to be the passive recipients of whatever is determined by their "personality trait" at any given time or place. For these individuals, no further understanding or explanation of their thoughts, feelings, or behaviors is necessary. The limiting and self-defeating consequences of this type of belief system must be challenged if more adaptive skills, such as communication and problem-solving, are to be learned.

Early Learning and Development

There is at least one additional way that people may learn to expect that they will stay the same and not change. They may be told, in a variety of ways, that they are the product of their early learning environment, and these experiences have formed their personality. Once a personality is formed, the logic goes, patterns of thinking, feeling, and acting are set for life. Adults are taught that they have passed the critical period for learning and further change is unlikely. A common variant of this belief is the idea, "Since I have been this way so long, it is unlikely that I could change now." Popular thinking in this culture reinforces these ideas, reflected in the teachings of some mental health professionals.

SUBSTITUTING ADAPTIVE BELIEFS

Because the concepts of biological determinants, diagnosis, trait labels, and fixed learning periods can have dysfunctional effects on clients, it is the therapist's duty to correct mistaken beliefs in these areas when they are present. When properly used and understood, the concepts of biology, diagnosis, and prior learning can be helpful to an individual by providing accurate understanding and useful information.

Biology

It is important that the client understand that biological makeup influences a person's thoughts, feelings, and behaviors. An individual's genetics and biology set certain limits to psychological functioning. However, it is also important for clients to know that few people function at the upper limits of their biologically determined capacity.

Diagnosis

Balanced information about diagnoses and traits is also important. An individual may be told that a trait is defined as stability of thinking, feeling, and behaving across different situations. However, it is important to indicate that traits are *descriptions,* not *causes,* of behavior. Traits may be well established but even the most ingrained one can be modified.

Early Learning

Similarly, it is likely that early learning is important in establishing the way an adult thinks, feels, and acts. However, new learning is possible regardless of prior experiences. The idea that biology or early learning precludes change in important and positive directions must be exposed as untrue.

To counteract some of the preceding beliefs, the practitioner should provide an alternative explanation to the client. A logical explanation of how people can learn and change will not instantly cause the individual to discard old beliefs and adopt new ones. It will, however, demonstrate that there is at least one different way to look at the situation.

Malleability and Lifelong Learning

A brief nontechnical explanation of why people can be expected to change may begin with the suggestion that the way a person interacts with others is determined by two factors: the situation and the person's "personality." The personality is the sum total of one's behaviors and associated thoughts and feelings. The way a person thinks, feels, and acts varies in different situations and has been learned through past experience. The capacity to learn continues throughout life as new situations and life experiences are encountered. Therefore, just as people establish current ways of relating to others by learning to think, feel, and act in certain ways, they can continue the process and learn more effective ways of thinking, feeling, and acting.

The argument presented in Chapter 2 about helping people understand that skills can be learned may be applied here. These ideas help people believe change can occur.

Differentiating Blame and Responsibility

The concepts of blame and responsibility also help people overcome beliefs that lead to passivity and the lack of motivation to learn and use new skills. Consistent with erroneous beliefs about their psychological problems, people frequently display a habit of "blaming" their patterns of thoughts, feelings, and behaviors on an illness, personality type, or prior learning. When people do this, they become passive and yield control to these external influences. A "blaming" style precludes the assumption of personal responsibility for thoughts, feelings, and behaviors.

One goal of treatment is to help the person move from a "blaming" cognitive style to one characterized by personal responsibility. The concepts of blame and responsibility help the person understand that much of the resistance to change may be due to the way he or she conceives the situation. Learning to conceive a situation in a different way may result in more adaptive conclusions.

Psychologically, the concepts of blame and responsibility have special meaning. As commonly used, these two concepts are often loaded with moral and value judgments. For example, it may be considered wrong or "weak" to blame someone, it takes "moral strength" to accept responsibility for one's actions, and a person "should" be held responsible for his or her actions. The use of these terms as advocated here eliminates the judgmental and moralistic aspects through the use of objective and value-free definitions.

To *blame* is to attribute the cause(s) of thoughts, feelings, or behaviors to (a) other people, (b) a characteristic of the self, or (c) external circumstances. Examples of blame statements include, "I don't want to go to the party because Linda called me at the last minute" (attributing what one wants to another's actions), "I am unable to make a request of another person because I am shy" (attributing behavior to a characteristic of the self), or "I am 'bummed out' (sad) because it is the weekend and it is raining so I can't play baseball" (attributing of feeling to external circumstance).

In these examples, the role of the individual is not acknowledged. When people habitually think this way, they attribute the cause of their thoughts, feelings, and behaviors to factors outside their control. In such instances, it is beneficial to help people recognize their own role in how they think, feel, and act and to take responsibility for their thoughts, feelings, and behaviors. This does not mean that a person has to take on the burdens of the world. Taking *responsibility* means attributing the cause of one's thoughts, feelings, and behaviors to one's own wants and/or expectations.

The examples given previously to illustrate "blaming" can be reexamined in the context of "assuming responsibility." In the first example, the person indicated he was not going to the party because of Linda's behavior, a blaming statement. Taking responsibility, the person would examine his own wants and expectations and would recognize that he wants something from Linda (to be invited well in advance) that he is not getting (he was invited at the last minute). His unmet want (and perhaps the anger associated with it) is the reason he is not going to the party. Perhaps he wants the "respect" that he believes comes with an early invitation. Obviously, it is only because he values being invited well in advance that he is not attending the party. The "responsible" statement about this situation is "I am not going to the party because I wanted to be invited well in advance and I was invited at the last minute." In this statement the person has "owned" his decision not to attend the party.

In the second example, the person said she did not make the request, because she was "shy." Again, taking responsibility requires the examination of wants and expectations. In this case, the "shyness" implies anxiety or fearfulness when interacting with another, and "avoidance" behavior (see TFB triad, Chapter 3). Thus, a responsibility statement is, "I did not make the request because I was feeling anxious and wanted to avoid interacting in a way I am uncertain about."

In the third example, the person attributed his sadness to the rainy weekend. When he evaluates his wants, he will come to realize that his sadness is because he has an unmet want (to play baseball) for which he has lost hope. In evaluating the unmet want, the person can take responsibility saying, "I am sad because I wanted to play baseball and now I cannot do so."

After learning to take responsibility, as illustrated, the people can do something about their thoughts, feelings, or behaviors, because they are no longer seen as due to external factors and thus out of personal control. Thoughts, feelings, and behaviors can be *evaluated* to determine if the wants and expectations on which they are based are realistic and reasonable. If they are not, people have the option of modifying them to be more realistic. Making wants more realistic often reduces the negative feelings associated with them. For example, the person who would not go to the party because the invitation was not timely might later determine that he is happy to be invited regardless of when it occurred. And, he might reject the idea that a late invitation is a sign of disrespect. Or, even if it is, he may choose to overlook it because he wants to go to the party.

Evaluation of wants may indicate they *are* reasonable. In this case, it is more adaptive to develop a plan of action to get what is wanted than to merely attribute the problem to forces outside one's control. In the preceding example, the person would make a request for behavior change of Linda, asking to be invited earlier to social events in the future.

Helping clients to understand the relevant issues will enable them to avoid the pitfalls that lead to passivity and acceptance of the status quo. They learn to see events as being within his or her control—not under the control of a trait, another person, or an external event. Clients will learn that, although they *can* blame their failure to engage in effective communication on an external event, they *can also* identify their wants and expectations, evaluate them, and devise a plan for achieving what they want.

In each case, we have commented on the person's thoughts, feelings, and behaviors as though these were well understood by the individual. This is not always the case. In fact, the skills described in Chapter 2 of this book are prerequisite to learning to attribute cause to factors within one's control.

UNDERSTANDING INHIBITORY
EMOTIONS IN EVERYDAY LIFE

The previous discussion has focused on generalized attributions that may reduce the individual's motivation for change and lower expectations of success. Attention to generalized attributions, however, is not always sufficient to enable people to perform the skills they have learned in therapy in real-life situations, even if they are motivated to do so and accept the rationale that doing so would be in their best interest. For these people, failure to exhibit effective communication and problem-solving skills is often due to inhibitory anxiety (fear of negative consequences). Here, the intensity of the interfering feeling becomes so great that there is loss of control over one's thoughts, feelings, and behavior, resulting in diminished ability to use new skills. The principle of the Yerkes-Dodson law (Yerkes & Dodson, 1908) is demonstrated here; that is, there is an optimal level of anxiety for effective performance. Performance improves as anxiety increases up to a point, beyond which performance deteriorates.

The excessive intensity of the feelings of anxiety may be attributable to biased thinking, possibly in the form of excessively negative expectations or unrealistic wants or expectations. For example, Jim started work last year in his company as a bookkeeper and is a graduate of an assertiveness training course. Jim is well liked, extremely competent, and reliable, which is acknowledged by the company owner despite her failure to offer him a raise. He believes he deserves a raise and knows the company is doing well financially. He, therefore, develops an assertive request (conflict request, Chapter 4) and starts to approach his supervisor's office on Monday morning. Jim proceeds slowly, however, and stops prematurely as he becomes overwhelmed with anxiety, experiencing "butterflies" in his stomach, trembling hands, palpitations, hot flushes, and the sweats. He is anticipating a negative response from his supervisor, thinking she will inform him that the company cannot afford a pay increase and suggest that he find employment elsewhere if his salary is not satisfactory. Before talking to his supervisor, he turns around and walks back to his desk, perceiving himself to be incapable of articulating his request clearly.

Here, despite Jim's *knowledge* of assertive skills, his ability to *execute* them is inhibited by the magnitude of his anxiety, which, itself, is produced by the unrealistic and extremely negative expectation regarding his supervisor's response.

Other intense feelings such as anger can also inhibit the use of assertive communication skills. For example, a woman is waiting at home for her boyfriend to pick her up at 8:30 A.M. to go to the beach. At 8:40, she starts to get annoyed, her anger increasing with his continued tardiness. At 8:50, she's pacing, cursing him under her breath, feeling the tension in her body, thinking what an inconsiderate lout he is. She composes a request for behavior change but continues to dwell on his selfishness. He rings the bell at 9:00, at which time she approaches the door fuming, feeling the blood rush to her head and her heart pumping hard as she throws open the door and starts yelling at him.

Here again, the magnitude of the feeling—anger in this case—became so great that control over behavior was diminished, in spite of adaptive skills being in the individual's repertoire. In these examples, the feeling (anxiety or anger) is charged by the perception that the expected negative event was *catastrophic*.

When either overwhelming anxiety or anger is experienced, the thought-feeling-behavior circle established is both maladaptive and self-perpetuating. Cognitive distortions or biases can produce the excessive feelings and physiological sensations that, in turn, disrupt behavioral performance. Feedback, especially from the latter two sources (i.e., physiology and behavior), then impacts on the negatively biased thoughts and feelings, serving to maintain and enhance them. Thinking becomes more rigid, with thoughts focused on unmet wants or negative expectations, physiological arousal increases, and unpleasant emotion strengthens. Unless one is responding to a stressful situation in which there is imminent threat of bodily harm, this reaction is maladaptive (Beck & Emery, 1985). Because of the interrelatedness of thoughts, feelings, and behaviors, a vicious cycle develops that perpetuates and exacerbates self-defeating thinking, uncomfortable physiological arousal, strong unpleasant emotion, and unassertive (maladaptive) behaviors.

To facilitate assertive communication and break the vicious cycle, two coping skills should be developed: (a) *thinking* needs to become more flexible so various options can be considered, and (b) *physiological arousal* needs to be decreased (i.e., brought under greater control). Clients should acquire *both* cognitive and physiological coping skills to provide the optimal opportunity to exhibit assertive behavior. Proficiency in these two kinds of coping skills requires regular practice, initially in a stress-free environment, then in gradually increasing stressful situations.

COPING WITH INHIBITORY ANXIETY

Cognitive Coping

Basic Principles

The notion that thoughts determine feelings dates back at least to the Stoic philosopher Epictetus (1890) who, in the first century, wrote, "People are disturbed not by things, but by the views which they take of them." Thus, when one reacts to an event with an extreme emotion, it is because one is focusing, or thinking, about some negative aspect of that event. When strong unpleasant emotions interfere significantly with one's ability to behave assertively, these feelings should serve as cues that biased, illogical thinking is likely to be a causal factor. In other words, if the severity of fear is so great that avoidant behavior is seen as the only real option, one should be alert to the probability that faulty thinking underlies this conclusion.

For example, *overestimating the probability of a negative occurrence* (arbitrary inference) and *catastrophizing* about an outcome (magnification) are two of the most common types of cognitive distortion associated with strong anxiety and passive (avoidant) behavior (Beck & Freeman, 1990; Michelson & Ascher, 1987). Commonly, the process of overestimation allows the person to predict a negative outcome even if there is no evidence or foundation.

Consider the case of a 19-year-old man who wants to ask an attractive young woman out to lunch but does not because he is fraught with anxiety over the prospect that she'll say no, brush him off quickly, chuckle under her breath, and laugh hysterically recounting the event with her friends. This expectation may exist in the absence of any evidence of its validity (even though this has never occurred).

Catastrophizing entails *magnification* of the *importance* or *severity* of a negative expectation. For example, suppose a young woman on an outing with friends wants to take part in the discussion but does not for fear she will say something uninteresting and boring. She shudders, thinking to herself, "Oh gee, what if these people think I am a bore?!" obviously reacting as though this would be a horrible outcome—it would be a "catastrophe" to be considered a bore.

Overestimating and catastrophizing both entail the expectation that something bad will happen. In overestimating, this expectation is faulty because there's no evidence to support it: The outcome predicted has not occurred under similar circumstances. Catastrophizing may entail a realistic expectation that an outcome will occur (because it has occurred with some frequency under similar circumstances). However, the expectation that its occurrence will entail severe negative consequences is irrational because it is exaggerated. These negative expectations, as predicted from the thought-feeling-behavior triad model presented in Chapter 2, produce intense fear and are associated with an increased probability of avoidant behaviors.

As discussed previously, thought-feeling-behavior triads are generally self-perpetuating, given the circular nature of the feedback loop and the reciprocal impact of the variables that compose the circle. Thus, somatic signals from avoidant behavior, and physiological sensations from autonomic arousal, also impact on the unrealistic expectations, serving to maintain, confirm, and intensify them. Obviously, inherent in the idea of the TFB circle is a mechanism for learning to escalate cognitive distortions such that overestimation and catastrophizing occur.

The task of changing self-defeating biased thoughts to more adaptive and realistic ones is variously called cognitive coping, cognitive modification (Meichenbaum, 1977), and cognitive restructuring (Beck, 1976). The following section will illustrate these approaches.

Imagine a situation in which a person wants to return an item of clothing to the store because it is the wrong color. He is well trained in the skill of the conflict request (Chapter 4) and other principles of assertive communication. However, he is concerned that the salesperson will act uncooperatively toward him and attempt to deny his request. He thinks he will forget what to say, and everyone in the store will look at him and think he is a troublemaker. "Oh," he thinks, "that would be terrible!" He is afraid he will be so nervous that he will stand there in silence and people will start laughing. He tells himself, "How utterly humiliating for others to see me so nervous!" His anxiety increases so much that he starts to sweat, and feels his heart pounding. Influenced by these somatic cues, he becomes convinced that he will not be able to make a conflict request and act assertively to the salesperson, so he decides not to return the item to the store but to keep it.

The Four Steps of Cognitive Coping

Cognitive coping consists of four steps: *R*ecognition, *E*valuation, *S*ubstitution, and *T*reat. These steps may be remembered with the acronym REST.

Recognition

The first step in cognitive coping is to *recognize the need* to do so. Self-awareness facilitates any change in behavior. As indicated in Chapter 2, thoughts, feelings, and behaviors often occur in triads. Therefore, it is important to monitor oneself for *cues* that signal the need to cope and to identify the appropriate TFB triad. The feeling of anxiety that inhibits assertive behavior may be recognized using two types of cognitive cues:

1. *Irrational Wants and/or Expectations.* As discussed in this chapter, irrational thinking is frequently the basis of inhibitory anxiety. Thinking is irrational either because of *overestimation* of the likelihood of negative outcomes or magnification of negative consequences (*catastrophizing*). The former is a defect in expectations and the latter overestimates the value of what is wanted.

2. *Physical Sensations (Feelings) and Reactions.* This includes rapid heartbeat, excess perspiration, nausea, "sinking" stomach, blushing, trembling, difficulty breathing, weak and shaky voice, dizziness, muscle tension.

Evaluation

In the scene described, both types of cues are present: For example, the person expects uncooperative behavior from the sales clerk and ridicule from the customers. Also, he is feeling sweaty and experiences a rapid heartbeat (irrational expectations, physical sensations). When people are able to recognize the need for cognitive coping through the identification of illogical expectations and the concomitant body sensations, they are ready for Step 2 of the process, which is to *evaluate self-statements.* As indicated, *evaluation* involves the *appraisal* of the validity of the irrational expectations.

Evaluating the validity of self-statements requires viewing each one as an hypothesis to be tested for its accuracy. The following two steps are performed to test self-statements.

First, determine whether the self-statements (that the salesperson will act uncooperatively, that people will think you're a troublemaker, that they will start laughing) are irrational due to *overestimating the likelihood of a negative outcome.* To make this determination, ask the following questions: *What evidence do I have* that the salesperson will be uncooperative? In previous instances when I've observed people speak politely to a salesperson and make a request, how frequently has the salesperson responded uncooperatively? Even if the salesperson was uncooperative, *how likely is it* that others in the store would think that *I* was the troublemaker? If they observed the whole interaction and heard that I made an assertive reasonable request, but the salesperson responded in a hostile manner, *how likely is it* that they would think *I* behaved inappropriately? *How likely is it* that others would laugh if they saw I was nervous and had trouble talking? How many times have I observed customers laughing at others?

Second, determine the presence of irrational thinking in the form of catastrophizing (believing that the negative outcome that is expected has exaggerated importance). To evaluate this possibility, you would ask the following questions: *"How terrible or important would it be if what I expected actually happened?"* "Does it really matter if some other customers thought I was a troublemaker or noticed I was nervous? Would that change my life in any way? Would I die, or lose my family, my job, my friends, or anything really worthwhile to me?"

Substitution

After questioning the likelihood of occurrence and relative importance of the expected negative outcomes, the person substitutes irrational expectations with realistic self-statements that help relieve the anxiety and permit the emission of adaptive, goal-directed behavior. In other words, after negative statements are appraised by questioning evidence for the (a) likelihood and (b) importance of expected negative outcomes, irrational thinking is substituted with the *answers* to these evaluation questions.

Continuing with our example, when evaluating the evidence by asking oneself about the likelihood of a hostile response following a polite reasonable request, the substitute coping self-statement could be: "It is highly unlikely that the salesperson would respond aggressively toward me if I asked to return the item. When I've previously returned something and treated the salesperson respectfully, I've gotten a cooperative response in return. Even if the salesperson did act aggressively, *I* would not be evaluated poorly by others, the salesclerk would be."

After questioning the actual importance of the negative consequences expected by asking oneself how horrible their occurrence would be, the following coping self-statements could substitute for the irrational originals: "Even if the other customers think I am a troublemaker, it's not the end of the world; I won't die, lose my family or friends, or anything really important. Even if my anxiety is apparent and people laugh, the worst that will happen is that I will feel uncomfortable for a few minutes in front of a bunch of strangers who mean nothing to me. In the long run, this will be insignificant." Stepping back from the situation enables a person to gain some perspective and realize that even a bad outcome won't affect life in any important way.

Treat

After the effective substitution of coping statements (and assertive behavior), the person should reward the effort by treating him- or herself well. A good attempt at substitution may also merit reward. Rewards with self-statements (as well as other, more tangible rewards) that acknowledge the specific things done well are highly recommended.

The acronym *REST* assists people in recalling the multistep process described. Another acronym, *REALIST,* may be employed if a person wishes also to recall the three questions that are part of the evaluation step. The acronyms are applied as follows:

*R*ecognition of anxiety cues.

*E*valuation of negative self-statements, which comprises:

    *A*ppraisal of the

        *L*ikelihood and

        *I*mportance of expectations, and

Substitution of coping self-statements for irrational ones (e.g., assertive for avoidant behavior).

Treating oneself with self-statements and tangible items that reward attempts at cognitive coping and competent assertive behavior.

Coping with Inhibitory Anger

Besides being useful for inhibitory anxiety, cognitive coping is similarly effective for anger control. The application to anger is very similar to that of anxiety. With inhibitory anger, identifiable kinds of faulty thoughts (i.e., irrational or unrealistic wants and/or expectations) also correspond to maladaptive feelings, (the intense anger, physiological arousal) and aggressive (negative approach) behavior. This process has been discussed elsewhere (Burns, 1980; Meichenbaum, 1977; Novaco, 1975; Walen, DiGiuseppe, & Dryden, 1992).

Nearly everyone will feel some degree of anger if a want is potentially attainable but not obtained. If the expectation intensifies, however, so that one *must* get what is wanted, and a particular want is not fulfilled, the intensity of the anger will be much greater and physiological arousal and aggressive behavior may be difficult to control. This is an example of *overestimating the necessity of having wants fulfilled,* which can lead to the kind of cognitive distortion known as *catastrophizing.*

The method of cognitive coping for irrational wants or expectations that produce anger is the same as that described for anxiety. The REST model would be applied to the anger-producing situation.

Physiological Coping

Slow Breathing

Although the cognitive coping procedures previously presented may be expected to impact on the high physiological arousal associated with maladaptive anxiety and anger (because of the association between thoughts and feelings), coping strategies that act directly on the physiological arousal are also available. Slow diaphragmatic breathing is one such technique.

Anxiety states are commonly accompanied (or even caused) by hyperventilation, or overbreathing. This increase in the rate and/or depth of breathing beyond metabolic demands creates an imbalance between carbon dioxide and oxygen, such that too much of the former is released. This decreases the pCO_2 (the partial pressure of carbon dioxide, with partial pressure defined as the force exerted by a gas in a liquid) in the lungs and blood, and increases blood alkalosis (pH). Although hyperventilation implies a higher intake of oxygen, increased levels are present in the blood alone because of constriction in certain blood vessels of the body and decreased ability of hemoglobin to distribute oxygen to the cells of the body.

The combined effects of all these processes include difficulty breathing, chest pain, paresthesia, palpitations, dizziness, and lightheadedness. Missri and Alexander (1978) report the multiple effects of hyperventilation on seven bodily systems (neurological, cardiovascular, etc.), with Ley (1987) stating it affects every bodily organ. Therefore, it is important to learn how to slow down and increase the efficiency of breathing.

Although the effects of hyperventilation are pervasive, they are not dangerous. Rather, they are the body's natural response to threat. When threatened with imminent harm, the body automatically prepares itself with the *fight/flight* response, with the changes produced by hyperventilation preparing the body for flight. That hyperventilation is a natural biological response that is not dangerous is an extremely important point to convey to people who may suffer from high anxiety (Barlow & Craske, 1989; Klosko & Barlow, 1989). This assurance helps reduce the fear response to initial anxiety cues.

A method of physiological coping that serves to increase breathing efficiency is slow diaphragmatic breathing. The diaphragm is a wall comprising muscle and membrane that separates the abdomen from the thoracic cavity. One can think of it as a plunger. During inspiration, it plunges/suctions downward and flattens, creating a vacuum that helps the lungs expand. During expiration, it relaxes back into its convex upward shape, reducing the vacuum, permitting the lungs to contract. Diaphragmatic, or abdominal, breathing accentuates this plunging movement, allowing maximal expansion of the lungs, facilitating breathing, helping to slow down the rate and counteract the multiple physiological effects of hyperventilation.

We have combined the diaphragmatic breathing procedure with "slow breathing" as described by Barlow and Cerny (1988), and Barlow and Craske (1989), which also incorporates a meditative component. Participants are taught how to take 10 diaphragmatic breaths in 60 seconds. They do this by inhaling for three seconds and mentally counting 1, 2, 3 and exhaling for three seconds while mentally counting 1, 2, 3. After each 6-second breath, they say to themselves "relax." The repetitive exercise promotes relaxation, with the word "relax" used to cue the relaxed state associated with exhalation.

During the years we have been treating persons with anxiety problems, clients have reported greater success with slow diaphragmatic breathing than with any other procedure.

Progressive Muscle Relaxation

A second method for reducing physiological arousal associated with maladaptive anxiety is progressive muscle relaxation. This technique was originally developed by (Jacobson, 1938). Jacobson demonstrated that tension in the skeletal muscles, which is a natural response to stress, is associated with activation of the central and autonomic nervous systems (CNS and ANS, respectively). During anxiety states, increases in the sympathetic arm of the ANS produce many of the physiological sensations and reactions, including increased heart rate, palpitations, increases in respiration and blood pressure, gastrointestinal disturbance, and sweating. Analogously, relaxation of the skeletal ("voluntary") muscles produces decreases in CNS and sympathetic arousal. Thus, any procedure that promotes the reduction of muscle tension is an effective method of relaxing away the physiological symptoms of anxiety.

Progressive muscle relaxation involves tensing, then relaxing, sequentially, various muscle groups of the body. Our protocol involves eight muscle groups, a focus on breathing, and exhalations associated with the word "relax." The purpose of tensing first is twofold: (a) to increase awareness of the sensations associated with muscle tension so that they can be more easily distinguished from those of relaxation and can be used to cue the need to relax, and (b) the sensation of release of tension is greater (especially with a novice) when muscles are initially tensed.

Once some proficiency has been gained (e.g., after two weeks), the procedure can be modified by having clients tense/relax combinations of muscle groups simultaneously. Combining muscles so that more of them can be tensed, then relaxed, together, attenuates the exercise, making it more time efficient.

After several weeks (according to individual progress), the tension component of the exercise can be eliminated. The assumption is that, by then, the contrasting sensations of tension and relaxation are known, and the latter state can be reached in an even more time-efficient and "portable" package. The user can practice the exercise anywhere, many times a day, without others being aware. As before, the self-instruction to "relax" is associated with the muscle release and each exhalation. "Relax" serves to signal, or "cue," the relaxation, so this procedure is aptly identified as "cue-controlled relaxation."

Relaxation is probably learned fastest in a quiet room with lights dimmed. However, if there is some extraneous noise or light, this may help promote generalization. Moreover, suggestions can be made to minimize the impact of these potentially distracting stimuli, which is exemplified in the relaxation protocol (Table 8–1).

To promote comfort, the participants should be wearing loose, nonrestrictive clothing. Shoes and eyeglasses may be removed and belt buckles loosened. A partially reclining position is probably optimal. If recliners are not available, however, participants should make themselves as comfortable as possible in standard chairs. Although a fully reclining position (lying down) may be most comfortable, we do not recommend it as it may promote sleep. Although this is one of the purposes for which relaxation is recommended, its use here serves a different function.

The facilitator should anticipate a participant who experiences relaxation-induced anxiety (RIA). Jacobson and Edinger (1982) found its occurrence frequent enough to label it a side effect of relaxation. Heide and Borkovec (1983, 1984), leading researchers in the field, found that 31% of subjects with generalized anxiety disorder reported increase in tension during the relaxation procedure. This was due primarily to fear of either losing control or the changes in sensory experience. In discussing this problem, Deffenbacher and Suinn (1987) mention four remedies: (a) giving clients a counterdemand or paradoxical instruction, informing them that it may take some time before relaxation comes under their control, and some individuals may initially experience increase in tension, (b) offering repeated exposure to relaxation, (c) changing to another relaxation technique, or (d) treating the specific fear with an alternative intervention (e.g., treating fear of loss of control with cognitive restructuring).

Regardless of whether or not the practitioner is treating an individual with RIA, it is always advisable to inform participants that the exercise is a means of *gaining,* not *losing,* control. Muscle tension contributes to anxiety by activating the nervous system. Releasing muscle tension deactivates nervous system activity and, thus, decreases anxiety. By releasing, or letting go, of tension, one is able to think more clearly, feel

TABLE 8–1
The Progressive Muscle Relaxation Protocol

The first muscle group that we are going to focus on comprises the muscles of your hands and arms. I want you to begin now to slowly form your fingers into two tight fists. Feel the tension as you do it. Make them as tight as you can.

As you do this, I want you to raise your hands up toward your shoulders as though you are forming two muscles. Feel the tension; feel how taut your fingers are. Hold them as tight as you can bear it. . . . Now relax, let your hands fall back to the chair. Relax your fingers . . . relax your forearms . . . let the tension leave your hands . . . let your hands sink into the arms of the chair . . . concentrate on relaxing the whole length of your arm . . . as you relax deeper, you can feel the warmth spreading in your fingers; as you relax further, the warmth will spread up your arms. . . .

What I want you to do is to raise your hands out in front of you . . . stretching them out in front of you, making the muscles of your arms and your fingers as taut as you can. Stretch your whole arm out in front of you. Hold it as tight as you can, feel the tension in the fingers and in your wrists. Now relax, let your hands fall back to your lap . . . let your arm be supported on your lap. Relax your fingers . . . let them sink into your lap . . . relax your wrists . . . let all the tension leave your forearms . . . as you relax, your fingers should be gently curled . . . just concentrate on relaxing your hands and your arms . . . let all the tension leave the muscles of your fingers and your arms. . . .

Now I am going to ask you to repeat the exercise again. I want you to form your fingers into a tight fist. As you do this, begin bringing your hands up toward your shoulders tensing all the muscles concentrating on the muscles that you are tensing, feeling the sensation of tenseness. Now hold it as tight as you can . . . now relax, let the tension leave your hands, relax your fingers, relax your wrists . . . you can feel the warm feeling, the tingling in your fingers. Concentrate on relaxing them further . . . relax your forearm, let the whole length of your arm relax. . . . Now I want you to raise your hands and your arms in front of you, stretching them out taut as you can. Spread your fingers holding them as rigid and as tight as you can. Feel the sensation in the muscle you are using. Now relax and let your hands fall to your lap . . . let your arm rest on your lap. I want you to concentrate on relaxing your fingers . . . let all the strain leave your arms and hands . . . relax them further. . . .

The next muscle groups we are going to work with are muscles of your legs and your feet. If you still have your shoes on, either kick them off or take them off. . . . You can put them down next to you on the floor. . . . Close your eyes and concentrate on the instructions that I am giving you. I want you to begin by pointing your toes up toward your face. As you do this, you should tense the whole length of your leg, your ankles, your arches, and your calves. Hold it as tight as you can. . . . Now I want you to point your toes in the opposite direction as though you were a ballerina. Feel the tension in your toes, in the soles of your feet, in your ankles, and in your thighs. Hold your feet far apart, relax your ankles . . . relax your toes . . . let all the tension leave your legs. Relax your calves . . . relax the whole length of your leg . . . concentrate on relaxing the soles of your feet, relax the toes. Concentrate on my voice and on

(continued)

TABLE 8–1 *(Continued)*

relaxing the muscles of your legs . . . relax them further. . . . Now I am going to ask you repeat the tensing and the relaxing the muscles of your legs again. I want you to begin by pointing your toes up toward your face, feel the tension, feel how rigid your legs are. Hold it. . . . Now begin to point your toes away from your body like a ballerina . . . make your legs as rigid as you can stand it . . . now relax . . . let your heels sink to the floor, let your feet gently fall apart . . . concentrate on letting all the strain and all the tension out of the muscles of your legs . . . relax your toes, relax your ankles . . . let your calves sink to the floor . . . let your legs become heavy and comfortable . . . relax them further. . . .

Now the next muscle group that we are going to focus on are the muscles of your neck. I want you to begin by pushing your chin into your chest. Now as you do this, feel the tension in the back of your neck. Push your chin down as far as you can stand it. Now hold it; now I want you to begin to lift your chin up and push your head back feeling the tension in the front of your neck. Jut your chin out as far as you can. Feel the change in the muscles with the tension that you are creating, hold it, now relax . . . relax the tension in your neck muscles, imagine your head is like a ball that's not at all attached to your body. You feel no sensation, no strain at all in your neck . . . relax the muscles further . . . concentrate on removing all stress and all strain from the area of your neck. When you are tense, when you are anxious, the first place it shows is in the muscles of your face. Now I want you to begin to focus on your facial muscles, begin by squeezing your face together as tight as you can stand it, hold it. . . . Now relax . . . now what I want you to do is to squeeze your eyes as tight as you can, not your forehead, not your nose, just your eyes, hold it as tight as you can. Now relax. . . . Now I want you to frown. I want you to put in all the displeasure that you've ever felt in it. A good frown will bring your eyebrows close together. Frown as hard as you can, hold it. Now relax. . . . Now I want you to squeeze your nose together as though you are smelling a particularly unpleasant odor, hold it. . . . Relax. . . . Now the next facial muscles are difficult to relax, these are the squeezing out of your cheeks. Begin by starting to smile, tighten the smile, I mean force out your cheeks . . . hold it. Now relax. . . . Now I want you to round out your lips as though you are pursing in a kiss, keep your teeth slightly apart. Now extend your lips outward. . . . Feel the tension and now relax. . . . Sigh deeply and sigh loudly. . . . As you sigh, you can feel your neck muscles and your shoulder muscles relaxing. Now relax your forehead, remove all the wrinkles from your face. . . . Concentrate on relaxing. . . . With your mouth open, gently relax your jaws. . . . Relax your facial muscles further . . . let all the stress and all the strain leave your mind . . . relax your forehead further. . . . When you tense the muscles of your face in this exercise, your face will slightly flush, this is good, this is a healthy flush; it will clear up in a few minutes, however, the wonderful feeling of relaxing will not. In order to control your breathing, I would like you to place your hands on your stomach. As you breathe, I want you to feel the rise and fall of your hands. And when I tell you to, I want you to take a deep breath and hold it. . . . Take a deep breath and hold it. . . . Feel the tension in your stomach, now relax with a sigh. . . . You can feel your stomach relaxing . . .

TABLE 8–1 *(Continued)*

you can feel the sensation within the pit of your stomach as you relax. . . . Relax your stomach muscles further. . . . You may put your arms back on the arms of the chair. . . .

Now take another deep breath and hold it . . . now relax with a sigh . . . let your breathing be very slow and very comfortable. . . . With each breath, I want you to let out tension and the strain within your body. . . . Concentrate on the rhythm of your breathing. Let your stomach muscles relax further. . . . Now relax your body, let your body sink into the chair . . . relax your arms . . . relax your mouth . . . let all the tension leave your legs . . . relax your fingers. As you relax, you can feel the warmth spreading throughout your body; let the pleasant feeling spread. Let your arms sink into the chair. Let your breathing be very comfortable and very relaxed. . . . With each breath, you will feel more and more relaxed. Relax your forehead, let all your worries and all the daily strain leave with each breath you take . . . let your whole body relax further. . . .

Now I am going to present a scene for you to visualize. I want you to imagine the scene as though it were taking place right this very moment. I want you to see everything as though it is happening right now. You will see, you will hear everything. I want you to imagine now that it is a warm spring day . . . you are out in the country . . . the flowers are all blooming. . . . You are lying on the soft grass. . . . It is very green and very comfortable. . . . Nearby is a small stream and the water is flowing very gently. . . . You can hear the bubbling as it flows. . . . The sun is beating down and the sky is blue. . . . Now I want you to stop visualizing the scene. Let the scene pass. Let your body relax. Concentrate on relaxing your arms. Relax your mouth, relax your breathing, relax your jaw. Let all the tension leave your hands and your legs. Look into the darkness of your eyes and relax. . . . Let your mouth open gently as you relax . . . let the warm feeling spread over your body, concentrate on relaxing . . . (5 minutes of undisturbed relaxation).

When I count three, I want you to open your eyes feeling very relaxed, very calm, and very refreshed. One . . . two . . . three! Now you can stretch, but again make no noise or no comment. . . .

It is very important that between sessions you practice the exercise that you learned today. . . . You should find a quiet spot where you can practice each day for about 15 minutes at a time. You will find that if you practice at nights you will soon learn to fall asleep rapidly. You will also find during the day that if you relaxed you will feel much better and your performance in school will improve. This is the end of our session. Thank you.

more positively, and behave in desired ways. An analogy taken from Goldfried and Davidson (1976) is that of floating in water, which one is able to accomplish only by letting go.

Prior to the onset of the relaxation induction, the therapist should ask participants if there are any remaining questions. After responding to these, the therapist should demonstrate the muscle groups involved in the exercise, and the manner in which they should be tensed and relaxed. Group members should participate in this practice demonstration. Goldfried and Davidson (1976) suggest that muscles be tensed to only 75% of their capacity so as not to strain them. Moreover, when the tension is released, it should be done at once, not gradually. Each muscle group should be tensed and relaxed twice.

There is a focus on breathing before the lower body is relaxed. To be consistent with the diaphragmatic breathing exercise, expansion of the stomach is suggested with inspiration, with the recommendation to say to oneself "relax" with each expiration. Through repeated association of the word "relax" with actual relaxation (release of tension from the body), it becomes the cue for this state.

After all the muscle groups have been sequentially tensed and relaxed, the facilitator may "deepen" the relaxation by counting from 1 to 5, with 3-second intervals between numbers, each number timed to an inspiration, the expiration following associated with the suggestion of deeper relaxation.

The therapist should conduct the relaxation procedure in a soft monotone, almost an hypnoticlike voice. The pace should be much slower than conversational speech.

Prior to the induction, participants should rate their level of relaxation on a 10 to 100 scale with 10 being minimally relaxed and 100 being maximally relaxed. Immediately after the relaxation session, participants should use this same scale to rate their level of relaxation at that time as well. This procedure provides a relatively concrete measure of change.

Once the procedure is terminated and everyone is alert with eyes open, and the evaluation of the degree of relaxation has been completed, participants should be allowed to acclimate at their own pace. After several minutes, the facilitator may ask if anyone would like to share his or her experience with the group. The relaxation ratings should be discussed in the context of a general discussion.

Audiotaped or written instructions of the relaxation procedure (Table 8–1) may be made for participants. Although clients generally prefer a tape, greater independence, generalizability, self-efficacy expectations, and sustained learning seem to occur without it. Moreover, as proficiency increases, the exercise will be modified and shortened, optimally two times, until "cue-controlled" relaxation is being practiced.

The written instructions (or tape) of the induction are distributed to each member, who is asked to practice the exercise at least once a day. The requirements for the physical environment in which it is first performed at home should be the same as previously described (dim lights, quiet, no interruptions). Initially, if possible, the exercise should be performed the same time each day, so a routine is established. At home, participants should record their pre- and postrelaxation/anxiety on the same 10 to 100 scale used in session. This record should be brought to the therapist for review.

As stated, and logically implied by the model of the TFB triad, there is a reciprocal beneficial effect of cognitive and physiological coping. As one decreases unrealistic expectations of negative outcomes occurring through cognitive coping, there is a consequent decrease in physiological arousal and fear. Physiological coping directly reduces the arousal and fear manyfold, which further decreases the cognitive distortions. Thus, through the use of cognitive and physiological coping, an adaptive reciprocal relationship can be established to substitute for the maladaptive one that inhibits the use of adaptive social skills.

EXPOSURE THERAPY: DEVELOPING A HIERARCHY OF SITUATIONS

Once participants have become proficient in cognitive and physiological coping, it is important they put these skills to use when attempting assertive behavior. We recommend using exposure therapy in which clients apply coping skills in increasingly stressful or progressively more demanding situations. A person who copes and behaves effectively in a low-anxiety/anger-provoking situation is ready to confront a slightly more provocative interaction. Continuing in this manner, a 10-item anxiety- or anger-provoking hierarchy can be established for each person.

Hierarchies can either be single-theme-based or a mixture of different but related themes. A single-theme-based hierarchy would include 10 items that describe variations of a particular type of stressful situation. For example, if the person is hesitant to make a conflict request, he might identify 10 different conflict request situations in which he would experience a range of anxiety. The least anxiety-provoking situation might entail making such a request to a supportive friend. The most anxiety-producing might be making such a request to a total stranger. The other situations composing the hierarchy could vary according to the perceived "friendliness" of the person to whom the request is to be made.

Another type of single-theme-based hierarchy focuses on one anxiety-provoking situation that is the target of treatment. At the top of the hierarchy is a situation such as asking for a pay increase, using a conflict request. Other items on the hierarchy include the sequence of events that culminate in the terminal event. For example, waiting outside the supervisor's office prior to making the request for the pay increase might be the second most anxiety-provoking situation. Until the person can cope with the anxiety in the waiting room, she will not be able to make the request for the raise. Several situations like this would be included in the hierarchy.

Other related situations are included in the hierarchy because they contain environmental cues that initiate anxiety that may escalate and contribute to the inability to perform the desired terminal behavior (in this case, asking for a raise). For example, the anxiety associated with calling the boss and scheduling a meeting to discuss the raise may initiate an anxiety reaction. This item would be placed on the hierarchy. Other similar items such as "walking down the hallway to the boss's office on the way to the meeting to ask for a raise" would also be included. The lowest item on the hierarchy might be "leaving for work on the day I am going to ask for a raise."

The idea of this type of hierarchy is to identify the sequence of anxiety-provoking stimulus situations that trigger anxiety, starting with the one that begins the process and ending with the terminal behavior. The irrational and unrealistic wants and expectations and bodily sensations that initiate and escalate the intensity of the anxiety are identified and the coping skills described in this chapter are applied to them. In addition, the client is exposed to these situations so he or she can obtain in vivo coping experience. Sometimes in vivo practice cannot be arranged (such as the opportunity to ask one's boss for a raise), and these situations are role-played as realistically as possible, based on the client's description of how he or she expects the situation to occur.

In other applications, a hierarchy can be a listing of situations describing any kind of assertive situation (e.g., making requests, responding to requests, expressing feelings), the sole requirement being that each is associated with a different intensity of stress that can be ranked in a hierarchy.

The hierarchy items result from the collaborative effort of therapist and client, and are evaluated on a 10 (minimum) to 100 (maximum) subjective units of distress scale (SUDS). Mastery of skills is expected to be greatest with a systematic exposure approach in which clients first master situations lowest in anxiety before progressing to more threatening ones.

A PROGRAM TO TEACH COGNITIVE COPING AND RELAXATION SKILLS

The following program of treatment is recommended for clients who are learning how to control thoughts, feelings, or behaviors that interfere with effective communication and problem-solving skills. This program includes cognitive coping, slow-diaphragmatic breathing, and progressive muscle relaxation. Teaching these skills is organized according to the four-part model of Instruction, Supervised Practice, Feedback and Independent Practice described in Chapter 1.

Lesson 1. Cognitive Coping

Instruction

The following is an outline of the skill concepts associated with cognitive coping. It may be presented in lecture form or the concepts may be discussed individually with clients.

1. Explain how factors such as anxiety can interfere with the performance of skills.

2. Provide overview of how cognitive coping, slow breathing, and progressive muscle relaxation can be used to cope with inhibitory anxiety.

3. Provide detailed explanation of cognitive coping.

    a. Explain overestimation.

    b. Explain catastrophizing.

    c. Present REST model (recognition, evaluation, substitution, and treat).

Supervised Practice

The group leader should distribute the "Record of Cognitive Coping" form (Table 8–2) and the Cognitive Coping Vignettes (Table 8–3). The leader then provides the following instructions for the exercise: "Read the first vignette and examine it for irrational expectations. Using the Record of Cognitive Coping, (1) describe the thoughts, feelings, and/or

TABLE 8–2
Record of Cognitive Coping

Situation	Recognize	Evaluate	Substitute	Treat
Describe	What are Cues? Thoughts Feelings Behaviors	Did I over-estimate likelihood? Y ___ N ___ Did I overrate importance? Y ___ N ___	What realistic appraisal could I make?	Positive self-statement

behaviors that you recognize as indicating the need for coping, (2) evaluate expectations by appraising their likelihood (to determine if the individual in the vignette is overestimating the probability of a negative occurrence) or their importance (to determine if the person is catastrophizing), (3) substituting rational alternatives for irrational ones, and finally (4) treat yourself with praise and tangible rewards.

"When everyone is finished, we'll go around the room and each member will get an opportunity to present his or her responses. After each response, feedback will be provided by the person sitting immediately to the right and then by the rest of the group."

TABLE 8–3
Cognitive Coping Vignettes

1. John was about to take a math test. After the papers were distributed, the teacher said, "No more talking." When he got his paper, though, he noticed a typing error that made one of the questions confusing. He wanted to raise his hand, but didn't, because of the teacher's request for quiet. He thought she would fail him if he attempted to talk to her.

2. Ed checked the restaurant bill and saw he was overcharged. He started to call the waitress, then changed his mind, shaking his head "no" when she began walking his way. He liked the waitress and the thought of ruining their friendship by pointing out her error resulted in his decision not to say anything.

3. Jill was about to open the wedding gift I bought her. I started to sweat, thinking how humiliating it would be if she didn't like it.

4. Jane was about to give a speech to the college freshman class. As she went up the auditorium stairs, her knees almost buckled under her as she thought of the possibility of forgetting some part of what she memorized.

5. Nicky lived in a nice neighborhood but stayed in her house lately just about all the time. She shook at the thought of going outside, afraid she would be assaulted.

6. David was invited to many class parties but never went because he thought he'd make a fool of himself by saying something stupid or tripping over something. Then his peers would reject him and no longer consider him an acceptable member of the group.

The first vignette should be done as an example with the group leader actively directing the patients in completing each of the various components of the process. We recommend using a chalkboard to record responses. If additional practice is needed beyond the six vignettes provided, the leader can develop additional situations using current experiences of the group members.

Feedback

Follow guidelines provided in Chapter 1.

Independent Practice

Distribute Record of Cognitive Coping (Table 8–2). Indicate to the group members that you want them to monitor the need for cognitive coping this week. On the Record of Cognitive Coping, they are to record two situations in which cognitive coping was needed. Provide the following instructions:

One of the situations should describe *successful* cognitive coping. In other words, you should describe one situation in which you were able to cognitively cope and then used effective communication or problem-solving skills.

The second situation should be one in which you had *difficulty* cognitively coping and behaving assertively.

For the successful situation:

1. Show how you evaluated your wants and expectations by asking about the likelihood and/or importance/severity of the expected negative outcome.
2. Record your substitute rational statements.
3. Describe your assertive behavior.
4. Record what you said/did to treat yourself.

For the situation in which you had trouble cognitively coping:

1. Specify the parts with which you had trouble.
2. Record what you would have done to turn this into an effective coping situation in which you behaved assertively. In other words, record the cues, your evaluation (the appraisal and substitute statements), the assertive behavior you would have liked to exhibit, and your self-treats.

This information is reviewed and feedback provided in subsequent treatment sessions. Areas of strength and weakness determine the focus of future instruction and practice.

Lesson 2. Slow Breathing

Instruction

Although cognitive coping is focused on the root of the problem (irrational thinking), there are also coping strategies that have a direct effect on overall physiological arousal. These physiological coping strategies can be used with cognitive coping to further decrease anxiety. An outline of the skill concepts follows:

1. Explain how overbreathing creates an imbalance between oxygen and carbon dioxide resulting in hyperventilation.

2. Describe how slow breathing helps to restore the natural balance of oxygen and carbon dioxide.

Supervised Practice

There are two parts to the exercise: learning the slow breathing technique, and learning the meditative component. Assemble clients in comfortable chairs. Demonstrate the procedure and have clients practice. The following procedure is suggested.

Slow Diaphragmatic Breathing.   "Slow diaphragmatic breathing emphasizes breathing from the abdomen, with minimal chest movement. Each time you inhale, the stomach area should 'balloon' out; each time you exhale, the stomach area should move inward." The group leader should demonstrate. "To help you observe yourself to make sure you're doing it correctly, place one hand on your chest, the other on your stomach. As you breathe, you should observe movement primarily in the lower, not the upper, hand. Breathing should proceed through your nose, evenly and slowly."

"If you have difficulty performing the movement, you can lie on your stomach, with head resting on hands, and you'll breathe through your diaphragm automatically. You can do this to help you learn the correct breathing movements. You can also practice by lying on your back with a piece of paper on your stomach and watching its movement as you breathe."

The procedure for slow breathing is explained and demonstrated. Participants are instructed to learn how to take 10 diaphragmatic breaths in 60 seconds. They do this by inhaling for 3 seconds and mentally counting 1, 2, 3 and exhaling for 3 seconds while mentally counting 1, 2, 3. Initially, a clock can be used to time the breathing so the clients' mental counting is accurate and produces a 6-second breath.

Meditative Component.   After each breath, the clients are instructed to say to themselves "relax." This repetitive exercise promotes relaxation, with the word "relax" becoming a cue associated with the relaxed state experienced with exhalation.

Clients are to practice the full procedure including the meditative component several times to establish the process. Once everyone understands the principle, and most are having some success with the breathing movement, the facilitator guides them through practice of the exercise for at least 10 minutes.

Before and after engaging in the relaxation procedure, clients evaluate their anxiety and tension. Participants rate their level of relaxation on a 10 to 100 scale with 10 being minimally relaxed and 100 being maximally relaxed. This rating provides a relatively concrete measure of the effectiveness of the procedure.

Feedback

Follow guidelines provided in Chapter 1.

Independent Practice

Follow guidelines for Lesson 3, Progressive Muscle Relaxation.

Lesson 3. Progressive Muscle Relaxation

Instruction

Present the following concepts to the clients:

1. Explain how tensing and relaxing muscles creates an overall relaxed state.
2. Explain progressive muscle relaxation.

Supervised Practice

The relaxation exercise will take about 20 minutes altogether. Instruct clients not to strain their muscles, and to only flex them to about 75% of their maximum potential. The therapist demonstrates the muscle groups involved and how to tense and relax them. The clients participate in this practice demonstration.

The leader conducts the relaxation exercise following the Protocol for Progressive Muscle Relaxation (Table 8–1) and the procedures described earlier in this chapter. The clients record their level of anxiety and tension before and after the procedure and discuss the experience of using progressive muscle relaxation.

Feedback

Follow guidelines provided in Chapter 1.

Independent Practice

The procedures described in this chapter can be broadly applied to situations in which the client is experiencing anxiety or other debilitating affect. They are especially useful when the client has learned a skill but has not been able to perform it in important areas of everyday life because of anxiety. Thus, these procedures can augment the Independent Practice activities associated with other skills such as making requests and responding to the requests of others. Also, many of the plans developed using the problem-solving process described in Chapter 7 should be supplemented by procedures to reduce anxiety and to identify and modify other inhibitory wants and expectations.

9

Applications of Communication and Problem-Solving Skills Training

There is widespread acceptance of the effectiveness of social skills training in mental health treatment. As indicated in Chapter 1, many research studies and a number of literature reviews attest to the value of this approach. This chapter describes a number of clinical applications of the social skills training procedures described in this book. There have been many applications over the years, and with each application, the materials have been adapted, revised, and improved. Therefore, the more recent applications are of materials precisely as they are described in this volume, while older applications are based on earlier versions that vary slightly in content and procedure.

Part of the reason for the wide range of applications over the years is the versatility of this program. It can be, and indeed has been, applied to many different client groups and treatment settings. Partly, the versatility is due to the focus on three fundamental social skills: self-awareness, communication of wants, and problem-solving. In our experience, it is rare to find an individual who does not benefit significantly from increased skills in these areas, regardless of diagnosis or treatment setting (outpatient, day treatment, partial hospital, and inpatient). Mental health professionals have also indicated personal growth as a result of learning these skills.

The following examples are taken from our experiences and represent the principal applications of the materials in this book. Many other applications are possible, but not yet tried. For example, we have yet to systematically demonstrate the effectiveness of these programs with couples experiencing marital conflict, an area of obvious application. Teaching these "assertive communication" skills to Latinos, Chinese, Koreans, and persons of other ethnic backgrounds has not yet been methodically performed and promises some interesting challenges. For example, what does it mean for a Latino or Chinese to be assertive? Do cognitive coping models based on mainstream America generalize to minority populations? We hope that the innovative practitioner, having read the examples in this chapter, will be inspired to create new and ingenious applications.

GROUP THERAPY

This program was developed for use in both time-limited and open-ended group therapy formats.

Time-Limited Groups

A time-limited group is created to achieve a specific set of goals in a specified period. Once these goals are accomplished, the group is disbanded. Social skills training groups easily fit this format of treatment.

When presented as a time-limited group, this program requires about 22 contact hours to teach self-awareness, empathy, communication of wants, principles of assertiveness, problem-solving, and coping with emotions that inhibit performance. The program follows the four-part model, which includes instruction, supervised practice, feedback, and independent practice. As the amount of time required for the independent practice assignments depends on the learning rate of clients being treated, total program time will vary somewhat as well. The theoretical and practical information in each chapter of this book is sufficiently detailed to guide the practitioner in the operation of a time-limited therapy group.

This program involves a substantial investment of time and energy. However, as the procedures described cover a wide range of skills and can easily be provided to a group of 10 clients, the practitioner can achieve substantial efficiency. In these times of managed care and cost containment, this is an important consideration.

A variety of more circumscribed time-limited groups can be developed from the material presented. Depending on the goals of treatment, it is appropriate to divide the total content of this book into smaller "modules" (Gordon et al., 1979). In fact, each of Chapters 2 through 8 could comprise an independent skill training module. For example, a group of clients receiving treatment in a mental health clinic may be evaluated and found to be lacking in self-awareness skills needed to progress in treatment. These clients would benefit from referral to a time-limited program of treatment lasting three or four sessions focused on the self-awareness skills described in Chapter 2. It would not be necessary to include the other skills covered in this text. Chapter 8 (coping with factors that inhibit use of skills) comprises the essence of cognitive coping skills and, therefore, can be the basis of a module for people with problems of anxiety, anger, and depression. Chapter 7 (problem-solving) is frequently conducted as an independent module to teach the basics of the problem-solving process. In addition, it would be appropriate to teach a brief module on empathy or assertiveness.

It is also useful to design time-limited treatment modules that consist of material from two or three chapters of this book. This is done when chapters address related and complementary skills that are best learned as a set. For example, it is beneficial to combine the material on self-awareness skills (Chapter 2) with empathy skills (Chapter 3) since, together, they address complementary issues regarding self and other. Such a module can meaningfully be further broadened by providing the information on assertiveness skills.

Experience has shown that the chapters on making and responding to requests combine to make a worthwhile module for clients who are not effective in these kinds of interpersonal situations. Some information on self-awareness and awareness of others is necessary for people to perform the request-making skills, so the information from Chapters 2 and 3 must be included in the training as well.

These are just a few of the customized, time-limited packages that can be developed to meet the varying needs of clients. The practitioner can use creativity to develop targeted and time-limited treatments.

Open-Ended Groups

An open-ended group has a broad agenda and operates for a long time. Because of its longevity, an open-ended group develops a stable, cohesive membership and new members are added to maintain the integrity of the group as old members terminate. The many therapeutic components and benefits of open-ended groups have been enumerated (e.g., Yalom, 1995).

Clients who complete a time-limited program of skills training, as described in the previous section, often benefit from subsequent participation in an open-ended group. Participation in an open-ended group allows clients to apply the skills learned in the time-limited group to real-life situations over a long period, while receiving supervision and support from a therapist and peers. An open-ended group should focus on real-life applications of self-awareness, empathy, communication, assertiveness, problem-solving, and coping skills.

An effective and interesting open-ended therapy group can be organized around the problem-solving format presented in Chapter 7. Such a group focuses on identifying problems, defining them in a solvable form, generating alternative solutions, evaluating the alternatives, selecting an alternative for implementation, and determining the effectiveness of the problem-solving plan. Descriptions of a problem-solving group based on the present model have been provided previously (Bedell et al., 1980; Bedell & Michael, 1985).

The problem-solving process (as described in Chapter 7) is naturally augmented by the other skills described in this book. For example, to be performed effectively, problem recognition and problem definition require a degree of self-awareness (Chapter 2) and awareness of others (Chapter 3). Also, many of the solutions require the making of assertive requests (Chapters 4 and 6). For example, the client who frequently has disagreements with a family member is likely to be called on to assertively express his or her wants, work toward compromise, and perhaps make a request for behavior change. The person who lives with a substance-abusing spouse will be guided to make clear and direct statements of what is wanted from the spouse in terms of treatment seeking, treatment compliance, and the consequences of continued substance use.

When attempting to implement solutions to problems, clients often experience anxiety that inhibits performance of effective behavior. Reference to the cognitive and physiological coping skills described in Chapter 8 will help to overcome these obstacles. On many occasions, the skills learned in the various time-limited groups become the foundation that, when applied to the process of the open-ended group, greatly enhance the effectiveness of the latter.

When conducting a problem-solving group, it is best to follow a structured format consisting of three distinct segments: socialization, "go-around," and in-depth problem-solving (Bedell, Provet, & Frank, 1994). We will describe each of these components.

A socialization period is used to start a problem-solving group. In a 60-minute problem-solving group, 5 to 10 minutes are dedicated to socialization; this is increased to 15 minutes for a group 90 minutes long. During this segment, discourage any discussion of treatment issues and psychological problems. Clients are to practice casual social interaction, which, ideally, does not focus on problems. After all, outside the therapy setting, who is going to want to socialize with someone who primarily talks about his or her medication and symptoms? The therapist joins in the socializing and facilitates discussion of recent activities or experiences, current news events, plans for future holidays, and social activities. In addition to providing practice in positive social behaviors, the purpose of this activity is to allow members (and the therapist) to become better acquainted with each other by learning about leisure-time pursuits, interests, friends, family, acquaintances, and other lifestyle information. This information is helpful in building cohesiveness, providing foundation material for use in problem-solving and, ultimately, the development of social support and networking among the group members.

Immediately following termination of the socialization period, a "go-around" is conducted. This activity gets its name from the fact that group members are usually gathered in a circle, and the focus of attention moves from one individual to another, around the circle. Each group member participates briefly in this activity (no longer than five minutes) during which the person provides a progress update implementing goals from previous meetings and new problems arising since the preceding meeting.

The go-around has several functions. First, it enables the group to follow up on the progress members have made in implementing problem solutions devised in prior therapy sessions. Follow-up continues on each problem presented to the group until it has been fully implemented or otherwise discontinued. The go-around also allows each person to briefly present a new problem with which he or she may want the group's help in applying the problem-solving process.

Following the go-around, the group selects one member's problem for in-depth attention. This problem is reviewed using the complete problem-solving process described in Chapter 7. This activity is time-consuming and generally occupies the rest of the session. It is extremely rare that more than one problem is given in-depth attention in one group session. It is recommended that the problem-solving worksheet provided in Chapter 7 be used in this portion of the group. A detailed description of this method of problem-solving has been presented (Bedell et al., 1994).

INDIVIDUAL COGNITIVE-BEHAVIORAL THERAPY

Although the concepts of skills training described in this book are organized into a group therapy format, they provide the foundation for individual therapy as well. The treatment components include self-awareness, awareness of others, methods of interpersonal communication, problem-solving, and cognitive coping strategies. These elements of treatment fit readily into a cognitive-behavioral and problem-oriented therapy format. Individual therapy almost always involves a component of self-awareness. The concepts and theories in this book focus the self-awareness process on identification of wants and expectations, relating wants and expectations to feelings and actions, and constructing TFB triads. The TFB triad can be a powerful foundation for self-awareness in individual therapy.

Also, the relative objectivity and simplicity of this model allows the client to understand his or her internal processes better and become a more skilled participant in therapy. For example, a client may come to his individual therapy session expressing feelings of sadness and depression. He is helped by learning that these feelings are associated with wants for which he has abandoned hope. The therapy may then be directed to evaluation of the wants and either acceptance of the loss or an increase in self-efficacy and ongoing pursuit of the wants. Similarly, the patient with chronic anger is helped to understand that these feelings are associated with desired but unmet wants. Therapy can be directed to evaluating the wants and applying the positive problem-solving process to determine how and if wants can reasonably be met. The anxious patient is guided to understand that his or her feelings imply perception that something "bad" is expected to happen. Therapy can then be directed to evaluating these expectations, which can lead to their reappraisal or positive problem-solving.

Once understanding of TFB triads leads to appraisal and positive problem-solving, it is often useful to have a framework for the assertive requests that are an inevitable part of individual therapy. The assertive philosophy and evaluation of the consequences of assertive behavior provide a useful framework within which to structure interpersonal interactions. Use of the REALIST model presented in Chapter 8 is well suited to an individual therapy format.

The problem-solving model also provides straightforward guidelines for individual therapy. In fact, individual therapy logically follows a process of first identifying the problem that brings the client to treatment, next clarifying it, then developing various possible solutions, selecting one for implementation and finally, following up on attempts to execute solutions. The problem-solving worksheet provided in Chapter 7 is a useful guide to individual therapy sessions. A similar problem-solving approach to individual psychotherapy has been presented by Nezu et al. (1989).

ACTIVITY THERAPY AND RECREATION THERAPY

Practitioners of activity and recreational therapies may see a lot of similarities between this program and their own. From the beginning of the development of this skills training model, it was obvious that the marriage of social skills training procedures with recreation and activity therapy was beneficial (Weathers, Bedell, Marlowe, & Gordon, 1978). The primary advantage of this marriage is that recreational and activity therapies provide an interesting and engaging way of facilitating repeated practice of skills during the learning process. They also promote constructive group interaction and allow clients with low levels of skill or significant levels of interfering symptoms to engage in skills training. Involving clients with these difficulties in active treatment is contrary to the usual supposition that social skills training is too difficult for low functioning or acutely mentally ill persons. In fact, Ward, Naster, Pace, and Whitaker (1994) describe applications of the present program that systematically link social skills to recreation and activity therapy for acutely ill persons. Similarly, Bedell and Ward (1989) describe how the integration of recreation and activity therapy with social skills training enabled acutely mentally ill patients to begin skills training therapy on the day they were admitted to an inpatient unit. Extensive use of therapeutic games for teaching the skills in this book has been described elsewhere (Bedell & Weathers, 1979; Cohen, Gordon, Adams, Bedell, & Weathers, 1979; Weathers et al., 1978; Weathers et al., 1981).

FAMILY THERAPY

There has been wide application of skills training to family treatment as described in Chapter 1. The self-awareness, empathy, and request-making skills described in this volume greatly facilitate adaptive communication and conflict resolution in families. The problem-solving and cognitive therapy approaches are also readily adapted for use with families.

Bedell et al. (1994) reported a recent application of the problem-solving program. They used problem-solving and communication skills in a multiple family therapy format. One of the goals of this treatment was that the clients, many of whom had severe mental disorders, participate in treatment on an equal footing with other family members. Therefore, the clients were provided 20 sessions of self-awareness and communication skills training prior to the commencement of problem-solving oriented multiple family therapy. The first task for the multiple family group was for the clients to teach the other family members the communication and problem-solving skills they had learned. Not only did this teaching have the very desirable result that family members and clients learned to communicate according to a common set of rules, but it also provided the client the opportunity to be more expert than the other family members. This expert status was an unusual and uplifting experience for the clients, and it gained them new respect from many family members. In most cases, this new attitude of respect for the client helped to change ingrained dysfunctional family patterns. There are many interesting and effective family therapy applications of the structured skills training programs described in this book.

VOCATIONAL REHABILITATION— SUPPORTED EMPLOYMENT

The development of adaptive social skills training has always been seen as relevant to vocational rehabilitation. Areas of functioning stressed in the present program (dealing with conflicts in wants and requests for behavior change) are particularly important since resolution of interpersonal conflicts with coworkers and supervisors is essential to job tenure. In fact, mental health clients are often well able to perform the technical duties of a job but do not obtain or maintain employment due to unassertive interpersonal skills.

The need for effective interpersonal skills is even more important in vocational rehabilitation with the advent of the Supported Employment (SE) model (Kregel, Wehman, & Banks, 1989). SE calls for the placement of persons with mental health disabilities in competitive employment without long periods of prevocational training. Rather, SE advocates immediate placement and on-the-job training utilizing a job coach. Another important goal of supported employment is full integration of the person with disabilities into the social aspects of work. Social integration is facilitated by assertive communication skills of the type presented in this book.

In recent evaluations of supported employment (Bedell, Gervey, & Draving, in press; Gervey & Bedell, 1994), clients' vocational training was supplemented with extensive skills training based on the program presented in this book. This training was provided daily during a one-month preemployment period after which clients entered the SE program. Since clients received communication skills training prior to job placement, job coaches helped clients apply these skills in the job setting to cope with difficulties. The results of an evaluation of this rehabilitation program indicated that the clients in the SE program, compared with clients in a program of paid prevocational training, were more likely to be placed in competitive employment and stayed on the job longer. While the independent effects of the self-awareness and communication skills training on these extremely favorable outcomes cannot be determined, they were considered to be a positive factor by job coaches. Undoubtedly, the use of assertive communication skills facilitated the integration of mental health clients into the social aspects of employment.

The importance of social skills and the ability to express wants and desires through assertive communication was also indicated by the results of interviews of persons in both SE and programs of paid prevocational training. In this research (Bedell, Guastadesigni, Parrish, Draving, & Gervey, 1995), 14 job stressors were evaluated including such factors as fear of physical injury on the job, concern about being overworked, boredom, relations with coworkers, and adequacy of job skills. Interestingly, concerns about maintaining a positive relationship with one's supervisor was the most stressful factor. Preservation of a positive relationship often involved requests for work supervision, adjustment of work duties and mediation of conflicts with other employees using assertive techniques. These results suggest that training in assertive communication should be included as a component of SE.

CASE MANAGEMENT

Case management is a system of treatment in which services are provided in the client's community, rather than a hospital, clinic, or other centralized mental health facility. Case managers link clients to services, assist in advocacy and teach adaptive social skills in the client's natural environment. Case managers and clients are better able to increase functioning in these three areas when they utilize the skills described in this volume.

The value of integrating skills training into case management services was demonstrated in a program entitled "Community Network Development (CND)" (Edmundson, Bedell, Archer, & Gordon, 1981; Edmundson, Bedell, Archer, & Gordon, 1982; Edmundson, Bedell, & Gordon, 1983). This innovative case management program used peer-counselors, who were also mental health services consumers, in conjunction with professional case managers, to maintain persons with severe mental disorders in the community. As part of the CND program, professional staff, peer-counselors and clients were all taught the same set of communication and problem-solving skills based on an earlier version of the models presented in this book. This training created a common mode of operation that united the efforts of this interdisciplinary team consisting of people with very different backgrounds, training, and roles in the program.

This program of case management proved to be very effective, reducing the frequency of clients' mental health hospitalizations and lengths of hospital stay. The paraprofessionals also indicated that they were able to function well within the social skills training framework of the program and found their role in the project fulfilling and meaningful. Although social skills training was only one component of this innovative treatment, it was a central unifying factor. Based on our experience with the CND program, it is recommended that skills training of the type described in this book be included in any case management program utilizing teams of professional and paraprofessional workers.

SPECIAL POPULATIONS

The program we have described has been the centerpiece of demonstration research programs dealing with clients experiencing their first hospital admission and clients being sent from community crisis treatment units to a state hospital. This program has also been adapted for use with persons who are cognitively impaired due to multiple sclerosis. These three applications demonstrate how the program can be used for a wide range of purposes.

First Hospital Admission

A person's first psychiatric hospitalization is significant for many reasons, not the least of which is its potential for initiating a process of institutionalization and overdependence on mental health professionals in lieu of natural supports. A deficit in social skills and the resulting lack of perceived control over the environment are also significant factors leading to hospitalization and institutionalization. Consequently, a program was established to both (a) identify clients experiencing their first mental health hospitalization and (b) provide a treatment focusing primarily on the development of clients' social skills, including self-awareness, assertive communication, and problem-solving (Archer, Amuso, & Bedell, 1980; Bedell & Weathers, 1979; Edmundson et al., 1981).

Clients who received this treatment program showed changes in basic personality trait structure. They became significantly more internal in locus of control (Rotter, 1966), indicating an expectation of more personal control over important reinforcers in their lives. They also showed a reduction in trait anxiety and depression and developed more effective problem-solving skills (Archer, Amuso, & Bedell, 1980). Components such as a peer-managed token economy (Bedell & Archer, 1980) and a self-medication system (Cohen et al., 1979) were linked to the skills training program. Because of the multifaceted nature of the treatment, it is not possible to determine the independent effects of each component. Nonetheless, the social skills training element provided the fundamental framework to which all other treatment elements were added.

Alternative to State Hospitalization

The skills training program described in this book was also the foundation of an intensive community-based treatment alternative to state hospitalization (Bedell & Ward, 1989). This program, entitled Intensive Residential Treatment (IRT), targeted clients who had been treated in a short-term (20 days) crisis inpatient unit and were due to be transferred to a state hospital for continued treatment. In lieu of transfer to the state hospital, clients were sent to the IRT program.

Based on skills training, behavioral management, and psychiatric rehabilitation models, this program provided 14 hours of active intervention each day, focusing on self-awareness, communication, and problem-solving. The treatment was structured into three progressive levels to which clients were assigned according to their functional abilities (Ward et al., 1994). This approach to inpatient treatment was found to be very effective. The program served over 300 patients each year with an average length of stay of 35 days compared with 165 days for a comparison group who received standard state hospital care (not based on social skills training). The rehospitalization rate was also less for clients graduating from the IRT program during the 42 months of postdischarge follow-up. And, the cost for an episode of treatment in the program based on skills training was only one-third of the cost for the state hospital treatment. The latter was a dramatic finding and one that is very relevant in the current age of managed care. The IRT program demonstrated that a social skills based inpatient service can be both clinically effective and cost-effective, even for patients with severe mental disorders.

Patients with Multiple Sclerosis

The application of the communication and problem-solving skills training procedures described is not limited to mental health clients. They are useful to any population that can benefit from a straightforward and readily comprehensible program of skills training. Foley et al. (1994) reported on its application to patients with multiple sclerosis (MS) who have cognitive impairments. As explained in this report, patients with MS experience difficulties in a variety of functions involving memory, cognitive flexibility, reasoning, and speed of information processing. Because of the straightforward and relative simplicity of the present model, it was selected for use with these patients. Although evaluation of treatment efficacy is ongoing, precluding any immediate conclusions, preliminary findings are positive.

Training Mental Health Professionals

Teaching mental health professionals how to conduct social skills training is an important application of the current material. Most professionals do not receive sufficient exposure to social skills training therapies. The profession of psychology, for example, emphasizes traditional psychotherapies, neuropsychology, and behavioral medicine (Stewart, Horn, Becker, & Kline, 1993).

To help rectify this situation, the National Institute of Mental Health (NIMH), during the years 1988 to 1993, funded a clinical training program to teach psychologists rehabilitation, cognitive-behavioral therapies, and social skills treatments. A description and evaluation of that training program, a facsimile of the one described in this text, has been reported (Bedell & Rivera, in press). In this evaluation, program graduates were asked, among other things, to rank-order the importance of 10 components that composed their training program. These components included individual clinical supervision, learning individual therapy techniques, and being taught seminars by expert faculty. The results of the rank-ordering indicated that the most highly regarded training experience was learning how to conduct social skills training groups. The program the students were evaluating was the one described in this book. Obviously, these trainees recognized both the importance of having these skills in their professional repertoire, and the deficits in social skills exhibited by many of the patients they treated.

So, it can be seen that the potential applications of the skills training described in this book are many and varied. They include the training of professionals and paraprofessionals, the treatment of seriously disabled clients and their families, persons being hospitalized for the first time, and persons engaging in individual and group therapy in an attempt to reduce symptoms and increase quality of life. The breadth of application of these treatment approaches is largely limited only by the imagination and creativity of mental health staff. We hope that the innovative practitioner, having been inspired by the examples provided, will create many new and ingenious applications for the benefit of a wide variety of clients.

References

Alberti, R. E., & Emmons, M. L. (1975). *Your perfect right: A guide to assertive behavior.* San Luis Obispo, CA: Impact Press.

Alloy, L. B., Peterson, C., Abramson, L. Y., & Seligman, L. E. (1984). Attributional style and the generality of learned helplessness. *Journal of Personality and Social Psychology, 46*(3), 681–687.

Anderson, C. M., Hogarty, G., & Reiss, D. (1980). Family treatment of adult schizophrenic patients: A psychoeducational approach. *Schizophrenia Bulletin, 6,* 490–505.

Anderson, C. M., Reiss, D. J., & Hogarty, G. E. (1986). *Schizophrenia and the family.* New York: Guilford Press.

Anthony, W. A., Cohen, M. R., & Farkas, M. D. (1990). *Psychiatric rehabilitation.* Boston: Boston University, Center for Psychiatric Rehabilitation.

Archer, R. P., Amuso, K. F., & Bedell, J. R. (1980). Time-limited residential treatment: Issues and evaluation. *Hospital and Community Psychiatry, 31,* 837–840.

Archer, R. P., Bedell, J. R., & Amuso, K. F. (1980). Relationships and characteristics of locus of control and trait anxiety among inpatients. *Social Behavior and Personality, 8*(2), 161–164.

Averill, J. R. (1975). A semantic atlas of emotional concepts. *Catalog of Selected Documents in Psychology, 5,* 330.

Bandura, A. (1969). *Principles of behavior modification.* New York: Holt, Rinehart and Winston.

Bandura, A. (1977). *Social learning theory.* Englewood Cliffs, NJ: Prentice-Hall.

Bandura, A., & Walters, R. H. (1963). *Social learning and personality development.* New York: Holt, Rinehart and Winston.

Barlow, D. H., & Cerny, J. A. (1988). *Psychological treatment of panic.* New York: Guilford Press.

Barlow, D. H., & Craske, M. G. (1989). *Mastery of your anxiety and panic.* Albany, NY: Gray Winds Publications.

Beck, A. T. (1976). *Cognitive therapy and emotional disorders.* New York: International Universities Press.

Beck, A. T., & Emery, G. (1985). *Anxiety disorders and phobias: A cognitive perspective.* New York: Basic Books.

Beck, A. T., & Freeman, A. M. (1990). *Cognitive therapy of personality disorders.* New York: Guilford Press.

Beck, A. T., Rush, A. J., Shaw, B. F., & Emery, G. (1979). *Cognitive therapy of depression.* New York: Guilford Press.

Bedell, J. R., & Archer, R. P. (1980). Peer managed token economies: Evaluation and description. *Journal of Clinical Psychology, 36,* 716–722.

Bedell, J. R., Archer, R. P., & Marlowe, H. A., Jr. (1980). A description and evaluation of a problem solving skills training program. In D. Upper & S. M. Ross (Eds.), *Behavioral group therapy: An annual review* (pp. 3–35). Champaign, IL: Research Press.

Bedell, J. R., Gervey, R., & Draving, D. (in press). Work stress in persons with severe mental disorders. In C. D. Spielberger & I. G. Sarason (Eds.), *Stress and emotion* (Vol. 16). Washington, DC: Taylor & Francis.

Bedell, J. R., Guastadesigni, P., Parrish, A., Draving, D., & Gervey, R. (1995, May). Work stress from supported employment programs. In R. Liberman (Chair), *Work and psychiatric disability in schizophrenia.* Symposium conducted at the 148th annual meeting of the American Psychiatric Association, Miami, FL.

Bedell, J. R., & Lennox, S. S. (1994). The standardized assessment of cognitive and behavioral components of social skills. In J. Bedell (Ed.), *Psychological assessment and treatment of persons with severe mental disorders* (pp. 58–71). Philadelphia, PA: Taylor and Francis.

Bedell, J. R., & Michael, D. D. (1985). Teaching problem solving skills to chronic psychiatric patients. In D. Upper & S. M. Ross (Eds.), *Handbook of behavioral group therapy.* New York: Plenum Press.

Bedell, J. R., Provet, P., & Frank, J. A. (1994). Rehabilitation oriented multiple family therapy. In J. R. Bedell (Ed.), *Psychological assessment and treatment of persons with severe mental disorders* (pp. 215–232). Washington, DC: Taylor and Francis.

Bedell, J. R., & Rivera, J. (1996). Antecedents and consequences of psychology training with the chronically mentally ill. *Professional Psychology: Research and Practice, 27,* 278–283.

Bedell, J. R., & Ward, J. (1989). An intensive community-based treatment alternative to state hospitalization. *Hospital and Community Psychiatry, 40,* 533–535.

Bedell, J. R., & Weathers, L. R. (1979). A psychoeducational model of skill training: Therapist and game facilitated appreciations. In D. Upper &

S. M. Ross (Eds.), *Behavioral group therapy: An annual review* (pp. 210–235). Champaign, IL: Research Press.

Bellack, A. S., Morrison, R. L., & Mueser, K. T. (1989). Social problem solving in schizophrenia. *Schizophrenia Bulletin, 15,* 101–116.

Bellack, A. S., & Mueser, K. T. (1986). A comprehensive treatment program for schizophrenia and chronic mental illness. Special issue: Systems aspects of chronic mental illness. *Community Mental Health Journal, 22*(3), 175–189.

Bellack, A. S., Turner, S. M., Hersen, M., & Luber, R. F. (1984). An examination of the efficacy of social skills training for chronic schizophrenic patients. *Hospital and Community Psychiatry, 35,* 1023–1028.

Benton, M. K., & Schroeder, H. E. (1990). Social skills training with schizophrenics: A meta-analytic evaluation. *Journal of Consulting and Clinical Psychology, 55,* 741–747.

Brady, J. P. (1984). Social skills training for psychiatric patients. II: Clinical outcome studies. *American Journal of Psychiatry, 141,* 491–498.

Brown, G. T., & Carmichael, K. (1992). Assertiveness training for clients with psychiatric illness: A pilot study. *British Journal of Occupational Therapy, 55*(4), 137–140.

Burns, D. D. (1980). *Feeling good: The new mood therapy.* New York: William Marrow.

Clore, G. L., Ortony, A., & Foss, M. A. (1987). The psychological foundations of the affective lexicon. *Journal of Personality and Social Psychology, 53*(4), 751–766.

Cohen, M., Gordon, R. E., Adams, J., Bedell, J. R., & Weathers, L. R. (1979). Single bedtime dose self-medication system. *Hospital and Community Psychiatry, 30,* 30–33.

Deffenbacher, J. L., & Suinn, R. M. (1987). Generalized anxiety syndrome. In L. Michelson & M. Ascher (Eds.), *Anxiety and stress disorders: Cognitive behavioral assessment and treatment* (pp. 332–360). New York: Guilford Press.

D'Zurilla, T. J. (1986). *Problem solving therapy: A social competence approach to clinical intervention.* New York: Springer.

D'Zurilla, T. J., & Goldfried, M. R. (1971). Problem solving and behavior modification. *Journal of Abnormal Psychology, 78,* 107–126.

D'Zurilla, T. J., & Nezu, A. M. (1990). Development and preliminary evaluation of the social problem solving inventory. *Psychological Assessment, 2,* 156–163.

Edmunson, E. D., Bedell, J. R., Archer, R. P., & Gordon, R. E. (1981). Integrating skills building, peer supports, and aftercare for adult mental patients. In R. E. Gordon & K. K. Gordon (Eds.), *Systems of treatment for the mentally ill* (pp. 251–284). New York: Grune & Stratton.

Edmunson, E. D., Bedell, J. R., Archer, R. P., & Gordon, R. E. (1982). Integrating skill building and peer support in mental health treatment: The early intervention and community network development projects. In A. M. Jeger & R. S. Slotnick (Eds.), *Community mental health and behavioral ecology: A handbook of theory, research, and practice* (pp. 127–138). New York: Plenum Press.

Edmunson, E. D., Bedell, J. R., & Gordon, R. E. (1983). The community network development project: Bridging the gap between professional aftercare and self-help. In F. Reisman & A. Gartner (Eds.), *Mental health and the self-help revolution* (pp. 195–203). New York: Human Services Press.

Egan, G. (1990). *The skilled helper: A problem management approach to helping*. Pacific Grove, CA: Brooks & Cole.

Ellis, A., & Grieger, R. (1978). *The handbook of rational-emotive therapy*. New York: Springer.

Ellis, A., & Harper, R. A. (1961). *A guide to rational living*. Englewood Cliffs, NJ: Prentice Hall.

Epictetus. (1890). *The collected works of Epictetus*. Boston: Little, Brown.

Falloon, I. R., McGill, C. W., Boyd, J. L., & Pederson, J. (1987). Family management in the prevention of morbidity of schizophrenia: Social outcome of a two-year longitudinal study. *Psychological Medicine, 17*(1), 59–66.

Farkas, M. D., O'Brien, W. F., Cohen, M. R., & Anthony, W. A. (1994). Assessment and planning in psychiatric rehabilitation. In J. R. Bedell (Ed.), *Psychological assessment and treatment of persons with severe mental disorders* (pp. 3–30). Philadelphia, PA: Taylor and Francis.

Fast, J. (1970). *Body language*. New York: Simon & Schuster.

Flowers, J. V., & Booraem, C. D. (1975). Assertion training: The training of trainers. *Counseling Psychologist, 5*(4), 29–36.

Foley, F. W., Dince, W. M., Bedell, J. R., LaRocca, N. G., Kalb, R., Caruso, L. S., Smith, C. R., & Shnek, Z. M. (1994). Psychoremediation of communication skills for cognitively impaired persons with multiple sclerosis. *Journal of Neurological Rehabilitation, 8,* 165–176.

Freud, S. (1942). *Beyond the pleasure principle*. London: Hogarth Press.

Fromm-Reichmann, F. (1950). *Principles of intensive psychotherapy*. Chicago: University of Chicago Press.

Gervey, R., & Bedell, J. R. (1994). Supported employment in vocational rehabilitation. In J. R. Bedell (Ed.), *Psychological assessment and treatment of persons with severe mental disorders* (pp. 151–172). Washington, DC: Taylor and Francis.

Goldfried, M. R., & Davidson, G. C. (1976). *Clinical behavior therapy*. New York: Holt, Rinehart and Winston.

Goldsmith, J. G., & McFall, R. M. (1975). Development and evaluation of an interpersonal skill training program for psychiatric inpatients. *Journal of Consulting and Clinical Psychology, 84,* 51–58.

Goldstein, A. A. (1973). *Structured learning therapy*. New York: Academic Press.

Gordon, R. E., Weathers, L. R., Patterson, R. L., Bedell, J. R., Bates, H. D., & Hatcher, M. (1979). Modular treatment and training. *University of South Florida Human Resources Institute Monograph Series* (Report No. 2).

Gottman, J., Notarius, C., Gonso, J., & Markman, H. (1976). *A couple's guide to communication.* Champaign, IL: Research Press.

Hall, E. T. (1959). *The silent language.* New York: Broom and Selznick.

Heide, F. J., & Borkovec, T. D. (1983). Relaxation induced anxiety: Paradoxical anxiety enhancement due to relaxation training. *Journal of Consulting and Clinical Psychology, 51*(2), 171–182.

Heide, F. J., & Borkovec, T. D. (1984). Relaxation induced anxiety: Mechanisms and theoretical implications. *Behavior Research and Therapy, 22*(1), 1–12.

Hersen, M., & Bellack, A. S. (1976). Social skills training for chronic psychiatric patients: Rationale, research findings, and future directions. *Comprehensive Psychiatry, 17,* 559–580.

Hogarty, G. E., Anderson, C. M., Reiss, K. J., Kornblith, S. J., Greenwald, D. P., Javna, C. D., & Madonia, M. J. (1986). Family psychoeducation, social skills training, and maintenance chemotherapy in aftercare treatment of schizophrenics: One-year effect of a controlled study on relapse and expressed emotion. *Archives of General Psychiatry, 43,* 633–642.

Hogarty, G. E., Kornblith, S. J., Greenwald, D., DiBarry, A. L., Cooley, S., Flesher, S., Reiss, D., Carter, M., & Ulrich, R. (1995). Personal therapy: A disorder-related psychotherapy for schizophrenia. *Schizophrenia Bulletin, 21,* 379–393.

Jacobson, E. (1938). *Progressive relaxation* (rev. ed.). Chicago: University of Chicago Press.

Jacobson, E., & Edinger, J. D. (1982). Side effects of relaxation treatment. *American Journal of Psychiatry, 139,* 952–953.

Jakubowski, P., & Lange, A. J. (1978). *The assertive option: Your rights and responsibilities.* Champaign, IL: Research Press.

James, W. (1987). *Writings 1902–1910 / William James.* In B. Kuklick (Ed.). New York: Viking Literary Classics of the United States.

Kagan, N. (1975). Influencing human interaction: Eleven years with IPR. *Canadian Counsellor, 9,* 75–97.

Kelly, G. A. (1955). *The psychology of personal constructs* (Vol. 1). London: Routledge.

Kemper, T. D. (1987). How many emotions are there? Wedding the social and autonomic components. *American Journal of Sociology, 93*(2), 263–289.

Klosko, J. S., & Barlow, D. H. (1989). Cognitive behavioral therapy. In C. Lindemann (Ed.), *Handbook of phobia therapy: Rapid symptom relief in anxiety disorders* (pp. 211–221). Northvale, NJ: Jason Aronson.

Kregel, J., Wehman, P., & Banks, R. D. (1989). The effect of consumer characteristics and types of employment models on individual outcomes in supported employment. *Journal of Applied Behavior Analysis, 22*(4), 407–415.

Ladd, G. W., & Mize, J. (1983). A cognitive-social learning model of social-skill training. *Psychological Review, 90,* 127–157.

Lange, A. J., & Jakubowski, P. (1976). *Responsible assertive behavior: Cognitive behavioral procedures for trainers.* Champaign, IL: Research Press.

Leff, J., & Vaughn, C. E. (1980). The interaction of life events and relatives' expressed emotion in schizophrenia and depressed neurosis. *British Journal of Psychiatry, 136,* 146–153.

Ley, R. (1987). Panic disorder: A hyperventilation interpretation. In L. Michelson & L. M. Ascher (Eds.), *Anxiety and stress disorders: Cognitive behavioral assessment and treatment* (pp. 191–212). New York: Guilford Press.

Liberman, R. P. (1982). Assessment of social skills. *Schizophrenia Bulletin, 8,* 62–83.

Liberman, R. P. (1992). Whither cognitive-behavioral therapy for schizophrenia? *Schizophrenia Bulletin, 18,* 27–34.

Liberman, R. P., & Bedell, J. R. (1989). Behavior therapy. In H. I. Kaplan & B. J. Sadock (Eds.), *Comprehensive textbook of psychiatry* (Vol. 5). Baltimore: Williams & Wilkins.

Liberman, R. P., DeRise, W. R., & Mueser, K. T. (1989). *Social skills training for psychiatric patients.* New York: Pergamon.

Liberman, R. P., & Green, M. F. (1982). Assessment of social skills. *Schizophrenia Bulletin, 8,* 62–83.

Liberman, R. P., Mueser, K. T., & Wallace, C. J. (1986). Social skills training for schizophrenic individuals at risk of relapse. 138th annual meeting of the American Psychiatric Association (1985, Dallas, TX). *American Journal of Psychiatry, 143*(4), 523–526.

Libet, J. M., & Lowensohn, P. M. (1973). Concept of social skill with special reference to the behavior of depressed persons. *Journal of Consulting and Clinical Psychology, 40,* 304–312.

McFall, R. M. (1982). A review and reformulation of the concept of social skills. *Behavioral Assessment, 4,* 1–33.

Mehrabian, A. (1972). *Nonverbal communication.* Chicago: Aldine-Atherton.

Meichenbaum, D. H. (1977). *Cognitive-behavior modification: An integrative approach.* New York: Plenum.

Meichenbaum, D. H., & Goodman, J. (1977). Training impulsive children to talk to themselves: A means of developing self-control. In A. Ellis & R. Grieger (Eds.), *Handbook of rational emotive therapy* (pp. 379–397). New York: Springer.

Michelson, L., & Ascher, L. M. (1987). *Anxiety and stress disorders: Cognitive behavioral assessment and treatment.* New York: Guilford Press.

Missri, J., & Alexander, S. (1978). Hyperventilation syndrome: A brief review. *Journal of the American Medical Association, 240,* 2093–2096.

Moreno, J. L. (1946). *Psychodrama* (Vol. 1). New York: Beacon House.

Morrison, R. L., & Bellack, A. S. (1984). Social skills training. In A. S. Bellack (Ed.), *Schizophrenia: Treatment, management and rehabilitation.* Orlando, FL: Grune & Stratton.

Nezu, A. M., & D'Zurilla, T. J. (1989). Social problem solving and negative affective conditions. In P. C. Kendall & D. Watson (Eds.), *Anxiety and depression: Distinctive and overlapping features* (pp. 285–315). New York: Academic Press.

Nezu, A. M., Nezu, C. M., & Perri, M. G. (1989). *Problem solving therapy for depression: Theory, research, and clinical guidelines.* New York: Wiley.

Novaco, R. (1975). *Anger control: The development and evaluation of an experimental treatment.* Lexington, MA: Heath.

Nunnally, J. C. (1967). *Psychometric theory.* New York: McGraw-Hill.

Penn, D. L., Van Der Does, A. W., Spaulding, W. D., Garbin, C. P., Linszen, D. H., & Dingemans, P. M. A. J. (1993). Information processing and social cognitive problem solving in schizophrenia: Assessment of interrelationships and changes over time. *Journal of Mental and Nervous Disease, 181*(1), 13–20.

Plutchik, R. (1994). *The psychology and biology of emotion.* New York: HarperCollins.

Rimm, D. C., & Masters, J. C. (1974). *Behavior therapy: Techniques and empirical findings.* New York: Academic Press.

Robertson, I., Richardson, A. M., & Youngson, S. C. (1984). Social skills training with mentally handicapped people: A review. *British Journal of Clinical Psychology, 23,* 241–264.

Rogers, C. R. (1951). *Client centered therapy: Its current practice, implications and theory.* Boston: Houghton Mifflin.

Rogers, C. R., & Sanford, R. C. (1989). Client-centered psychotherapy. In H. I. Kaplan & B. J. Sadook (Eds.), *Comprehensive textbook of psychiatry* (Vol. 4, pp. 1482–1501). Baltimore, MD: Williams and Wilkins.

Rotter, J. B. (1966). Generalized expectancies for internal versus external control of reinforcement. *Psychological Monographs: General and Applied, 80*(1), 1–28.

Ruesch, J. (1961). *Therapeutic communication.* New York: W. W. Norton.

Sacks, A. W. (1985). *The man who mistook his wife as a hat and other clinical tales.* New York: Summit Books.

Salter, A. (1949). *Conditioned reflex therapy.* New York: Farrar, Straus, & Giroux.

Spielberger, C. D. (1988). *Manual for the state-trait anger expression inventory (STAXI).* Odessa, FL: Psychological Assessment Resources.

Spielberger, C. D., Jacobs, G., Russell, S., & Crane, R. S. (1983). Assessment of anger: The state-trait anger scale. In J. N. Butcher & C. D. Spielberger (Eds.), *Advances in personality assessment* (Vol. 2, pp. 161–190). Hillsdale, NJ: Erlbaum.

Spielberger, C. D., Johnson, E. H., Russell, S. F., Crane, R. J., Jacobs, G. A., & Worden, T. J. (1985). The experience and expression of anger: Construction and validation of an anger expression scale. In M. A. Chesney & R. H. Rosenman (Eds.), *Anger and hostility in cardiovascular and behavioral disorders* (pp. 5–30). New York: Hemisphere.

Stewart, J. A., Horn, D. L., Becker, J. M., & Kline, J. S. (1993). Postdoctoral training in severe mental illness: A model for trainee development. *Professional Psychology: Research and Practice, 24,* 286–292.

Sullivan, H. S. (1953). *The interpersonal theory of psychiatry.* New York: W. W. Norton.

Taylor, S. E., Wayment, H. A., Heidi, A., & Collins, M. A. (1993). Positive illusions and affect regulation. In D. M. Wegner & J. W. Pennebaker (Eds.), *Handbook of mental control: Century psychology series* (pp. 325–343). Engelwood Cliffs, NJ: Prentice-Hall.

Trower, P., Bryant, B., & Argyle, M. (1978). *Social skills and mental health.* Pittsburgh, PA: University of Pittsburgh Press.

Truax, C. B., & Carkhuff, R. (1967). *Toward effective counseling and psychotherapy: Training and practice.* Chicago, IL: Aldine.

Ullmann, L. P., & Krasner, L. (1965). *Case studies in behavior modification.* New York: Holt, Rinehart and Winston.

Ulrich, R., Stachnich, T., & Mabry, J. (1966). *Control of human behavior.* Glenview, IL: Scott Foresman.

Walen, S. R., DiGiuseppe, R., & Dryden, W. (1992). *A practitioner's guide to rational emotive therapy.* New York: Oxford University Press.

Wallace, C. J. (1982). The social skills training project of the mental health clinical research center for the study of schizophrenia. In J. P. Curran & P. M. Monti (Eds.), *Social skills training: A practical handbook for assessment and treatment* (pp. 57–89). New York: Guilford Press.

Wallace, C. J., & Boone, S. E. (1984). Cognitive factors in the social skills of schizophrenic patients: Implications for treatment. In W. D. Spaulding & J. K. Cole (Eds.), *Symposium on Motivation 1983: Theories of schizophrenia and psychosis* (pp. 283–318). Lincoln: University of Nebraska Press.

Wallace, C. J., & Liberman, R. P. (1985). Social skill training for patients with schizophrenia: A controlled clinical trial. *Psychiatry Research, 15,* 239–247.

Wallace, C. J., Liberman, R. P., MacKain, S. J., Eckman, T. A., & Blackwell, G. A. (1992). The effectiveness and replicability of modules to train social and independent living skills. *American Journal of Psychiatry, 149,* 654–658.

Wallace, C. J., Nelson, C. J., Liberman, R. P., Atchison, R. A., Lukoff, D., Elder, J. P., & Ferris, C. (1980). A review and critique of social skills training with schizophrenic patients. *Schizophrenia Bulletin, 6,* 42–63.

Ward, J., & Naster, B. (1991). Reliability of an observational system used to monitor behavior in a mental health residential treatment unit. *Journal of Mental Health Administration, 18*(1), 64–68.

Ward, J., Naster, B. J., Pace, J. E., & Whitaker, P. K. (1994). Recreational and activity therapies in multilevel psychoeducationally oriented social skills training. In J. R. Bedell (Ed.), *Psychological assessment and treatment for persons with severe mental disorders* (pp. 121–138). Washington, DC: Taylor and Francis.

Weathers, L. R., Bedell, J. R., Marlowe, H. A., Jr., & Gordon, R. E. (1978). Psychotherapeutic games. *Journal of the Florida Medical Association, 65,* 891–896.

Weathers, L. R., Bedell, J. R., Marlowe, H. A., Jr., Gordon, R. E., Adams, J., Reed, V., Palmer, J., & Gordon, K. K. (1981). Using psychotherapeutic games to train patient skills. In R. E. Gordon & K. K. Gordon (Eds.), *Systems of treatment for the mentally ill* (pp. 109–124). New York: Grune & Stratton.

Whitely, J. M., & Flowers, J. U. (1978). *Approaches to assertive training.* Monterey, CA: Brooks/Cole.

Wolpe, J. (1958). *Psychotherapy by reciprocal inhibition.* Stanford, CA: Stanford University Press.

Wolpe, J., & Lazarus, A. A. (1966). *Behavior therapy techniques: A guide to the treatment of neuroses.* New York: Pergamon Press.

Yalom, I. D. (1995). *The theory and practice of group psychotherapy.* New York: Basic Books.

Yerkes, R. M., & Dodson, J. D. (1908). The relation of strength of stimulus to rapidity of habit formation. *Journal of Comparative and Neurological Psychology, 18,* 459–482.

Zigler, E., & Phillips, L. (1961). Social competence and outcome in psychiatric disorder. *Journal of Abnormal and Social Psychology, 63,* 264–271.

Author Index

Subject Index